The Ultimate Book of
Decorative
Knots

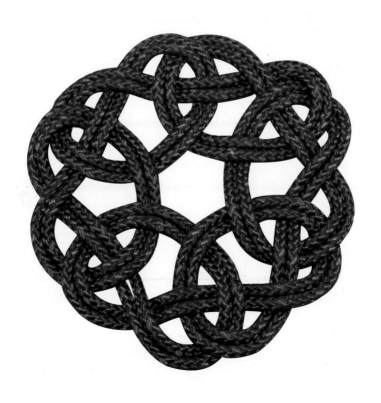

The Ultimate Book of
Decorative Knots

LINDSEY PHILPOTT

Skyhorse Publishing

Skyhorse Publishing books may be purchased in bulk at special discounts for sales promotion, corporate gifts, fund-raising, or educational purposes. Special editions can also be created to specifications. For details, contact the Special Sales Department, Skyhorse Publishing, 307 West 36th Street, 11th Floor, New York, NY 10018 or info@skyhorsepublishing.com.

Skyhorse® and Skyhorse Publishing® are registered trademarks of Skyhorse Publishing, Inc.®, a Delaware corporation.

Visit our website at www.skyhorsepublishing.com.

10 9 8 7 6 5 4 3 2

Library of Congress Cataloging-in-Publication Data is available on file.

Cover design by Jane Sheppard

ISBN: 978-1-5107-6377-7
Ebook ISBN: 978-1-62873-415-7

Printed in China

Contents

Acknowledgments

The author sincerely thanks his fellow knot-tyers for having shared their knowledge and skills so freely. Whether they are members of the International Guild of Knot Tyers, KnotHeads Worldwide, or simply the folks who stop by any of the demonstrations and displays in which I have taken part, their knowledge has been invaluable in providing pointers and answers to the questions that plague each of us when making a knot for the first time. Without the available knowledge of those who have gone before, each of us would be forced to start from scratch and would undoubtedly find the process less inventive and more a simple search for whatever truths knot-tying brings—it has charms to soothe the savage breast [William Congreve: *The Mourning Bride;* 1697 originally: Musick has charms to sooth the savage breast] or it may be that it shows the person just how much their persistence may be stretched.

By standing on the shoulders of giants we see farther, and may even be able to contribute by deriving a simpler tying method, perhaps a new knot, or even make some meaningful contribution to the store of knot knowledge.

I wish to thank my editor, Abigail Gehring, and all the staff at Skyhorse Publishing, for having put up with my poor English, punctuation, prosaic turns of phrase, and Photoshop efforts, making this book a contribution worthy of the name. In particular, I wish to thank publisher Tony Lyons for his forbearance and for being willing to remain steadfast to the ideals of publishing. Among the names of people whom I wish to thank on this page, if I have not already done so

many times in person, are Brian Field, Harold Scott, Georg Schaake, Gary Sessions, and Bud Brewer, all of whom have now passed away—thank you all for your great contributions to an ongoing craft that is still alive and well, thanks to your efforts. Finally, and with the hope that she will forgive my putting her name last and by no means least on these pages, my wife, Kim. Without your support and encouragement this would not have been possible—thank you!

This book is dedicated to the memory of all great knot-tyers and to all who have trodden this rare and exotic path—the journey continues!

Preface

Practical knots (and books about how to tie and use them) are commonly found in the company of sailors, campers, mountaineers, rock-climbers, fishermen, firefighters, rescue workers, linesmen, riggers, and others who regularly use line for work or leisure. Many books of knots include some decorative knots. However, books entirely about decorative knots from around the world are hard to find. *The Encyclopedia of Fancy Knots and Rope Work* by Graumont and Hensel (1939) was probably the first large book in English to classify decorative and functional knots together in one volume. It is a single volume containing 311 black-and-white photographic plates illustrating knots and attempting to describe their construction. The book's value as a reference work is evident to those who have some mastery of knots and knotting.

Frontispiece   ROPE ANCHOR   Description on Page 438

Since that time, there has been no single work collecting decorative knotting from different cultures around the world, a void I now hope to partially fill.

In this book I hope to share my passion for decorative knotting by teaching you how to make such knots yourself. Provided here are step-by-step instructions, illustrated with photographs. If I succeed in this endeavor, it is because you have joined with me in seeing the overall pattern and sense of the knot, aided by photographs showing critical stages in their construction. Where I do not meet your expectations, I welcome your feedback for further and future improvements at www.theknotguy.com.

While there are several distinct styles in which decorative knots may be fashioned, this book will focus strictly on the use of cord, avoiding other elements of decoration that rely on knotting, like beadwork,

*Frontispiece from Graumont &
Hensel's Encyclopedia
of Knots and Fancy Rope Work,
published by Cornell*

Following the publication of Graumont & Hensel's *Encyclopedia*, Clifford W. Ashley wrote the somewhat encyclopedic *Ashley Book of Knots* (1944), known to knotters as ABOK or the "bible of knots." It contains 3,854 knots and knot descriptions and more than 7,000 drawings prepared by Ashley himself—no mean feat considering that World War II was not yet over and paper was scarce!

*Opening page of Ashley's Book of Knots,
published originally by Doubleday Doran Co.
The drawing, along with thousands of others in
the book,
was made by Ashley himself.*

ornaments, or pearls. I have tried to include as many types of decorative knots as are known. However, I cannot describe every decorative knot; the craft is constantly evolving, and so instead I have attempted to classify decorative knotting by the style of knotting, thereby enabling you to find which style most appeals to your sensibilities. I then provide information concerning the background and construction of some better-known knots of each style. The list of knots is, of course, incomplete because no single book could possibly effectively show all decorative knots that could be made.

There are as many classifications of decorative knots as there are individual knots.

To simplify things, I have classified knots into the following general types:

Flat Knots	Ornamental Knots
Sinnets	Braids & Plaits
Purely Decorative	Covering Knots
Turk's Head	Knob Knots

In the beginning of this book I provide a brief history of knotting. You will also find information about the tools and materials used to craft decorative knots. You may be able to use this information to create your own individual style, and even a few new knots, helping to ensure the continuation of this growing art.

FIG. 684.—Stafford Knot.

FIG. 685.—Wake or Ormonde Knot.

FIG. 686.—Bourchier Knot.

FIG. 687.—Heneage Knot.

Getting Started

KNOTTING TODAY

To some people, decorative knotting is an art, enjoyed for its simplicity or complexity and for the wide variety of textiles, lines, and textures present. For others, decorative knotting is a legacy of folk craft that exists for others to practice, and for all to enjoy. For a third group, decorative knotting is a skill to be mastered and learned, so that the art and craft may be passed on to others. Scientists enjoy the descriptive possibilities that knot topology provides for understanding the universe. Manual therapists like the repetitive motions inherent in tying knots, which may be good therapy for mending minds and bodies. Your interest may be artistic or practical, manual,

⁂ *A square knot that cannot be undone, garnishing the cape on a marble statue of Ferdinando d'e Catolico at the Palacio Real, Madrid, Spain. Note also the tassels.*

or mathematical. There are challenges and opportunities for all in decorative knotting. Above all, decorative knotting is something to be enjoyed, whether in the making, using, admiring, or in passing on to others.

USING
DECORATIVE CORD

Cords come in a variety of types, sizes, materials, and colors. Different types of cords produce one effect; different thicknesses produce another, even in the same knot. The straightforward "over-under" style of weaving cords has many applications, including braids, sinnets, simple mats, rail coverings, and so on. By varying the "over-under" to include more than one crossing, or more than one cord, we start to see the possibilities for an even greater set of choices. By understanding this basic premise, we can then proceed to develop specific shapes in the finished article, producing knob knots, buttons, stars, roses, or more complex mats.

Going beyond the production of articles for practical purposes that have a decorative finish, we then look at ways in which we may create works of knotting that are purely decorative, having no other purpose than to look elegant. Now we explore realms of possibility of cord choice in fabric, color, and texture. We can start to explore some of the knotting used for weddings and other ceremonies. We start to look at haute couture and fashion, where the use of cord is becoming ever more prevalent. Here are some unusual uses of decorative knotting.

WHERE DECORATIVE
KNOTS ARE USED

I have placed decorative knots in the unlikeliest of places, such as on a hiking staff, on a kettle handle, and as a doormat, so nothing would surprise or puzzle me about where to place or how to use a decorative knot. Some decorative knots lie flat, others are round. Some make solid shapes, others exist in ropelike forms, such as braids or sinnets. Decorative knots can cover, they can embellish, they can be a sole decoration, or they can add to a previous decoration. They may be made of humble stuff or made of gold and other precious metals. They may be colorful, stark white, or even the natural color of the plant fiber from which the material or cord was derived. I can no more tell you where to use decorative knots than I can tell you how to dress yourself, but I *can* provide some examples of where others have used them, in order to help stimulate your imagination. Here is one example of a particularly fine piece of knotting:

⚘ *Knot design as a Mandala[1] by Leonardo Da Vinci, recreated in cord by Colin Grundy, IGKT*

⚘ *Trees trained into a latticework known as pleaching, in Barcelona, Spain*

One of the most obvious places to use a decorative knot is on an object hanging around your neck, like a necklace or a key-card lanyard, or suspended as a brooch. Knots may be used as attachments to the ends of pens or as bookmark tabs. Sailors used them to create knife lanyards that were the envy of their shipmates. Key-ring tags made from decorative knotting are something of a craze among knot-tyers—and even non-tyers have started to use them, preferring the hard-to-lose knobby feel of the key-ring tag in their pocket or purse. Wherever decorative knots are used, they heighten the awareness of beauty that exists in even the simplest of objects, so that, literally, "a thing of beauty is a joy forever," (opening line from *Endymion*, by John Keats, 1795 – 1821).

Thinking of fashion and fashion accessories, Hollywood stars are quick to start trends and drop them almost as quickly. Recently stars and starlets have taken to using knots tied in fabric or silken cords around their necks or waists or over their shoulders to emphasize some particular feature or to de-emphasize some particular shape. Among dedicated knot-tyers, the use of decorative knots is somewhat simple – used in picture frames, bell ropes, and horse tack, decorative knots give plenty of rein (pardon my pun!) to the imagination. It is among the decorative knotting artists that the greatest range may be expected, where the mundane is put to exemplary use in creating the best use of space, material, and weave.

---

[1] Mandala . . . . is from the classical Indian language of Sanskrit. Loosely translated it means "circle" & "tis found in all of nature." A Mandala represents wholeness that can be a vision of the world as it extends beyond and into our bodies and minds.

*≈ Butterfly Knot from
the author's own hand
in his personal collection*

*≈ A decorative Rose Knot and a
silk necklace made by the author,
incorporating old Chinese coins*

Materials, Methods, Measurements, and Tools

MATERIALS

Materials! I usually field many questions about materials when I demonstrate knotting. What should I use and where will I find some? Surely they don't still make that, do they? What do I do with it when it is finished? Where should I store it? Does this stretch, shrink, burn, fade, or do anything else in reaction to stressors? What colors, finishes, types, and thicknesses are available? Are there special glues, lacquers, varnishes, or coatings that I should or should not use? These are all typical questions, and are proper for those starting out.

There are many materials one can use to create knots and knotted articles. Artists have used everything from carbon fiber to hempen cord. A few of the more common materials are examined here. These are leather, cord, wire, line, plastic, and natural fibers. You will learn what to use them for and where to get them, how to treat something you've made with them, and any potential problems their use implies.

A word about the construction of cords and lines: Some are known as *laid* cords or line. These are cords made by twisting the original fibers into yarns. Those yarns are subsequently twisted in the opposite direction into strands. Then the strands are twisted together, again in the opposite direction, into lines or cords. The final twist may be described as left laid (known in the trade as S-laid because a left-laid cord's strands appear to follow the stroke of the letter S) or they may be right-laid, which is the most common form (also known as Z-laid). You should note that cords may be simply described on the store shelves as twisted; you should examine this yourself to determine the way in which they were constructed.

When a cord is described as braided, or as "braid on braid" (or even as single or double braid), again this refers to the form of construction. Braided lines and cords are made with twisted fibers that have been paired, tripled, or quadrupled in groups as yarns, after which the yarns are braided

« Manila Z-laid line (right-laid) on left and hemp S-laid line (left-laid) on right »

over and under each other in two directions, one group to the left, and one group to the right. The expression "braid on braid" refers to the fact that a braid lies inside the hollow core of another braided line. A fibrillated cord is made from shorter fibers that have been artificially created out of a normally continuous piece of extruded polymer. A similar description, spun cord, is used for lines made from normally continuous extrusions that have been made into shorter fiber lengths for spinning into cord. Fibrillated and spun cords have a softer feel to the hand

Let's take a look at the types of materials with which you will be making your decorative knotting!

LEATHER

Leather, specifically split leather hide, is one of the oldest cords used for practical

« Single braid on the left in AmSteel Blue UHMWPE and double braid on the right in polypropylene. Notice the over-two under-two structure of the yarns. »

lashings and for decorative work. Leather is the hide of an animal, such as a cow, deer, or kangaroo (serious leatherworkers prefer kangaroo leather, which ranks first in workability and durability). The gauchos of South America and the cowboys of the American West used rawhide instead of the tanned hide to produce some very strong leathers. However, rawhide requires special lacquer or wax finishing to preserve the leather because, if it is water-soaked, it will frequently soften and deteriorate quickly. The thickness of the hide will determine where it is used and how much wear it can take. When tanned, leather is both pliable and strong. It can even be carved, which is a separate subject area and one that we do not cover in this book. After constructing a decorative knot with tanned leather one should treat it with neatsfoot oil for conditioning, and mink oil for waterproofing. Varnish or other hard finishes are usually not appropriate for tanned leatherwork. Seen here are photographs of leather strips in suede, sold in craft stores for beading, but eminently suitable for beginning decorative knotting.

Where to get it:

Here are the names of a few leather craft stores in the USA that stock quality product:

Tandy Leather Stores
LeatherSkills.com
Leather Unlimited
Wylie Leather Works

Each can be found by a web search or searching the Yellow Pages under "leather." If your area does not have a leather supplier you can buy supplies from Internet stores or catalogs. If you are only able to buy from the Internet, be sure that you get a

recommendation from an experienced leatherworker about the quality of the products sold by the supplier you've chosen, and be prepared to accept defects from time to time. Remember, this is a natural fabric. Also note that most general craft stores stock leather lace, a thin ribbon of leather cut from a hide, sometimes as treated tanned leather and sometimes as rawhide.

How does it work?

Leather laces and straps are sliced in a continuous ribbon using a strap-cutting tool that is run around the outer edge of a hide. The width of this ribbon can vary from an eighth of an inch to two inches wide or more.

There are two principal types of leather laces and straps. The first is straight-cut lace, which in cross section is perfectly rectangular. It has no beveled edges. Professional knotters find straight-cut lace more difficult to work with because it can leave unsightly bulges in their work. However, straight-cut lace is cheaper, and also less prone to breaking when pulled through a piece of braiding. This makes it a good choice for beginners to work with. The second type, beveled-edge lace, will break if pulled too eagerly and takes more care in working, although the end result is absolutely marvelous! Using leather requires patience, both in drawing up the work (tightening the strands as they are woven through the piece) and in adapting the piece if some widths and thicknesses are not optimal. The use of beveled edges is essential if you want the piece to look clean, not lumpy and misshapen.

> **Tip:** Be very careful to avoid dirtying long lengths of light-colored lace. If necessary, use white cotton gloves for handling.

What works:

Leather cut in a continuous ribbon is subject to natural thinning in sections, so be aware that sometimes the lace will break when you are partway through a project. Also, because it is a natural fabric and therefore subject to natural blemishes, you should be prepared to cut away sections that don't meet your standards or tastes. When a break happens or cutting becomes necessary in a neat piece of work (as opposed to work that is not intended for close up inspection), you can add a new section by skiving a new length of lace on to the existing piece and then hiding the join under a crossing section. Skiving is a term used to describe the action of paring away two overlapping pieces of leather in opposing slopes, gradually tapering each side of the joint, and then gluing them together so that the overlapped thickness appears not to have changed. Ask your local leather store for a glue to use in skiving. I sometimes use cyanoacrylate glue (CA or Superglue®) and sometimes rubber cement—it just depends on what I am making.

Leather also stretches during the making of a knot, and may show up as an unusually thin section if pulled too hard. To get the best results, be patient and pull leather through by hand using a gentle tugging motion and, when dealing with a small gap, by inserting a lifter or other tool under the strip. Saddle soap is also very useful in easing the tension. Practice with a spare piece if you are at all concerned.

What doesn't:

Leather does not take well to exposure to water unless treated specifically to resist its effects. Leather also does not react well to heat or age. It becomes dry, stiff, and brittle over time. Maintenance is important if you want your piece to last. Use an appropriate finish for the kind of leather you have chosen, whether it is suede, vegetable-tanned, oil-tanned, or has some other special finish or appearance. Leather will stand up to sunlight quite well if it is treated with oil. Suede leathers will fade, however, particularly dye-colored suede skins, and you should be prepared to re-color your piece if the color is important. Remember also that every piece of leather has a "good" side and a less desirable side. The edges of a cut piece of lace will also show up stark white or brown against the piece. Some of this can be colored out; some must be beveled to assure that it does not show.

CORD

Cord, also known as twine or string, refers to all long and flexible fiber-based materials that come in thicknesses (diameter) ranging from fine silk thread up to 3/16 of an inch (5 mm). Be aware that seine twine sometimes has a different scale size than tatting cord which is different again from cotton cord. Cord usually comes in 300-foot lengths or greater wound on spools. It is a very versatile material that can decorate anything from a dress to a ship. Cords are manufactured from both man-made and organic fibers. They may be twisted (also known as laid) or braided, usually in single braid, although there are also some very good double braids and braid-over-parallel cords. Cords come in a wide variety of colors. The cords in the photograph are twisted, colored, hard-laid cotton. You can also purchase cords made from Kevlar, polyester, nylon, or polypropylene.

Where to get it:

Cord may be obtained from most craft stores, art supply houses, chandlers, hardware stores, and fishing supply stores. A few of my favorites are:

Home Depot, Orchard Supply Hardware, Lowe's Hardware, USA
JoAnns Fabrics, USA
Michaels Art and Crafts Supplies, USA

R & W Rope Warehouse of New Bedford, MA, USA

If you have a favorite place, why not drop me a line at www.theknotguy.com and let me know? Cord can also be found at Wal-Mart or at some framing stores. Keep your eyes peeled for special deals on cord, particularly on eBay, or other auction houses. Macramé stores also have some good selections of cord. One of my favorite white cotton cords was supplied by Marty Combs through his Internet site at www.angelfire.com. His business has now been seconded to KnoticalUSA.com (Daniel Noel), who supplies very similar white cotton cord of great quality. Marty also had some spectacular knotting books and useful tools for cords and tying, which may still be available through Daniel's site. When visiting your favorite local chandlery at the marina, ask about their supplies of braided nylon or polyester cord and look for twisted fine lines in boating stores and in fishing, camping, marina, and chandlery outlets. There are many more stores listed in your

clean. Use a very small amount of cleaner on a damp cotton cloth or a clean new sponge. You may have to repeat this process many times, but in the end you will be rewarded with a pristine piece that will look good for many years. You will find more about fabric care later in this chapter.

Cord is hardy and can generally stand some pulling, much more so than leather or

local telephone directory to search through —try them for yourself and enjoy this part of your hobby!

How does it work?

Cord is usually supplied in 300-foot spools, in hanks of about 120 feet, or in 200-foot balls enclosed in plastic wrap. When I find a cord I like, I usually buy more than I need, so that I have some left over for the next project. Some spools that I bought several years ago have not been used yet—I keep spare supplies in a cedar chest so that natural fibers do not get attacked by moths, silverfish, or other pests. I also keep a list of suppliers in a spreadsheet on my computer. This can be very useful if you are selling your work and get an order for a repeat of something you made some time ago.

What works:

White cotton cord is very good at picking up dirt and grease from your hands, so if you want it to remain clean, either clean it after you have finished the piece, using an art gum eraser or a wool washing liquid like Woolite®, or wear white cotton gloves to keep the work

silk. However, keep sharp objects away to avoid snags to the finished surfaces, and be sure that the cord's diameter does not shrink because you were pulling too hard on one section or strand. When tightening a knot, it is essential that you keep the tension even throughout the piece (unless you want a differently tensioned piece). This comes with practice and may take several tries before you are satisfied. A word to the wise—if it looks right on the first try, you should try to remember the tension you applied, because it may not look the same in the second piece you make. If you are making multiple pieces for, say, a picture frame, you will want to lay

S-twist. Left laid is much less common in the USA than in Europe, where these pieces came from. The left-laid is made of Hungarian hemp, which is very good fiber.

WIRE

Stainless steel, copper, aluminum, gold, and silver are all suitable metals for use as

the pieces side-by-side, to check that the tension is even all the way through each piece and that the cord size (thickness) and color matches throughout.

What doesn't:

Cords, particularly laid cords, are apt to twist when pulled too fast, or too often, through a narrow gap. Try using a hollow Swedish fid to make a small gap through which the cord can first be passed. The cords can then be tightened individually using a pricker or some other flat-bladed tool (see the section on tools). As noted above, cord can snag, which may ruin the appearance of a piece. If you get snags in your cordage, try gently twisting or rolling the offending length by hand to put the snag underneath the finished surface after trimming away the snagged fibers. If using laid cord, be sure to twist in the direction of the lay of the line. Lay is the term used to describe the direction in which the cord was twisted when originally made. A finished piece of laid cord will have a surface that has diagonal strands along the length of the cord. See these diagonals in the photographs here. The earlier photographs show right-laid or Z-twist and left-laid or

wire. Normally it is necessary for the wire to be ductile (able to be deformed without losing toughness). After a knot is formed from ductile wire it can be heat-treated and quenched, which hardens it, preventing it from losing its shape. Sometimes a hard metal, such as stainless steel, can be annealed, or softened, so that you can flex it into a shape that holds without too much loss of function.

Where to get it:

Craft stores, marine suppliers, hardware stores, catalogs, Internet.

How does it work?

Wire is made either by drawing or by extrusion. "Drawing" describes the process of taking a rod of metal and physically pulling (drawing) it through a set of dies to make it progressively thinner, until the desired thickness is achieved. As you might imagine, this is a very heat-intensive process and the wire becomes softer for having been drawn in this way. However, after treatment, it is usually much stiffer than regular cord. After

you've cut a length of wire, beware of the sharp edge left on its end. Using a piece of coarse emery paper, fold it in two and grip the end with the paper. Then rotate the wire in the fold of the emery paper, making a temporary bend in the wire to act as a handle if needed—don't use pliers to grip it unless you have a pair with flat surfaces and no teeth, otherwise you may mar the surface of the wire.

> **Tip**: When passing one piece of wire past another in the knot you're building, push rather than pull, so that you can feel your way through.

What works:

Pulling (or pushing) wire with rubber gloves or leather gloves works well, as does using flat-bladed pliers, cutting by working to and fro at a bend, and having sharp cutting nippers. Wire is a material that can be pushed as well as pulled. It does not take well to bending, however. Once bent, a piece of wire will seldom go back to being perfectly straight again.

What doesn't:

Repeated bending puts a permanent crimp in a piece. Scratches in the surface of a piece of wire can very seldom be smoothed away. Colored wire will lose its anodized color surface if you twist it too much. Colored wire has a painted or oxidized surface that may or may not be able to take some rough treatment. If the color of a piece of wire you're using is important, try to treat the wire with kid gloves (literally) so that you do not abrade the surface and so that bent pieces can be gently massaged back into a reasonable shape.

LINE

If cord is a fiber bundle that is less than $3/16$ of an inch thick, line is every other long, fiber-based flexible bundle. This includes rope, braided line, laid line, and more. You can find most lines in marine hardware stores, regular hardware stores, ironmongers, horse and farm animal feed supply houses, and, sometimes, craft stores. There is a terrific variety of lines available, from the hemp shown previously (obtained from Europe) to manila available almost everywhere you look, to jute, sisal, inorganic fibers (such as nylon, polyester, and polypropylene), and more. At left (below) is a photograph of a hank of coir (pronounced *CAW-R*) which is made from the husk of the coconut seed. It is the only natural fiber to float without treatment. The cells are hollow, to help the seed float the world's Southern and Indian Oceans.

The photograph of natural fibers (right, below) is of a hank of raw sisal. Sisal fibers are very white and quite coarse when made into rope. The rope tends to be weak in comparison with manila, but it is much lower in cost.

The horsehair (top left of next page) is taken from a horse's mane and tail. It tends to make soft but prickly braids and is found ready-made principally in South America, although some dealers of horse tack sell horsehair by the pound.

Where to get it:

You can buy hemp line from suppliers such as R & W Rope Warehouse in New Bedford, MA. Manila and sisal lines are available in home supply outlets such as Wal-Mart, Orchard Supply Hardware, or Home Depot. Horse tack dealers and supply stores usually have sisal, manila, cotton, and

horsehair. Inorganic line is available almost everywhere you look, from feed stores to craft suppliers to marine stores—plenty of choices of colors, textures, and thicknesses to be had!

How does it work?

For organic lines, fibers from the living plant are first cut and then rotted in ponds of lye to remove the pith in which the fibers are embedded. After a suitable length of time the fibers are removed from the lye, rinsed, and then dried in the sun. They are

then hackled by being drawn repeatedly in bundles through a series of metal combs and brushes (that use nails instead of rubber teeth) to straighten the fibers and to remove any rubbish, like bark or thick stem growth, that may still be around. The fibers are then spun by being twisted into yarns, the yarns are twisted into strands, and the strands are twisted into ropes or lines. Each twisting is done in the opposite direction to the one previous. The fibers for a piece of right-laid line are twisted to the right to form yarns, these yarns are combined and twisted to the left to form strands, and the strands are combined and twisted to the right to form the finished piece, balanced and ready for use. Cotton line is also made from raw fibers, but the treatment (lye) is not as harsh as it is for the other vegetable fibers and the spinning is done almost entirely by machine.

Inorganic fibers are made by extrusion (pushing out of a hole like toothpaste), pultrusion (pulling out of a hole like toffee), or spun from a melt through a spinneret (like a spider uses to make its silk), and then combined to make the final line. This spinning process is quite fascinating and involves the gyration of opposite twist threads on large spools twisted around each other on a carousel that has many pairs of spools dancing around each other. The process is kept under rigid tension control by computer and produces a very even-thickness line of uniform color, weave, and strength.

What works:

Lines made from natural fibers are attractive and will form a touchable surface. Natural fibers also have ecological benefits and are replaceable by growing new fibers or collecting more horsehair or coir. They also have an attractive odor that is all but impossible to find with inorganic lines. Organic lines are more heat-resistant than inorganic fibers. They may char, however, so do not assume that they resist all heat. Organic fibers also have an attractive color variation throughout that some prefer to the uniformity of color in an inorganic line. Strength is not a consideration in decorative knotting, so most reasons for using inorganic line are reduced when considering this factor. Lastly, organic lines are very inexpensive and usually lighter in weight when compared with inorganic lines. Inorganic lines are very useful if you must occasionally run the item through a wash cycle. Certain inorganic lines will also withstand abrasion quite well, although it is hard to beat the durability of coir rope. Inorganic lines are uniformly colored and may withstand sunlight better than organic lines, although do beware of polypropylene lines—they turn to powder with excessive exposure to sunlight!

What doesn't:

If you're not willing to replace the fibers from time to time, don't put your organic line work where people can touch it. You can coat natural fibers to protect them, but any coatings you use will inevitably change their characteristics. If you wish your work to be preserved, install it behind glass, Perspex®, or some other laminated, clear surface that prevents human contact. Note also that natural fibers will eventually lose their elasticity. They also dry out over time, particularly if the temperature is not controlled carefully. Once dried out they cannot be restored to their former state and must then be protected from further damage. Inorganic fibers can be washed, so the protection needed is not as great. Heat is not a problem for most natural fibers, as long as no flame is involved and the temperature is not high enough to char the fibers. Water, however, will rot the fibers out from the inside if they are not thoroughly dried through. Another element that will damage organic line is sunlight, which will fade colored fibers (note that all colors will fade with time). Manila will turn gray; hemp may yellow; sisal will get more brown, and cotton picks up dirt. The last item to watch for when using natural fibers is shock loading. Natural fibers do not react well to shock loads. However, since most decorative knotters are not concerned with the shock load-bearing capabilities of their pieces, this is less of a concern.

Heat is a very good way of permanently ruining a piece of inorganic line. These lines are technically made of plastic and will not survive high temperatures. Three hundred degrees seems to be the upper limit for most. Inorganic lines will not suffer from rot and so do not need to be kept away from water. However, untreated polypropylene lines require protection from the sun or they will turn to dust. Nylon made into mats will stiffen with time and exposure to sunlight.

PLASTIC

Plastic cord (like Gimp®) is one of the fastest-growing materials used in decorative knotting. The colors are endlessly varied and bright, and the surface is usually shiny, which makes it attractive to children and young people. Plastic cord comes in half-moon, round, flat, rectangular, tubular, and triangular shapes (cross-section).

Where to get it:

Craft stores, catalog sales, Internet supply houses.

How does it work?

Plastic Gimp®, also known as Rex Lace® or by several other trade names, can come in hollow plastic straw, a half-round shape, or round cord. The colors are usually vivid. Most plastic cords are extruded (pushed through a die) and cooled immediately, although some are cast, which makes them harder and more brittle.

What works:

You can fuse two pieces of plastic cord by applying gentle heat, such as with a match or a lighter, if you find yourself in need of extra length. Most pieces made with plastic do not need great lengths of cord. However, it is good to know they can be extended when necessary. Plastic is also washable and will withstand a great deal of wear.

What doesn't:

Plastic may melt if pulled too quickly through a piece of braid, or, of course, if left on a hot surface. If you finish a piece made with plastic cord by applying heat to it, then do not touch the melting plastic

been dipped, so be careful when using it with other materials if you do not want them to be marked with tar. Tar marks may be removed with oils such as olive oil or canola oil or any other 100-percent vegetable oil. Other natural fibers (hemp, manila, sisal, coir, cotton, henequen, and silk) are used frequently in decorative work. Polished hemp twine is particularly sought after because it feels soft, wears well, and is strong enough to resist normal wear and tear. Sisal is quite coarse and may act roughly on skin, but it looks effective when used in a natural setting such as a swing set or in some location where it will be set against bamboo or other natural materials. Sisal is also extremely durable when used as a cat toy or as a covering for cats to clean their claws, instead of using your furniture! Coir is also very rough but has the added benefit of being able to take rough treatment and so is used frequently for doormats and other places where hard-wearing characteristics are needed. Henequen and seagrass are frequently used when making stools or seats—these very good-looking fibers have

with your skin until the plastic has solidified and cooled. Gimp® also has a further slight disadvantage in that it stretches! You have to be very careful to pull on each piece steadily and with the same strength, or you may find some pieces over-extended and others quite distended (fat).

OTHER NATURAL FIBERS

Hemp, manila, cotton, henequen, seagrass, sisal, coir, silk—all are natural fibers that are made into cord and into line. Shown here is a roll of something known as marline, which is made from jute fibers, although most marline used to be made from hemp. Marline is quite strong and was used, tarred, to cover lines onboard old, square-rigged ships to prevent chafe. When marline is twisted tightly around a piece of standing rigging (the shrouds and some stays that hold up the masts) it is called service. Tarred marline will sometimes release the tar in which it has

great, hard-wearing characteristics! Silk is well-known as hard-wearing also (not so good in mats, however!), and in cord form can add bright hues to a favorite dress, jacket, hat, shirt, or fashion accessory.

Where to get it:

Craft stores, specialty stores, builder's stores, agricultural feed stores, horse tack stores, and through catalogs and the Internet.

How does it work?

Natural cord, twine, rope, and line is sold on spools or in balls of about one pound and upward. Hemp twine is also sold in craft stores in small bundles of twenty yards to eighty yards for crafters to use in making jewelry or beading work.

What works:

Natural fibers are at their best when their natural color is used to enhance the appearance of something like a wall-hanging, a purse or shoulder bag, or even a jacket. I have seen natural fibers in many applications, some of the best being outdoors in sunny climates for path control, indoors as a rope handrail, or as a decorative embellishment to a rail or a deck of a ship.

What doesn't:

When natural fibers get wet they start to rot if not dried out effectively. They will also char and burn if exposed to extremes of heat (more than about 400 degrees Fahrenheit). Other care notes are shown above in "line."

METHODS

The question I'm asked most often is "How can I make these beautiful pieces?"

First-time or novice knotters will say, "I have never done it before," or, "You must have so much patience!" when they see finished works by others. Each of us starts at the exact same point—the point of being interested in what you see and wanting to make something like it for yourself. Experienced knotters are not blessed with any superhuman skills or abilities, we simply apply ourselves for the time it takes for us to get bored, tired, or annoyed with what we are doing and then we stop—just like everyone else! It is really not about patience, although having patience does help. It is more a question of determination, doggedness, and whether you want an end result that is perfect, near-perfect, or an interpretation. Do try to remember that this is supposed to be fun. Once it stops being fun, you can stop and come back to it later. The second most popular question is "How long did it take to make that?" This is an important thing to think about when making something for sale, but can be a little insulting when asked of someone who has just spent over forty hours making something for display. If you are making it for yourself or for a demonstration, the question is not quite as important, but for a novice, it is important to know how much time making something takes. Time is a common measure for many people and the question of how long it takes to make something can be translated to "How much time will this take away from something else I want to do?" so that the person asking can relate to what involvement they want to have or whether it is better to have someone else make the piece—maybe you! It also enables the person to place a value on what is being offered—if it takes an expert ten minutes to make something then some people will relate that to what they consider an appropriate hourly rate to be for the craft or art and determine what value they would place on the finished article. Something that took you eighty hours to make may not have the same value for the buyer, because they perhaps do not realize the time it takes to make something like this and they may be unaware of its complexity.

Here are some common terms you should know that appear regularly in this book:

C/C: Counterclockwise.

C/W: Clockwise.

O/U: Over-Under, referring to the working end's movement in relation to the cord it meets.

w-end: Working end—the end that is doing the majority of movement through the knot.

st-end or s-part: Standing end—the part of the cord that does not move when forming the knot.

Bight: Generally a 180-degree bend in a line. However, not all bights are 180 degrees.

Loop: An immediate crossing of one part of a line over itself.

Crossing: Where one line crosses over a different line, or different length of the same line (such as later in a knot's construction).

Knot: Any confusion such as crossings, bights or loops in a piece of line, creating an object or shape.

Strand: A single section of line, cord, fiber, plastic, leather, wire, or other flexible material.

Working Surfaces:

Buy a board with a clip mounted at the top. This will serve as an excellent working surface. Another useful surface is corkboard or very firm fiberboard, to which

you can anchor your work using T-pins. If you have to keep your piece under tension, try setting a temporary clamp or vise on the edge of a table (use cardboard or folded newspaper to protect the table surface), and use that vise to pull against to keep the tension even. You might even try adding a clamp to your belt and then attaching your piece to that clamp so that you can lean a little of your body-weight against it. I use a piece of 18x24-inch fiberboard when I must (most of my pieces I make in hand), which is large enough so that I can just prop it on my lap and lean it against a table with a good light over my shoulder. The chair I use is an upright dining room chair with nothing on it (arms, finials, leg-braces, etc.) to snag the line (VERY important). This type of chair is just comfortable enough for me to sit in for about forty-five minutes before I have to get up and stretch, walk about, and perhaps have a cup of tea before getting back to work. If I am working on a rail or a wheel rim on a boat or anywhere outdoors, I try to make sure I have an umbrella, hat, or some other shade to keep me out of the sun and rain. Whatever you use, make sure it is comfortable and that, no matter how comfortable it is, you get up and stretch at least once an hour.

TOOLS TO USE

A pricker is probably THE most useful tool. It is used to pull line, rope, cord, or twine through your knot work so that the tension on each piece is sufficient to ensure a smooth appearance. It will certainly save your nails from being chipped, cracked, and broken from trying to grip and pull a piece of cord

≈ *Note the thumb on top of the cord and the pricker tip under the cord. The pricker is held by the remaining fingers of the right hand.*

through a tight spot. There are a number of ready-made prickers you can buy. I have several that I use, depending on what I am working on. All of them share a single feature: They are not sharp enough to penetrate the fiber I am working with, unless I really stab at it. The ends have a radiused or tapered point, but it is never sharp. If it were, it would pick up stray fibers and could even snag fibers that then could not be smoothed down again, which could wreck the finished look of the piece. To use a pricker, insert just the tip parallel to the cord you want to pull and then slide the tip under sideways, place your thumb on top of the cord, and, using the rest of your hand to grip the tool, press down with your thumb-tip enough so that you can grip the cord and pull it through. Try not to pull from too far away in the piece; instead, pull directly adjacent to the length that requires your attention. Pulling from too far away can stretch the cord without getting the piece you want in place. Above is a photograph of a pricker in use.

If you are making anything with particularly long cords in it, make the cords up into a bundle (or knittle, as it was once called).

Start with the cord in your sub-dominant hand, palm facing you, with the tip of the cord at the pinky side of your palm. Make a turn up and around your outstretched thumb, counterclockwise if on your left hand, clockwise if on your right hand. Stretch out your pinky finger and wind the cord in the opposite direction around the pinky, making a figure-eight twist across your palm. Keep making figure-eight turns until you have enough cord for the work you are going to do, then finish it off by slipping the coils from your thumb only and putting a Half Hitch around the center of the bundle before taking it off your pinky finger. Add a second Half Hitch in the same direction (making a Clove Hitch) around the center of the bundle. Now, find the end you started with and you can begin the work with that end. As you start to use up the cord, pull out one or two twists of the figure-eight bundle and retighten the Clove Hitch around the middle, to keep the bundle in place. You could use elastic bands if you do not know how to make a Half Hitch, but always start your piece with the end you started on your palm prior to winding around your thumb and pinky. You may even want to add a slip of paper or tape with a number or letter on it under the Clove Hitch or elastic band, to identify which knittle it is for later reference.

The ends of cords can be easily confused with each other, particularly if you are making something with multiple cords of the same color. Wrap the end with a piece of differently colored electrician's tape or, using a piece of drafting tape, add a letter or number to each end of each cord, so that you can tell which one is which. For some cords, tape will not work, so try adding a dab of cyanoacrylate glue (also called CA glue or super-glue) to the end of your cord and allow it to set

« *Final knittle:
Note the
starting thread
is pulled from
the coil turn
by turn with
no hindrance.
Be sure to
tighten the
Clove Hitch
occasionally.*

hard before beginning your work. Color or identification can then be added with a colored pen or marker.

Tip: When passing the end of a cord through a piece, it is sometimes better to insert the doubled end rather than the very tip, so that the tip does not become worn out.

I have one last piece of advice about the ends of cords and lines. Once you have faired your piece and are preparing to apply sizing or a clear finish or to mount it in a shadow-box, you will have at least two ends of which to dispose. Do not simply cut them off. If the piece is such that you can work these ends back in underneath something already tightened and fair, then that is preferable, provided you do it so that the ends cannot be

seen or picked out of place by little fingers. The best way to do this is to make a bight in the end of your cord, and slide a piece of fine doubled wire underneath where you want the cord hidden, starting its travel at the point where you will cut the cord. The wire should be clean and snag-free. Tuck the bight of the end of your cord into the wire loop and pull the wire loop back through, dragging the cord with it. Give a small but firm tug to the cord to stretch it just a little. Then, using the sharpest scissors you have, place the scissors flat on top of the work, blades each side of the cord to be cut, and snip. As the cord relaxes the tension it will suck back under your already tight work (you might even give it a shove). When done properly, this technique will cause your ends to all but disappear. NOTE: This wire method works well when you are making a solid sinnet, braid or globe; it will not work on a flat knot.

Other methods of hiding ends include splicing them into a prior cord, sewing them together with whipping twine, covering them with glue and holding them in place until the glue dries (I find that either a 75/25 mix or a 50/50 mix of white glue and water leaves very little trace on the finished piece and that a hot glue gun can be very helpful), or simply taping them in place. The important thing is to determine what kind of exposure your cord ends will have. If this is to be a doormat, you will want to splice or sew the ends in place. A display piece behind glass may need no more than a piece of tape or some light glue that will not mark the finished cord (be aware that some CA glues will leave a yellow mark on white cord). Also, if you are using an inorganic line, it may be possible to melt the ends back into the other cords. If you can think of a better way or you come up with something that works for you, do write me and let me know [www.theknotguy.com]!

MEASUREMENTS

Another frequently asked question is: "How much line/cord/string do I need to make this?" We have the perfect answer. It depends! For some knots it is possible to provide you with a formula (yes, some mathematics!) that enables you to compute the precise length of cord needed (though most people will pad or increase this number with a bit of extra length). But for most works, the length of the cords you use will be determined by the type of knot you're making

and the style of knotting, as well as the materials from which you wish to construct it.

However, there are some knotting types for which approximate cord length measurements are useful:

Macramé: About three or four times as long as the length you want the finished piece to be, depending on the knots used.

Netting: About twice as long as the finished net, depending on where and how you measure it.

Sinnet: About four times the finished length, depending again on the knots used.

Flat Knots: There are too many patterns here for any general recommendation to be useful.

Following is the best advice I can give you for measuring how much cord you need.

Covering Cylindrical Objects:

When you are covering something with your work, such as a rail or a rod, knot up a sample length of about one inch or so in your chosen cord and style. Mark the beginning and end on the cord used (assuming you have used the appropriate tension), then take it apart and measure how much cord you used. Multiply that length by the length or diameter of the thing you wish to cover. If you used fourteen inches of cord to create one inch of knotting, and your rail is twenty inches long, you will need 280 inches (20x14) for working and coverage. Last, add a foot or so extra to this figure, so that you'll have a bit of breathing room when creating your piece.

Covering Spherical Objects:

When you are covering a ball, wrap the ball with a single piece of cord, using enough turns to completely cover it, then mark the beginning and end of that cord and multiply that length by three. If you are using multiple cords, you will need the total length of all cords to cover the ball completely.

Making Mats:

When you are making a mat, lay your cord in ever-decreasing circles, starting at approximately the outside size of your finished mat, until you reach the center. Measure the total length of all line laid this way, then increase that length by one-third for a loose weave and one half for a tight weave. Last, add a foot to give yourself some working room.

Making Jewelry:

When you are making a piece of decorative jewelry in dozens of pieces, make a test piece using more cord than you think you'll need, then take it apart and measure how much was used, always adding a little extra to work with. If the material you are working with is expensive, such as gold, silver, or some other high-cost material, make a sample using inexpensive cord or wire of the same thickness, then take it apart and use that as your measure.

For all other measures, it is largely up to you to practice and find how much tension you apply, what cord you can consistently get, and whether or not you make the article with severe bends or long slow bends in it! Many cords are also relatively inexpensive on a cost-per-foot basis, so overly long pieces may not matter as much; pieces that are too short, however, are a different matter. Allow plenty!

TOOLS

Here is a list of the tools that I have found useful in making knotted pieces:

Shears, the sharper the better
Sharp scissors in various sizes
Tape (drafting tape is best)
T-pins made of stainless steel
Squared pin-board used for macramé
Marlinespike, not essential but helpful
A hollow, steel fid
Flat-bladed and needle-nosed pliers
Medical forceps or hemostats
A small butane torch or lighter
CA glue, refrigerated
Clamps in assorted sizes
A vise that fits a table edge
Paper, pencil, and eraser, for drawing
This book!

Here are some photographs to help you to see what I use—your collection may include all sorts of different items and I would be very interested to hear what you use.

The first is a marlinespike, with a lanyard attached—not very decorative, but very practical! Notice that it has a slightly bent

tip, which is useful as a lever when pulling cords through a piece of tight decorative stuff. Put your thumb on the cord, with the tip of the tool underneath, and then press down on the cord to grip it against the tool. The same technique can be used with the pricker, shown earlier.

This next tool is a pusher, commonly sold with a Samson® double-braid splicing kit. Basically, it is a stiff wire rod, which can be used to make a small hole under some previously tightened cords, that is large

found them to be invaluable for all kinds of cord and they are a staple of my personal toolbox. The orange clip in the center holds the spring-action scissors closed, so that you won't cut your fingers accidentally.

The Swedish fid, or hollow fid, is a vital tool in my toolbox, useful for any time when I want to make a hollow space to insert a cord. A word to the wise: Don't ever use the tip of this tool as a lever unless you want a bent tip! For some work you can use a drinking straw or a pen tube as a hollow fid. However, note

enough to pass a subsequent cord through. This is not the most used tool in my box, but it's helpful just the same!

The third tool in the list is a pair of very sharp, spring-action scissors, which are sold at fabric stores and normally used for sewing. These can be used to cut thin cord very close to the place where you want it to end. I have

that the hollow fid sold by rope companies for splicing hollow braid is not the same thing as this hollow Swedish fid. Their fid actually has a closed body and a hollow end.

The pricker of which I spoke earlier is photographed here. It is one of my particular favorites, not only for its shape, but also for the weight distribution in my hand, which helps to balance the tool when in use, and the helpful tip, which slides so easily under cords. You can also use a flat-bladed screwdriver as a pricker (you don't have to buy everything especially for this hobby!).

The next essential tool is a pair of shears. This particular pair is made in Germany and has very sharp blades and a short blade length in comparison to the handle, for best leverage.

When you have finished your piece you will have to sew the ends of the cord or glue them out of sight. If you are sewing, these needles are made by Smith of England and are perfect for those small jobs requiring a stiff needle that will pass readily through rope, cord, or sail cloth. The cross-section of the needles is triangular, so they are not as greatly impeded by passing through whatever

you are sewing. They are, of course, larger in size than the regular sewing needles, so they can be used for jobs requiring a little stiffness and leverage.

The next object, masking tape, is not often thought of as a tool, but it is exceedingly useful when you want to apply a temporary whipping to the end of a cord, when you want to stiffen a cord for passing it through a

piece, or when you need to use a permanent marker to identify which of several cords you are using. Masking tape holds well temporarily and can be pulled off and discarded after it is no longer useful, or when you have finished your piece. Don't leave it in place for too long or it will leave a nasty adhesive residue behind!

This is polyester whipping twine. I use a waxed polyester twine, which is very strong and available in multiple colors, for whipping

the end of my cords and for constrictor knots to hold sections of cords in place.

The next tool is a wooden fid, a tapered tool used to part strands when making splices in three-strand or four-strand fiber lines. It is also very useful when you want to make a small space in a decorative knot through which to pass a piece of cord.

These round-nose and chain-nose pliers are useful tools for working in wire. Their side cutters can clip lengths of wire, and the pliers can be used with both wire and cord because they do not have teeth that will mark either material. You may have to twist cord around

round-nosed pliers because it is easier to pull that way. The chain-nose pliers are very helpful when it comes to using finer cords or for use with trimmings to embellish your knot-work.

A good pair of hemostats is essential if you want to pull a cord through a small gap. The hemostats shown are a great pair, made in stainless steel, and can be locked in the closed position while gripping an end or a bight of cord.

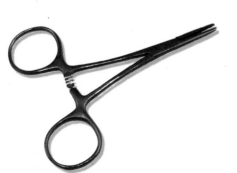

Flat Knots

F lat knots are just what they sound like—flat. They are made in two dimensions and come in round, square, or other geometric plane figures. Cruciform (cross-shaped) knots are covered in Chapter 11, but all other flat knots are in this chapter. Flat knots of course are not really flat—they are made so that there is only one intended depth, that of the crossing of one line over another.

ROUND-SHAPED FLAT KNOTS

One of the first round flat knots to try is a mat using one variety of the Turk's Head Knot. Turk's Head Knots are described by the number

CHAPTER

3

of bights around the perimeter, the number of leads or crossings they make from the outside toward the center, and the number of times the original length of cord is doubled, tripled, or doubled again! The following instructions describe how to make a Turk's Head Knot of seven bights and six leads. This means there are seven bights or "bumps" around the perimeter and six parts crossing each other around the inside of the knot. The leads are

ROUND TURK'S HEAD FLAT MAT

« **STAGE 1** – In the center of your cord, make a counter-clockwise turn over (a loop), forming bight #1.

» **STAGE 2** – Pass the working end under and then over the loop, then under the upper limb. You have now completed bight #2.

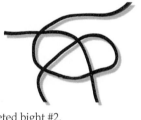

⌃ **STAGE 4** – Notice the cord pulled tighter to the center and then continuing under, over, under, over, under, over to the right side of the mat, forming bight #4 at the upper left position.

⌃ **STAGE 3** – Continue c/c under, over, over, under bights #2 and #1. This will form bight #3 on the outer left side here. Note how these bights take shape in a clockwise direction. Take care to pull the cord toward the center so that the center bights are formed at the same time.

⌃ **STAGE 5** – To form bight #5, pass through bight #4 under, over, under, over to the center, then over, under, over, under to the lower right, and pull through carefully.

the pieces that make up the crossings from outside to inside. The leads may be doubled, as they are here, or they can be tripled, or doubled and doubled again—whatever fits the size of cord you are using. More bights would result in a greater roundness, but would also cause there to be more bights on the inside, making the knot somewhat more open in the center for a flat mat (many bights in the center results in a crowded and bulky center).

» **STAGE 6** – From bight #5 there are three "ladders'—distinct sections of the knot that, when identified, help simplify these directions. For the first ladder, go under bight #5, then over, under, over, under, over.

≈ *Here we show the finished shape, with ends still not hidden (see top center) and with all passes doubled. Dress or fair the passes to make them even and there you have it! For a slightly different appearance, make an over-two, under-two Spanish Ring Flat Mat, a form of Turk's Head mat, by following the pattern in the photograph:* ≈

« **STAGE 7** – Pass the second ladder under, over, under, over to complete bight #6.

» **STAGE 8** – Add the final bight #7 and pass the third ladder, under, over, under, over to rejoin the start cord.

This round flat mat, using the Turk's Head pattern, took fifteen feet of ¼-inch cord and ended up being quite tight and about six inches across, just to give you some idea of scale. Take a look at other Turk's Head Knots throughout the book, particularly in Chapter 9, where Turk's Head Knots are also made cylindrically instead of flat.

Thump Mat

This round mat is seen in Ashley's Book of Knots, number 2360, which he refers to as a thump mat. It is used on ships, with blocks through which lines are passed to change the direction of the line, fastened near the deck. It is made as a mat around a deck fitting in such a way that the block may "thump" against the mat instead of thumping the deck, which could mark and/or damage deck and block both. One of the features about its style that I like is that it forms a pleasing round mat but has half the number of bights in the center that one would see in a Turk's Head flat mat of the same size. The Turk's Head mat would have the same number of outside bights as inside bights. The thump mat uses a less lumpy center, which makes it ideal for coasters or other uses in which you need outer ring support.

« Stage 3 – bringing it over itself to complete a second round turn, and then make one tuck under the bottom of the original turn.

Stage 4 – Pass the working end over, over, under to upper right. **»**

Stage 1 – Start with a clockwise overhand round turn. **»**

« Stage 2 – Bring the working end over the round turn, c/w . . .

⌐ Stage 5 – Then move up the ladder over, under, over, under, over, under to rejoin the standing end.

Here is the completed thump mat, where you can see the small triangular crossing in the center and the six bights arranged neatly around the perimeter. The ends are not finished, just whipped and tucked underneath. These other coasters are examples of finished works: »

« Coasters made from two-colored polypropylene cords— outstanding!

DECORATIVE ROUND MAT

The next variety of round flat knot to try is one of these. The style is that of the thump mat, but with added Half Hitches, which are also used elsewhere in making mats, to add a touch of interior interest—a good technique that can readily be applied for many shapes of mat. The pattern here appears at first to be complex, and yet, if you study it closely you will observe that it is similar to the thump mat, though amended to include an additional interior twisted loop. The thump mat contains twice as many bights to the outer rim as it does to the interior rim. In the case of the above mat, however, the number of exterior bights is four times as many as those of the interior (24 outer bights and six inner bights), because of that extra interior loop. Copy the blank pattern to a sheet matching the size you want your mat to be. Try using T-pins to pin the line down to a board as you proceed, as shown below.

STAGE 1 – Start your line in the middle and work both ways, one strand to each loop, making one outside loop and one inside. »

≈ STAGE 2 – Following the pattern, continue to make another exterior loop and form the first interior pass.

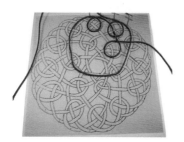

STAGE 3 – Add two more interior passes »

≈ STAGE 4 – Then add two more inside loops, bringing the inside loop total so far to four, with six outside loops.

Stage 5 – With two more interior passes and two more outside loops, we near the end of the first passes. »

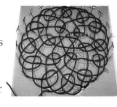

» Stage 7 – The last of the outer loops and one interior pass bring us to the first round of our final shape, ready now for doubling or tripling.

« Stage 6 – Now we add two more interior loops and we are ready to finish the last interior pass.

« The completed pattern in cord, doubled and with the ends hidden underneath.

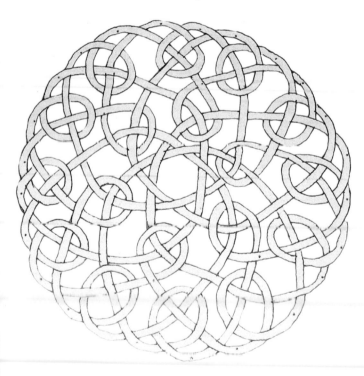

« The pattern without cord, showing overs and unders. The dots are from sticking T-pins through the line!

SQUARE-SHAPED FLAT KNOTS

SQUARE MAT

The square flat knots are really a category unto themselves. Square is a relative term in knotting, as these knots" shapes are usually only approximately square when made with one cord. When made with two cords they are squarer. Square Turk's Head Knots are those that have one less or one more part than bights. So Turk's Head Knots with five parts and four bights as well as those with four parts and five bights are both "square." (See Chapter 9 on Turk's Head Knots for more explanation of the terms used here if you need it). A true square knot is not possible as a Turk's Head Flat Knot because Turk's Head Knots are made with only one cord. The loops and turns for true square knots require more than one cord, just as you will see in Celtic

Knots, which are designed more for carving or for calligraphy. Here is a Celtic Knot design of a single cord, as well as a square knot requiring two cords, from Aidan Meehan's book *Celtic Design: Knotwork*, which book and designs I find intriguing:

 ≈ *A square knot of two cords, again from Aidan Meehan's book.*

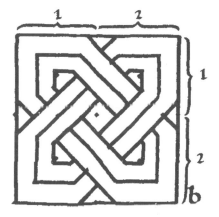

To make a square knot mat you should first determine how many bights or bumps you want on each of the knot's sides. You'll also need to identify the number of passes you want to make. Note that in square knot mats made from a single cord, both ends of your cord will finish in the same place, so you can easily double your mat using the same cord. (Some of the mats presented in the oval and "other shapes" sections can only be made with one pass of a single cord because the ends finish in different places on the mat, effectively preventing a follow-around to make a doubling. Doubling these mats requires adding a second cord.)

 ≈ *16 spiral knots, from Aidan Meehan's book*

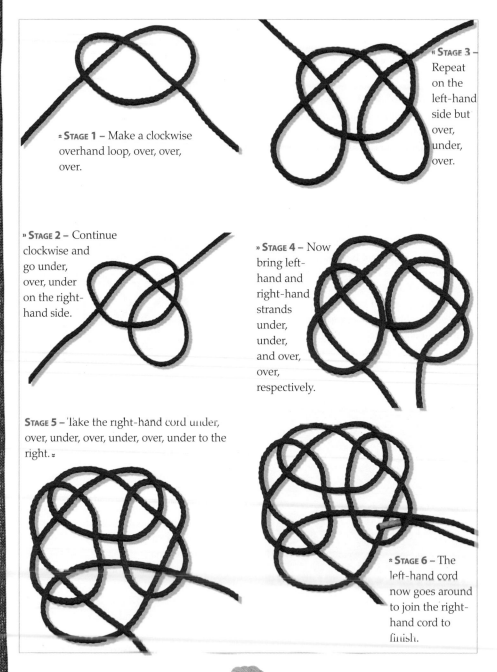

⩓ **STAGE 1** – Make a clockwise overhand loop, over, over, over.

« **STAGE 3** – Repeat on the left-hand side but over, under, over.

» **STAGE 2** – Continue clockwise and go under, over, under on the right-hand side.

» **STAGE 4** – Now bring left-hand and right-hand strands under, under, and over, over, respectively.

STAGE 5 – Take the right-hand cord under, over, under, over, under, over, under to the right. ⩔

⩓ **STAGE 6** – The left-hand cord now goes around to join the right-hand cord to finish.

The finished square mat knot, with four passes

(Near) Square Mat

This next shape is also somewhat square, but has one less bight on the top edge than the side edges. The formation is a little different, but, as a series of bights and loops across and back, it makes for a rectangular pattern that is quite pleasing to the eye. Have fun with it and perhaps expand it by adding one or two more bights to each side.

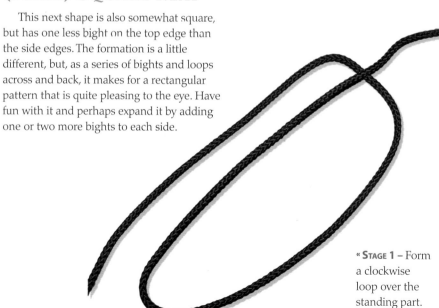

« Stage 1 – Form a clockwise loop over the standing part.

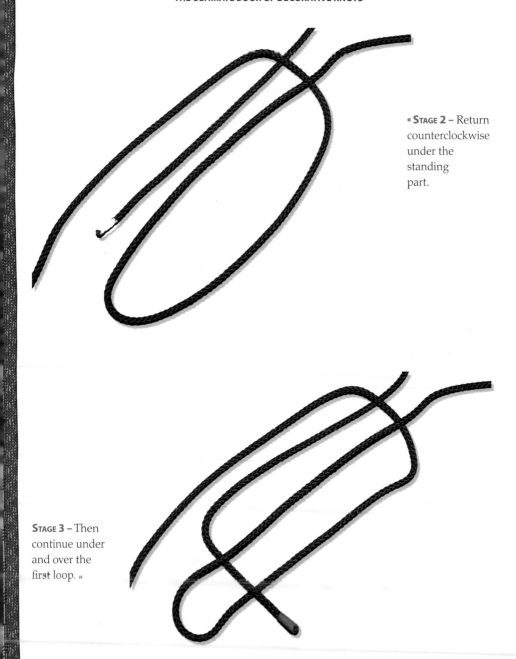

« Stage 2 – Return counterclockwise under the standing part.

Stage 3 – Then continue under and over the first loop. **»**

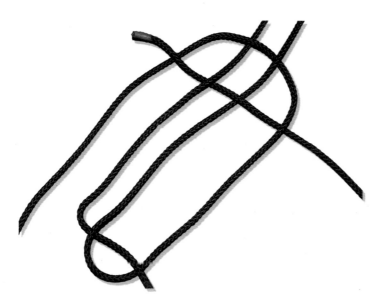

« Stage 4 – Then make a 180-degree turn and pass under, over, under, over.

Stage 5 – Continue c/cw under, over, under, over, under. »

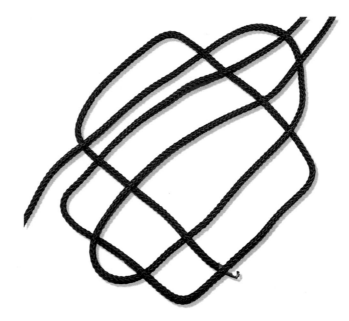

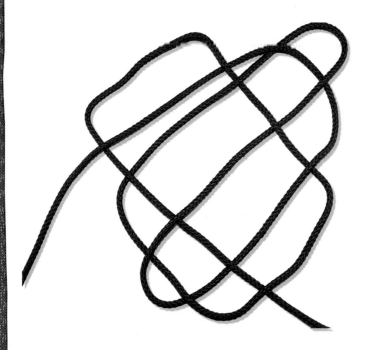

« **Stage 6** – Square up the knot a little to maintain the shape . . .

Stage 7 – and then take the other end under, over, under, over . . . »

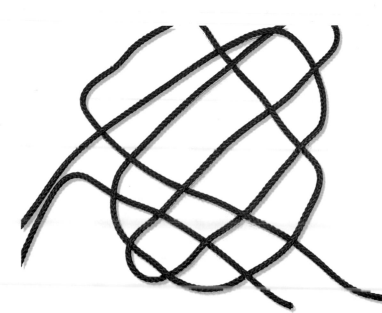

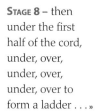

Stage 8 – then under the first half of the cord, under, over, under, over, under, over to form a ladder . . . »

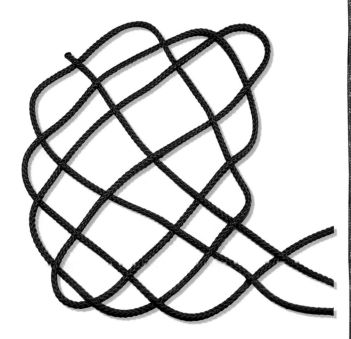

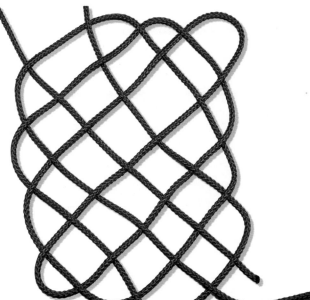

" **Stage 9** – returning down the ladder, u, o, u, o, u, o, u to meet the other end . . .

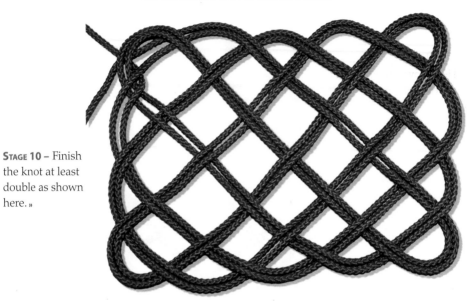

STAGE 10 – Finish the knot at least double as shown here. »

« Finish the mat with triple or more passes, being sure to even out the bights to each side.

OTHER SHAPES

Other shapes, naturally, include anything not strictly round or square. Hence, oval, long rectangle, triangular, and more. Try these shapes and see which you like best!

OVAL MAT

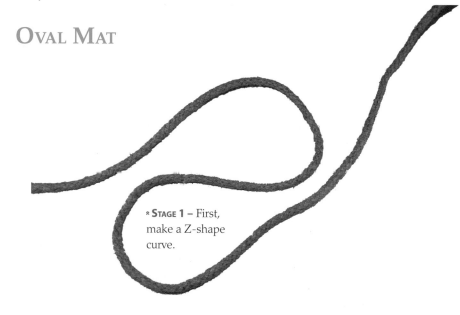

⌃ **STAGE 1** – First, make a Z-shape curve.

» **STAGE 2** – Close the top of the Z and move the loop this makes over the tail of the bottom of the Z.

41

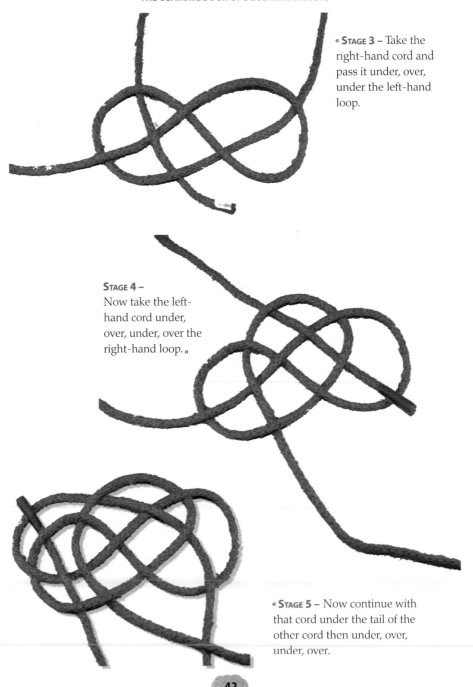

« **STAGE 3** – Take the right-hand cord and pass it under, over, under the left-hand loop.

STAGE 4 – Now take the left-hand cord under, over, under, over the right-hand loop. »

« **STAGE 5** – Now continue with that cord under the tail of the other cord then under, over, under, over.

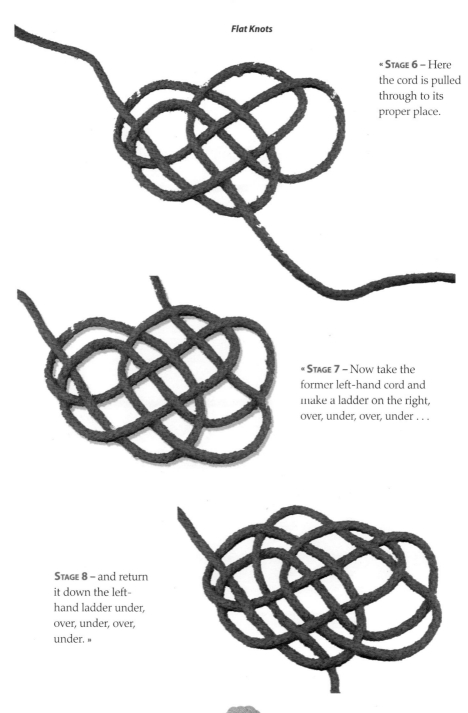

« **STAGE 6** – Here the cord is pulled through to its proper place.

« **STAGE 7** – Now take the former left-hand cord and make a ladder on the right, over, under, over, under . . .

STAGE 8 – and return it down the left-hand ladder under, over, under, over, under. »

Stage 9 – Take the remaining cord under, over, down the newly formed right-hand ladder. »

The finished oval mat, doubled for a more open look. You may decide to triple it to close all the small gaps.

LONG RECTANGULAR MATS

The two mats that follow are, respectively, an Ocean Plait Mat and a Prolong Mat. Note that the Prolong Mat has a different start than the Ocean Plait, and yet adds only two bights to the outer edge. Try making one with two more bights added to each side and see what happens!

STAGE 1 – Tie a LH Overhand Knot in the middle of the cord. »

« **STAGE 2** – Extend the two lowest crossings to make two bights about as long as the desired length of mat.

« **STAGE 3** – Twist both bights a half turn each to the left. If you tied an RH overhand to start, turn each bight a half turn to the right (and reverse the handedness of the following directions).

STAGE 4 – Slide the left-hand bight over the right-hand. »

« **STAGE 5** – Weave the
LH cord over, under,
under, over to trap the
lower bight . . .

STAGE 6 – then
weave the RH
cord under, over,
under, over, under
to finish at the
bottom bight. »

« **STAGE 7** – Bring the
other cord around
to follow it back up
through the whole mat
to finish.

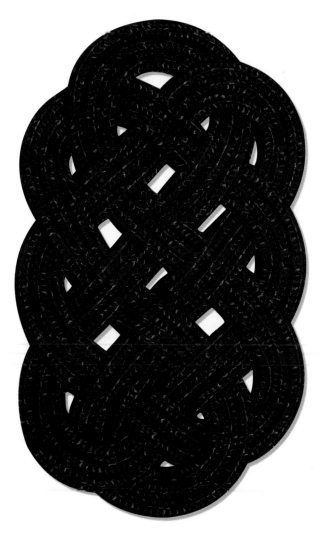

* *The finished Ocean Plait Mat, tripled and with eight bights around the perimeter*

Note that if you extend the original bights in Stage 3, then twist each of the lower loops immediately after completing Stage 6 and re-cross them and thread the ends of the cords through (as you did in Stages 4, 5, and 6), you can increase the number of bights around the perimeter of an Ocean Plait Mat from eight to twelve, producing a longer mat.

PROLONG MAT

The Prolong Mat is a similar mat to the Ocean Plait, but has at least ten bights along the perimeter. Here is the sequence for this rather longer-length mat, which may be expanded in the same manner as the Ocean Plait by adding another twist to each of the loops before feeding the ends through.

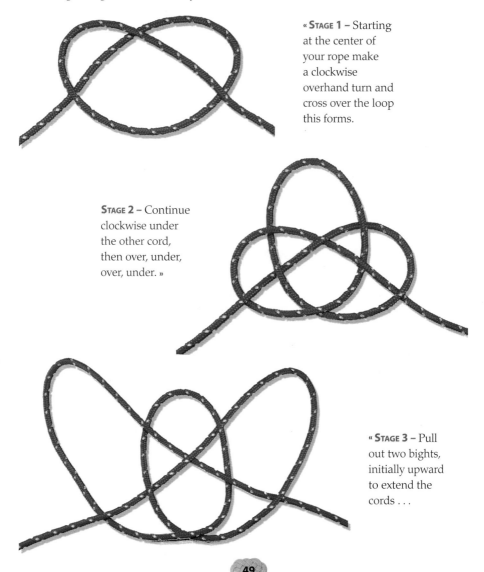

« **STAGE 1** – Starting at the center of your rope make a clockwise overhand turn and cross over the loop this forms.

STAGE 2 – Continue clockwise under the other cord, then over, under, over, under. »

« **STAGE 3** – Pull out two bights, initially upward to extend the cords . . .

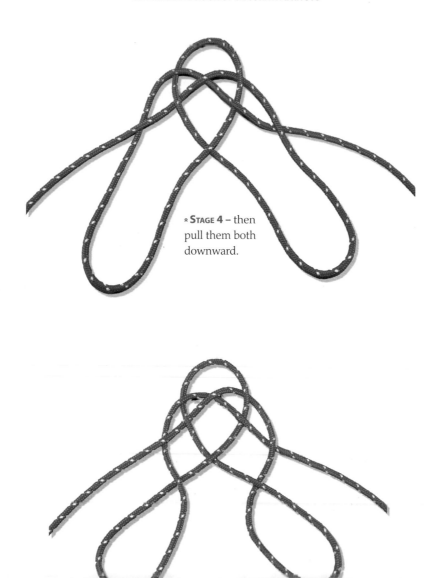

⋩ **STAGE 4** – then pull them both downward.

⋩ **STAGE 5** – Flip the RH and LH loops over to the right, to form a clockwise underhand turn.

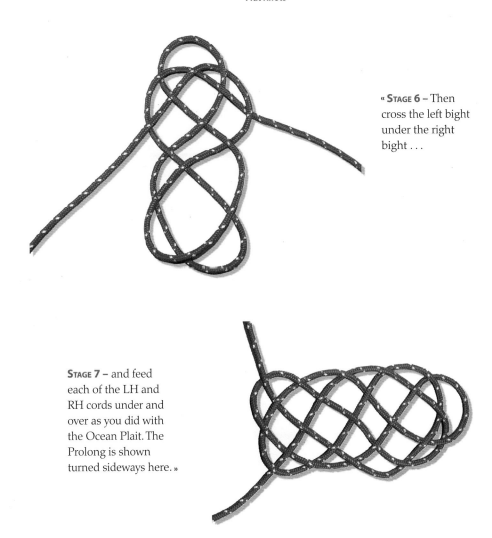

« **STAGE 6** – Then cross the left bight under the right bight . . .

STAGE 7 – and feed each of the LH and RH cords under and over as you did with the Ocean Plait. The Prolong is shown turned sideways here. »

Fair up the bights, make the other passes as desired (tripled cords here) and complete the knot by sewing, gluing, or splicing the ends together underneath. Adjust to finish.

A friend of mine recently announced that he had made a mat according to the instructions in a book. He very proudly showed me the result of his labors, shown in the photograph on page 53 as shown to me.

≈ *A Prolong Mat of ten bights*

≈ *A Prolong Mat of
sixteen bights*

I pointed out that this was the first and only example of a nine-bight flat mat I had seen made in this form (there are other forms of nine-bight mats)—it turned out that he had made a small adjustment when following the instructions for an Ocean Plait Mat and ended up "inventing" a new mat! It is a most unusual and eye-catching piece and I asked that he not change it—it makes a wonderful addition to the lexicon of decorative knotting. Maybe you also will "invent" a unique piece, whether by accident or deliberate action!

KRINGLE (CRINGLE) MAT

Next, we turn to the Cringle mat—a favorite of Nordic regions and Nordic people it seems. The Cringle mat was not named after Kris Kringle, but because the loops with which it is made bear some loose resemblance to the Danish cringle, a rather tasty pastry filled with cream cheese or jam. In Germany the word for a cross-knot or cross-hitch mat loosely translates to kringle, probably because of its resemblance to the pretzel knot, which in turn resembles the Danish kringle that was brought to Denmark by Roman Catholic priests in the thirteenth century. It is made with a series of interlocking clockwise overhand loops (note that the example shown is developed counter-clockwise, just for fun). This Kringle mat has only six inside bights and twelve outer bights. However, you could make this mat with as few as two to as many bights as you like. This is a handsome mat, particularly when tied in manila or sisal to work as a welcome mat at your front door or in cotton as a trivet under a hot dish at the table.

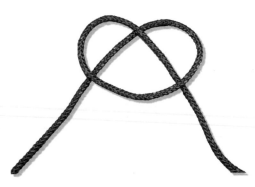

« STAGE 1 – Form a counterclockwise overhand loop and lay it over the working part of the line (in this case the left-hand end). Note how the standing part (the right end) is now temporarily tucked under, and will remain so until Stage 9.

STAGE 2 – Continue counterclockwise with the working end over, under, over . . . »

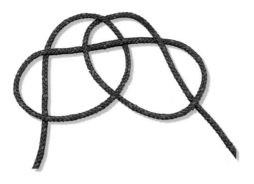

« STAGE 3 – and pull through the rest of the line, forming a pass under the loop this forms . . .

STAGE 4 – and then again over, under, over this second loop . . . »

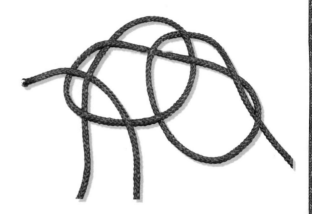

« STAGE 5 – Pull the line through again and put the working part under the third loop.

« **Stage 6** – Repeat Stage 4, but with the third loop, over, under, over again.

Stage 7 – Pull through the line and put the working end under the fourth loop. »

« **Stage 8** – Repeat Stage 4, but with the fourth loop.

« STAGE 9 – Make the fifth loop, pulling all the working-end line through and tucking it under this loop. Remove the tucked portion of the standing line from Stage 1.

STAGE 10 – Cross the standing part over the right half of the first loop . . . »

« STAGE 11 – then tuck the working part under, over, under the first loop, making the sixth loop.

STAGE 12 –Finally, tuck the working part over, under, over the fifth loop to complete the sixth loop—voila! Start doubling or tripling the line around the mat from this point around the whole mat by following this pattern. »

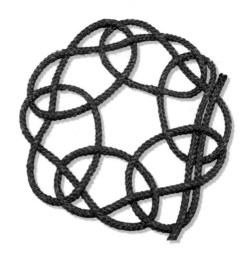

» *The finished Cringle mat, doubled, and the ends sealed under*

HALF-HITCH MATS

Next we look at the Half Hitch Style Mat. This style of mat uses Half Hitches in succession to form a very handsome interweave. The mat may be called something different, depending on who made it. Because I work based on structure, I call the series Half Hitch Mats, because they have clear Half Hitches to start each one, each interlinked with its preceding and succeeding Half-Hitch, and overlapping in the center of the mat. Look at the stages where I describe this below. For the superstitious among you, the largest mat shown here has thirteen bights around the edge, so take care! We start with a single Half Hitch Mat, which has five bights to the edge.

Single Half-Hitch Mat

↗ **STAGE 1** – Form an overhand clockwise loop . . .

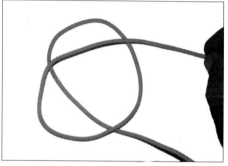

↗ **STAGE 2** – Bring the working end over the loop clockwise . . .

STAGE 3 – continue clockwise over, over, under. ↘

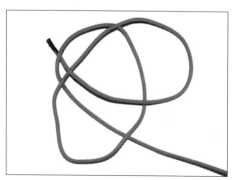

STAGE 4 – Now reverse and go counterclockwise over, under, over, under, over to the start. ↘

Here is the Single, Hitch Mat, tripled. »

Two Half-Hitch Mat

Next, we move to a Half Hitch Mat with two Half Hitches and find we have seven bights to the perimeter—one more Half Hitch equals two more bights. Take particular note of the pattern in the center of the knot—a square or four-sided series of passes of the line with a triangular-shaped series of passes to the upper left and the lower right. Keep this in mind when studying the patterns for the other Half Hitch Mats.

« **STAGE 1** – Form two underhand counterclockwise loops, place the second (RH) on top of the first (LH).

STAGE 2 – Bring the working end counterclockwise under, over, over, under. ⸕

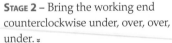

⸕ **STAGE 3** – Reverse to clockwise and bring the working end under, over, over, under, over, under.

« STAGE 4 – Here the line is pulled through to show the shape so far.

≈ STAGE 5 – Reverse the working end to counterclockwise, going over, under, over, under, over, under to finish, and then continue counterclockwise to double or triple the line.

≈ STAGE 6 – The shapes in the center are highlighted in red.

The next in this series of hitch mats, the Two-Hitch Mat, again tripled »

The third mat in the series is made with three Half Hitches, again using the same idea of placing the Half Hitches over each other to start and then traveling clockwise, counterclockwise, then clockwise to finish. Do be careful of the center—sometimes it takes a little practice to get the pattern just right here. Again, increasing the Half Hitches by one and the bights by two, we now get three Half Hitches and nine bights. Based on your observation from the previous mat, do you now see a square with a triangle to the top and one to the bottom of the center? The oval mat and this Triple-Hitch Mat have some similarities that may now be apparent to you in making the knot by building structures. Finish the mat by sewing or gluing the ends as described in Chapter 2.

Three Half-Hitch Mat

⌃ **STAGE 1** – Form three counterclockwise underhand loops, then tuck the far right-hand loop's left edge under the far left-hand loop's right edge . . .

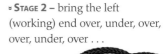

⌄ **STAGE 2** – bring the left (working) end over, under, over, over, under, over . . .

⌃ **STAGE 3** – then pull the cord through like this.

⌄ **STAGE 4** – Now reverse to go over, under, over, over, under, over, under, over.

▲ STAGE 5 – Pull that loop through like this.

▲ STAGE 6 – Now, counterclockwise, pass under and then over four times from the top left to the last loop formed and pull through. Double, then double again if you desire.

« STAGE 7 – The noted square and two triangles—did you see them?

The finished Three-Hitch mat, tripled or doubled and doubled again. Handsome, isn't it? »

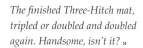

FOUR HALF-HITCH MAT

Now for a mat of four Half Hitches. Reviewing the patterns above you can see that for every Half Hitch after the first we add two bights to the perimeter. We started with a Single-Hitch Mat, which has five bights around the perimeter. The Two-Hitch Mat had a total of seven bights around the outside. The Three-Hitch Mat had nine outer bights. This means that our Four-Hitch Mat should have eleven bights on its perimeter. Again, take note of the two triangular-shaped crossings and the square crossing between them, just as for the Two-Half-Hitch Mat.

« **STAGE 1** – Form three Half Hitches counterclockwise and underhand and tuck the left edge of the far right loop beneath the right edge of the far left loop, as in Stage 1 of the Three Half-Hitch Mat . . .

STAGE 2 – form a fourth Half Hitch, again counterclockwise and underhand, and pass the loop over, under, over . . . »

« STAGE 3 – pass the left cord over, under, over, under to make a turned-back clockwise loop . . .

STAGE 4 – then pass it under, over, under, over, aiming down and to the right . . . »

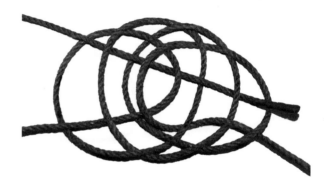

« STAGE 5 – turn back on itself c/c and pass over, under, over, under . . .

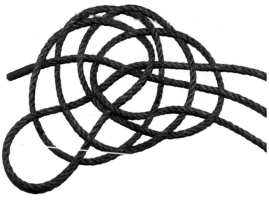

« **Stage 6** – cross under itself, then pass over, under, over, under . . .

Stage 7 –turn back on itself again and go counterclockwise, splitting the ladder over, under, over, under, over through the center of the first turned-back loop (from Stage 3). »

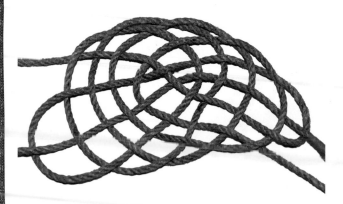

« **Stage 8** – Finally pass under, over, under, over, under, over to finish up where the right cord started . . .

STAGE 9 – pulling through and then fairing the knot to the desired shape (here, left ovate) until ready for doubling. »

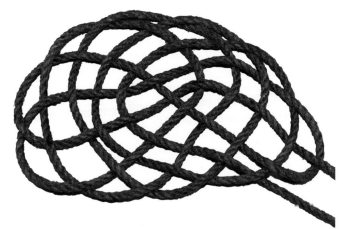

⚹ *The completed mat, made with three passes*

There is a square crossing pattern in the center, as you can see—but wait, there's more! Notice how ovate or egg-shaped the mat is? This is because there are more parts on each end of the mat than there are parts along each side of the knot. Count them to check for yourself. These uneven parts can be smoothed out by more purposeful fairing or dressing, just like we have done with the Five Half Hitch Mat below. The eleven bights should be faired up to make them even in shape and make a more rounded shape of

the mat overall, although, of course, there is nothing wrong with an ovate mat, as long as that is what you want!

Five Half-Hitch Mat

The last of the mats shown here is the Five Half-Hitch Mat. You have seen the pattern of development from one to four Half-Hitches and the corresponding increase in the number of perimeter bights from five to eleven. This last mat gives you thirteen outer bights. Maybe you would like to try for fifteen

bights, or perhaps even more? The mat shape is good and deserves added colors or added bights, or both, just to show off!

Here is the last of the Half-Hitch Mats included in this book, in its finished form. Do you see the pentagon in the center, with two triangular-shaped crossings above and one below? The next in the series will have fifteen bights and begin with six Half Hitches—give it a try!

The same mat with an added color between, just for fun—try it, you may like it!

Braids and Plaits

Braids, plaits, and sinnets—what's the difference, if there is one? This chapter is my attempt to distinguish between the terms (although we cover sinnet in another later chapter). Some very eminent and sensible people have tried to make sense of these differences before, but there does not appear to be a consensus. We will explore their thoughts further below. Still, whatever the terminology, braiding and plaiting are wonderful arts that bring beautiful cords together. The braids and plaits illustrated in this book include:

Braids

Three through eight strand, and others.

Plaits

Four through six strand, and others.

In addition, we look at how to make and use looped braids, sometimes (at risk of raising more confusion) referred to as loop sinnets.

Let's start by looking at the differences and similarities between braids, plaits, and sinnets. First some definitions (and guesses?) from past and current experts such as G. Budworth, C.W. Ashley, R. Graumont, J. Hensel, H.G. Smith, C.L. Day and the OED:

Geoffrey Budworth, author of several prominent knotting books, states "Captain John Smith (1626) called plaits "sinnets." So did Manwayring (1644), Blanckley (1750), and Dana (1841), with Ashley following suit (1944). Falconer (1769) insisted upon the alternative spelling "sennit'. And both of these maritime terms are still in use today."

Clifford Ashley says, "The word braid appears to have been applied almost exclusively to Flat Sinnets." He goes on to describe how "the word plat or plait, besides meaning braid, also means a fold in cloth. It is often spelled pleat, but is always pronounced plat at sea. Sailors use the word when platting a mat."

Graumont & Hensel, authors of the *Encyclopedia of Knots and Fancy Rope Work*, state that Plait is the "same as braid and plat."

Hervey Garrett Smith, author of *The Marlinespike Sailor*, first published in 1956, does not address any difference that may exist between the two.

Cyrus Day, author of *Knots and Splices*, speaks in his book of the term "plaited rope,"

referring to eight-strand lay, and "braided rope," and referring to the fact that it has a greater number of yarns instead of the eight-strand construction of plaited rope.

The Compact Oxford English Dictionary (OED) refers to the origin of the word plait as having come in written form from about 1440: "*Promptorium parvulorum sive clericorium, lexicon*" being their quoted source. Also, "A contexture of three or more interlaced strands of hair, ribbon, straw or any cord-like substance."

The OED also describes a braid as "anything plaited, interwoven or entwined," which indicates the possibility of it having been formed from a single strand or perhaps two strands. They, too, refer to Captain Smith's Seaman's Grammar (1627) directing the seaman to "brade up close all them sailes."

I got no further ahead with examining this set of similarities, so I set about trying to define braids, plaits, and sinnets based on differences in common usage. When I hear others speak of braiding or forming a braid, it is with respect to a person's hair. Hair braiding may be performed with three or more strands of the hair caught up in bundles, perhaps being twisted as it is formed. When I hear people talk of plaits they mostly refer to three-strand intertwining and not more, and maintaining a flat structure to the individual strands or bundles of hair as well as a flat structure to the finished product. Almost nobody I know speaks of sinnet or sennit, because they do not know the term, or have only heard it in reference to sailor's work and cannot define it differently than braiding or plaiting. So, here is my tentative view, used in this book to try to make sense of some very mixed terms:

A braid is an over and under intertwining (or an over and back, or a mixture of the two) of three or more strands, cords, ribbons, or pieces to produce an interwoven structure capable of working flat as a ribbon or round or other-shaped as a cord or rope.

A plait is an intertwining of four or more strands, cords, ribbons, or pieces to produce an interwoven, mostly flat in finished shape, and moderately complex surface-textured structure. It is normally used as a belt or a ribbon or as a decorative object over a generally flat surface.

A sinnet is an over and under intertwining that has a definite shape in cross-section. This shape varies and includes half-round, round, square, oblong, triangular, and other more complex shapes. Sinnets are comprised of more than three separate strands, cords, or ropes. They have a complex surface texture and pattern, and are used as a decoration or decorative ornament.

Braids then, generally, are simple structures having the same surface appearance, plaits have a generally flat cross-section and may have a more complex surface structure and cross-section, and sinnets are complex structures with complex patterns and usually a larger number of strands or parts than either braids or plaits. Sinnets are also more likely to be solid shapes.

Let's start with braids and see what we can develop. Before making any braid or plait, it is useful to set up a station at the workbench, table, or wherever you are comfortable working. When I am working on a piece of braiding or plaiting, I use this clamp, which is itself clamped at the edges to a table. This kind of clamp, with wood screw-tightened jaws and a brass frame, is very helpful for holding the braid as you complete it. A simple bench-top vice with soft jaws (you can get these as inserts of plastic from your local handyman store) will also work well.

BRAIDS

THREE-STRAND BRAIDS

This form of braid is the one you remember from your time as a child, when your, your sister's, or a favorite relative's hair was "done up" in a braid. Split your three strands into even-bulk groups or, if using cords, three cords laid alongside each other.

Ribbons must be laid flat and so are usually sewn to something else temporarily. The three strands are laid out with one in the center and one to each side. Here are some photographs of the process of braiding by passing the cords over from the front. You can also braid by passing the cords under from behind, as shown in the second set, which just produces the back of the first set.

STAGE 1 – Start with 3 strands . . . »

« **STAGE 2** – and take the right strand over the middle, between the middle and the left strand.

STAGE 3 – Take the left strand over the new middle one and make it the latest middle strand . . . »

« **Stage 4 –** repeating Stage 2 over from the right . . .

« **Stage 5 –** and again over from the left.

« **Stage 6 –** Repeat as needed for length, keeping the braid as tight as you need for the appearance you want.

≈ *This is the tightened Three-strand braid.*

Second Set (Set 2):

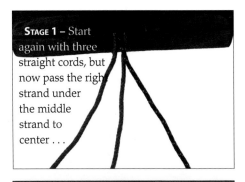

STAGE 1 – Start again with three straight cords, but now pass the right strand under the middle strand to center . . .

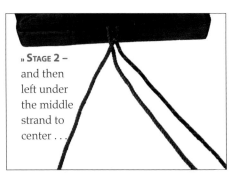

» **STAGE 2** – and then left under the middle strand to center . . .

» **STAGE 3** – then right under middle to center . . .

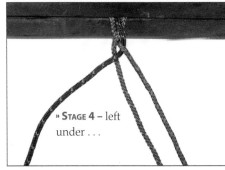

» **STAGE 4** – left under . . .

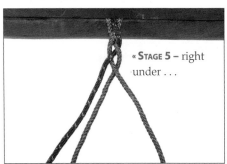

« **STAGE 5** – right under . . .

« **STAGE 6** – and complete to length.

FOUR-STRAND BRAIDS

This form of braid starts with two strands on each side of center. It makes no difference to the final piece whether or not you start with two of the same or two different colors on either side—the end result will look the same. Having decided what colors you want, set up your braid-clamping attachment with the strands firmly gripped. From this point it is usual to braid from behind, but you may also try braiding from the front. Note that this braid is very similar to the four strand sinnet (described in Chapter 5), but the action required to create the pattern evenly is somewhat different. The braid also usually ends up being a little looser than the sinnet. Try to keep even tension on both sets of cords so that you produce a nice regular braid. Finer cords will also help!

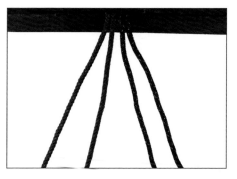

⌃ **STAGE 1** – Lay out the cords with two on each side of center.

⌃ **STAGE 3** – Cross the far left cord over the left-most arm of the crossing from Stage 2 . . .

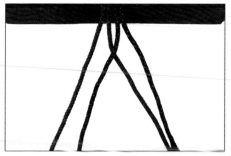

⌃ **STAGE 2** – then cross the middle two, right over left (or left over right if you prefer, in which case you should reverse the following instructions) . . .

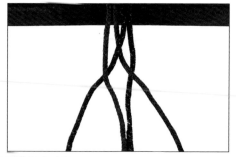

⌃ **STAGE 4** – then cross the right-most cord of the left-hand pair over the rightmost cord of the right-hand pair.

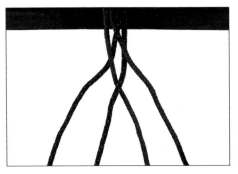

⌃ **STAGE 5** – Cross the middle two cords, right over left . . .

⌃ **STAGE 6** – then cross the left strands of each pair again, here shown loosely, so that you can see the pattern. Maintain tension evenly throughout to get the desired length of your braid, and then tie off with a Constrictor Knot.

⌄ *Here is the finished braid seen from the front . . .*

⌃ *. . . and again from the back.*

FIVE-STRAND BRAIDS

Five-Strand Braids take a little more managing, but the shape is still very elegant. These braids require one further step of crossing over and under the next two strands in the grouping, using the three-strand as the basic model. Because this number of cords in a braid requires manipulating a more bulky set of strands, it does not work as well with thicker cords or rope, but it can be made quite readily with finer cords. Here are more photographs of the process.

⋆ **STAGE 1** – Lay out five cords flat . . .

⋆ **STAGE 2** – then take the right cord under, over, under, over to the left . . .

⋆ **STAGE 3** – and then repeat with every "new" right-hand cord, under, over, under, over until you have the length you need. Be sure to apply even tension throughout. This is very important!

⋆ The finished tightened braid

SIX-STRAND BRAIDS

The six-strand braid is next in the progression. After the first pass over from the right, the strand is passed under the next strand and then over the fourth and under the fifth strand to finish over the sixth strand. This method follows the same pattern we have seen before, so you will see only the finished article below.

⯎ Method 1, over, under succeeding strands, is seen here for six strands.

Another method introduces a slightly different tucking pattern, which may be followed as shown below:

⯎ **STAGE 1** – Six strands laid flat . . .

⯎ **STAGE 2** – left outer cord moves over one, under one to the right set . . .

« **STAGE 3** – right outer cord moves over one, under two to the left set . . .

⁂ **STAGE 4** – then the new left cord over one, under one to the right set . . .

⁂ **STAGE 5** – and again take the right cord over one, under two to the left.

⁂ **STAGE 6 & 7** – Repeat to length desired.

⁂ *The six-strand braid as seen from the back (L) and the front (R)* ⁂

This second method is a little more complex but produces a very flexible braid that is slightly heavier and narrower.

SEVEN-STRAND BRAIDS

Now, extend the five-strand with two more strands, which is about all most people can handle at first. Some people cannot "get" this type of braiding—it is difficult to keep straight and flat but, with practice, it can be mastered. Try putting a weight on the top of the braid as you complete it and maintain the tension off to each side rather than pulling everything tight down the center of

the braid, because the braid is made with the same start from the right each time. There are also two methods of constructing this braid. First is shown a finished seven-strand braid created using the normal method of over one, under one across the full range of cords.

These instructions detail how to use the second method to construct a seven-strand braid.

ᴗ *This is the front of the seven-strand braid, worked looser so that you can see the pattern.*

⚮ **STAGE 1 –** Start with all strands laid flat, three on the left and four on the right.

⚮ **STAGE 2 –** Move the first cord on the left, over one, under one.

STAGE 3 – Move the first cord on the right under one, over two, and then under the next left . . .

STAGE 4 – back to the left side, over one, under one . . .

STAGE 5 – and then again from the right, under one, over two, and under one to the left. Continue this pattern until you reach the length you need. »

The back and front of a more open seven-strand braid—it may be cinched down further if you like it tight.

Eight-Strand Braids

The eight-strand braid is the final extension of braiding in this style, and for this chapter. Follow the pattern laid out for the six-strand braid, but be careful that you do not slip into the eight-strand round sinnet. This braid is best applied to a completely flat surface, or one with a very slight curve to the upper surface. When making it try to ensure that you keep tension out to the sides rather than down the center. Pulling the cords down the center will end up bending the braid upward in the middle. The first photograph below shows an eight-strand braid constructed using the standard method (over one, under one, from the right). The second was created by starting with four strands each side, passing the left outer strand over one, under one, over one from the left in to the center, leaving five strands on the right and three on the left. We started with four left strands and four right strands so, having passed the outer left strand from the left to center, we pass over one, under two, over two with one strand from the right outer side to the center. Go back to the left side and repeat.

≈ *The eight-strand braid using the standard format*

≈ *The eight-strand braid using the under two format, seen from the front (LH) and back (RH)* ≋

SIMPLE CHAIN BRAIDING

Chain braiding is straightforward but, if you need to join it to form a circle or bracelet, pay attention to the last few photographs. This simple chain braid is also known as Monkey Braid.

‹ STAGE 3 – Tighten the first loop around the second one . . .

‹ STAGE 1 – Form a clockwise overhand loop.

‹ STAGE 4 – then bring another loop up through and tighten the last previous.

» STAGE 2 – Bring a loop from the working end up.

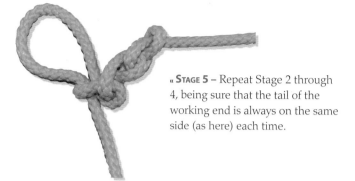

« STAGE 5 – Repeat Stage 2 through 4, being sure that the tail of the working end is always on the same side (as here) each time.

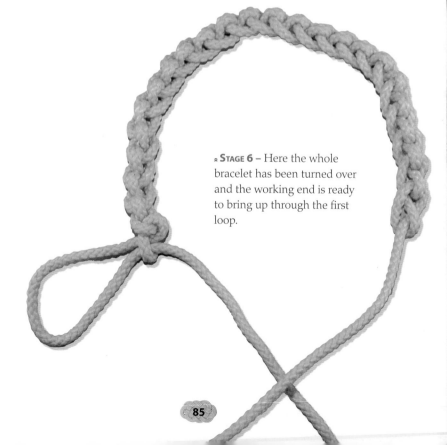

≈ STAGE 6 – Here the whole bracelet has been turned over and the working end is ready to bring up through the first loop.

STAGE 7 – Here the working end has been brought back through its own loop in the same direction it did previously, only now brought through by itself instead of as a loop. »

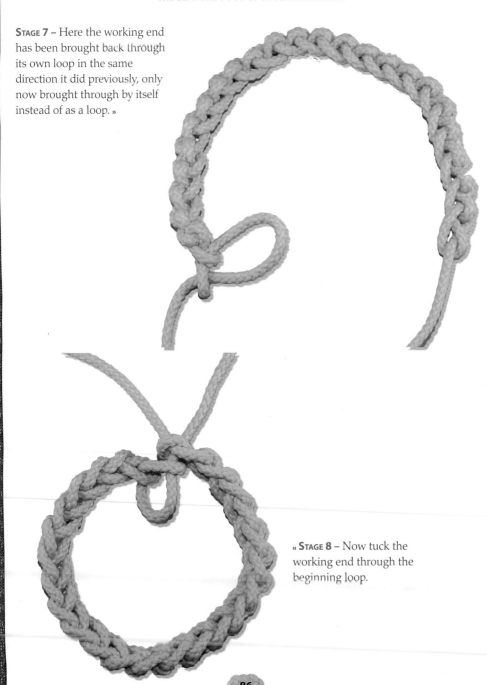

« **STAGE 8** – Now tuck the working end through the beginning loop.

« **STAGE 9** – Follow the working end back along itself.

« **STAGE 10** – Back the standing end you began with up through, ready to tie the two together.

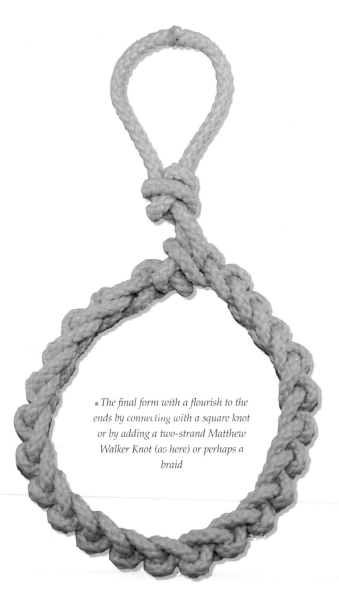

≈ *The final form with a flourish to the ends by connecting with a square knot or by adding a two-strand Matthew Walker Knot (as here) or perhaps a braid*

The single chain is very elegant, so perhaps a double chain is doubly elegant? No need for greater superlatives, of course—this braid speaks for itself.

DOUBLE-CHAIN BRAIDING

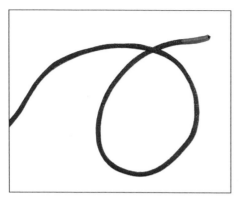

≈ **STAGE 1** – Form a counterclockwise loop, overhand, starting here with the standing end at top right.

STAGE 3 – Pull through a loop of the working part, being sure to keep the tail to the lower side as shown here. ≈

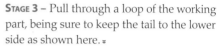

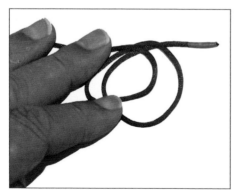

≈ **STAGE 2** – Follow with a second loop, placed atop the first, again counterclockwise.

STAGE 4 – The second and all subsequent loops are pulled through in turn. Make sure to tighten each PREVIOUS loop after putting in the next one. ≈

Double-Chain Braiding with the ends left pulled through at start and finished to prevent unintended unraveling ⊱

When you have completed a length of double chain you may want to consider linking the two ends, just as you did for the single chain. The double chain is very attractive as a curtain tieback or as a sewn-on embellishment to evening wear. The braid is also sometimes referred to as Trumpet Cord or Bugler's Braid, on account of its use as an embellishment on brass instruments. It may also be seen in other, typically gold-colored embellishments to military dress wear.

PLAITS

Four strand
Five strand
Six strand
Others

For plaiting, I have tried to steer away from simpler forms, branching out into more interesting weaves. As more cords or strands are incorporated, some startling and beautiful patterns appear that can stand alone or be incorporated into a larger work. There are many, many patterns that are available in plaiting, especially with leather thongs for making straps or other leather items.

Four-Strand Plait

There are at least a couple of methods of making plaits, particularly for larger numbers of strands. We'll start with two methods for plaiting four cords. Each way produces a distinctly different look. The first look is a straight line of bights to each of four faces, each bight having the same color

as its straight-line (180-degree) opposite. This differs from a four-strand braid which has a twist along its length, although a four-strand plait can also have a twist of colors that spiral down the piece if you start with the placement of colors as suggested in the caption to the second photo below.

Plait One

Stage 1 – Start with four strands, evenly spread.

Stage 3 – and then wrap it back to the left, over one, and settle it below its former mate.

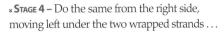

Stage 2 – Tuck the outer left under two to the right . . .

Stage 4 – Do the same from the right side, moving left under the two wrapped strands . . .

☙ **STAGE 5** – . . . and wrap it back over to the right, finishing below its former mate.

Overall, take each strand in turn, the outer one from each side, wrapping it behind and between the two on the opposing side, and then return it below its former pair-mate.

☙ *Here is what happens with two blue on the left, two green on the right.*

☙ *Here is what happens with a start of alternating colors, one blue, one green, one blue, one green—spiraling colors!*

PLAIT TWO

The second method of plaiting is to create a pattern of chevrons on the surface. This gives an unusual look to the edge, reminiscent of a rope. The difficulty I have found with it is that it wants to twist as you make it, because it has more strands packed in to one side than the other. Be sure to set up your workspace so that you maintain tension on your anchor as you proceed with the work.

STAGE 1 – Start with four strands . . .

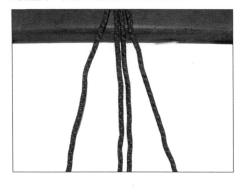

STAGE 2 – tuck the right under two and over one . . .

STAGE 3 – tuck under two again from the right and over one . . .

STAGE 4 – under two and over one again for as long as needed.

⌃ *Side view (right side) . . .*

⌃ *Final view (left side)*

FIVE-STRAND PLAIT

There are at least three ways to make the handsome Five-Strand Plait. Notice what happens in the third set below, where the tension is deliberately altered a little along its length, making one end of the same plait half-round and the other end made flatter—the effect is rather interesting.

PLAIT ONE METHOD

⌃ **STAGE 1** – Five strands are clamped together.

STAGE 2 – Take the right cord under three and over one . . . ⌄

« **STAGE 3** – and then take the next right cord again under three and over one, being sure to pull it tight to the left.

STAGE 4 – Repeat with outer right cord as necessary for length, being sure to pull the cord hard to the left. »

≈ *Here we see the plait from the front . . .*

≈ *. . . and here we see it from the side, with an interesting "ropelike" texture.*

PLAIT TWO METHOD

This pattern is also plaited using strands from one edge, but goes under and over a different number.

STAGE 1 – We start, of course, with five strands clamped together, and then pass under two, over one, under one.

STAGE 2 – Again we pass the right cord under two, over one, under one as before, being sure to pull the previous cord tight to the left and then wrap it tightly down over the current working cord to lock it in place (shown loose here).

The five-strand plait viewed from the front or worked side

The five-strand plait viewed from the underside—note the slight half-round texture.

Plait Three Method

This is another half-round plait, which may be woven tightly or loosely. Note the effect on each half of the plait in the photo below to see which is better for your application.

⚞ **Stage 1** – Lay the five strands out and pass the right cord under one, over two, under one.

⚞ **Stage 2** – Repeat with each of the other strands as they in turn become the right-most strand, being sure to pull each one tight to the left and then wrap the last cord down over.

⚞ **Stage 3** – Repeat until you reach the length you need.

⚞ *Here we see the front of the plait. Note that the left half has been flattened and left a little looser than the right half, which has a distinct half-round shape to it.*

⚞ *The view from the back—note the ridge on the section at the right.*

Six-Strand Plait

The six-strand plait shown here may have some similarities to the six-strand braid. However, a brief study shows them to have different structures, including, for the plait, a very pleasing chevron on one side. Here are two methods/patterns for you to try.

Method One

↟ **Stage 1** – Take all six strands and lay them out evenly, then take the outer right (or outer left) under one, over one, under one, over one, under one to the left and cinch up tightly.

↟ **Stage 2** – The same as for Stage 1, under, over, under, over, under. The last pass under can be easier if you cinch up after the fourth strand only, pulling down and holding the first four strands in your right hand, and then twist the final fifth strand to the right down over the passed strand (the #1 strand) and hold it again with the right hand.

↟ **Stage 3** – Repeat as needed, being sure to pull tight after each pass.

↟ Final stage: Even up tension on all the strands on both faces by carefully taking each cord in turn and tugging until it sits fair.

⚜ *The finished plait from the back, with a handsome long double slash*

METHOD TWO

« **STAGE 1** – Insert six cords in the clamp, three left and three right.

STAGE 2 – Cross the two center cords, right over left. »

« **STAGE 3** – Bring the outer left cord under one, over one to the center.

Stage 4 – Bring the outer right cord over one, under one, over one to center. »

« Stage 5 – Bring the new outer left cord under one, over one to center.

Stage 6 – Bring the new outer right cord over one, under one, over one to center. »

« Stage 7 – Repeat Stage 5.

⇌ **STAGE 8** – Repeat Stage 6 and continue repeating Stages 5 and 6 as long as needed to complete length. Be sure to tighten as you go—the open weave here is so that you can see the form of crossings.

⇌ *The finished plait seen from the back*

⇌ *The finished plait seen from the side*

⇌ *The finished plait seen from the front*

SINGLE-STRAND PLAITS FROM SINNETS

These two plaits form distinctive patterns even though they're made with only a single strand of cord. The two examples shown here are ideal for covering larger base materials and are derived from sinnet patterns – hence Plaits From Sinnets.

FRENCH SINNET

STAGE 1 – Temporarily fix one end of the strand you are winding onto the material you wish to cover.

STAGE 2 – Pass the strand behind, then form an underhand loop; tuck the loop under the first strand.

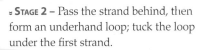

STAGE 3 – Form a Half Hitch around the base material below the tucked loop.

STAGE 4 – Pass the working end under, over, under the first tucked loop.

⌣ **STAGE 5 –** Pass the working end over the loop's standing part and under the Half Hitch.

⌣ **STAGE 6 –** Pull the cord through as shown.

⌃ **STAGE 7 –** Form another Half Hitch around the base material below the last pass.

⌃ **STAGE 8 –** Pass the working end under three, then over one, and tuck the working end under the previous Half Hitch. Repeat Stages 7 and 8.

⌃ *The faired and finished single strand French Sinnet as a plait on the base material. Note the single chevron in the center as a series of X's.*

Next is the Single-Strand Sinnet Plait, which has a slightly different finish than the French Single-Strand Plait. Note that both of these plaits employ only one strand and yet the finished article has a great intricacy that belies its simple base. For a complete project, try adding a Turk's Head Knot at the beginning and end to cover the start and finish.

« STAGE 1A –
Pass the line around the base material and over itself.

STAGE 1B – Make a second pass in the same direction, just below the previous pass . . . »

« STAGE 1C – around again to the right and downward . . .

STAGE 1D – around over and under to the right, passing the working end under the previous pass . . . »

« **Stage 1E** – around again to the right, making a start on the third pass around.

Stage 1F – Over, under, over for the third pass to the right . »

« **Stage 1G** – around again . . .

Stage 1H – over, under, over so that we have now set up our three passes above and three passes below center. »

STAGE 2 – Now, we insert a steel loop, or add a hollow needle to the end of the line, and pass it under the five crossing parts in the center as seen here. Tuck the working end under these five strands. »

« **STAGE 3** – Here the line has been pulled through to the left . . .

STAGE 4 – again, over, under, over the three lower strands, to the right. »

« **STAGE 5** –
Around again
and then over
itself to the right
and under the
next . . .

STAGE 6 – and again,
pass under five strands
with the needle or
loop. Repeat Stages
2 through 5 for the
length needed. »

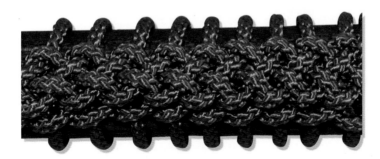

⌃ *Single-Strand Sinnet Plait, very similar to the French Single-Strand Sinnet Plait but having
a double chevron in the center, instead of a single chevron*

Sinnets

S innets—what exactly are they? To paraphrase a statement about the bo'sun on an old-fashioned sailing vessel, they are neither fish nor fowl. What is meant by that, in the case of the bo'sun, is that he is neither an officer nor a seaman, but rather that he sits somewhere between. Sinnets, similarly, are somewhere between braids and plaits. A sinnet is a woven structure, frequently having several cords or strands, and usually adaptable to incorporating several colors and patterns. Sinnet is variously defined elsewhere as braided cord, plaited cord, or simply cords woven over and under each other—I like the latter definition much better and I hope that I can clarify it for you as we progress. The term

CHAPTER

5

was used in written language as early as the seventeenth century (Oxford English Dictionary entry: a nautical term of obscure origin: 1611 Contgr. *Trene*: a three-fold rope, cord, string or twist, called by Marriners a Sinnet) and includes, variously, descriptions as two-, three-, four-, five-, up to twenty-five- or thirty-part twisting or braiding of separate cords into a sinnet. So—why do I let you know this? Simply put, it allows you to gather more information if you need it concerning the origins of the terms and to possibly reference other written material that has reference to those terms. If you don't need it, no harm done.

What seems important to me to understand is that sinnet (also spelled sennit, cinnet, or sinnate) is woven by making alternating passes of one cord (or several cords as part of a bundle) over and under the remaining cords in the bundle to form a flat, round, or other-shaped cross-section rope or long piece of ropework that is decorative, especially if made with several colors. A sinnet is therefore a structure that lends itself to multiple strands being woven together into multiple patterns and shapes, with a relatively simple repetitive activity of over and under. As with all seemingly simple pieces however, there are cautions. It can be easy to "drop a stitch" in making multiple-strand sinnets, which, if you want your sinnet to look right, means you may have a lot of undoing to do if you want to correct it. For that reason I highly recommend that you number or otherwise mark the ends of your strands, so that you will always be able to see which strand is going to be passed next.

There is almost no limit to the number of strands that can be made or braided into a sinnet by hand. Asian braiders use a table tool with a hole in the center to braid complex

patterns with hundreds of colored silk strands into beautiful braided cord for decorative purposes on kimonos, dresses, pillows, and other decorative items of clothing and furniture. The strands are weighted and the finished braid is brought through the center of the table, which is known as a *marudai* in Japan. The center (finished) braid has a weight attached to it so that it can be pulled naturally through the *marudai* to produce even tension in the finished braid as the individual packets of colored strands are being passed over and under each other. The name for the practice of making these braids or sinnets is *kumihimo*.

There are many forms of sinnet throughout the world, depending on the fibers used and the final purpose of the sinnet. Fijian islanders have a version called *magimagi*, named for coconut fiber grown on the Lau group of islands in Fiji (*magimagi* means "thrifty," which seems appropriate because the sinnet uses an otherwise discarded fiber). These sinnets are used to cover the poles that form huts called *mbure* with a woven series of braided strands. Sinnets are also used to suspend jewelry like carved wood, horn, ivory and bone fragments by both Fijian and other Pacific Islanders. At the bottom of page 109 is a photograph of a main beam intersection to the roof framing of an *mbure* in Vulaga, one of the islands in the Lau group of Fiji. (Photograph by Vernon Cox, from Wikipedia, assigned to public domain use.

This photograph shows the individual pieces of sinnet that are woven from the **niumagimagi** *coconut fibers around the junction of the main beams of the* **mbure***, to hold the beams in place.)*

When you are making a sinnet for your own use, it may take a few practice sessions first to ensure that you produce an even amount of tension in the finished piece's strands. Remember that the cord surface will exert friction on the other cords and that friction is overcome by the amount you pull on the individual cords. If you pull unevenly your sinnet may look lumpy and crooked and will vary in thickness. Overall you want to achieve an even appearance for most decorative work, because the sinnet is not really the center of attraction; instead, it is being used to enhance something else.

⚓ *A typical macramé screw clamp of wood on a metal frame.*

If, however, you are making the sinnet the center of attention it will be perfectly acceptable to have an uneven appearance, so that you can highlight some feature of the sinnet more artfully.

The close-up on the previous page shows some of the eighteen-strand flat sinnet work, with Turk's Head coverings, French Whipping, Crowning, Over-two Crowning, Solomon Bar and Square Knot Covering made by one of the ship's crew on board Gloria, the steel barque square-rigged training ship of the Colombian Navy.

As with most decorative work, it is your skills that will show through in the finished piece, so take your time to do a thorough job and do make sure to practice first, so that you can become used to the way the sinnet works for you. Although Graumont and Hensel include more than 400 types of sinnet in their *Encyclopedia of Knots and Fancy Rope Work*, I have included only three in this chapter: flat, round, and other shapes. There

are many more forms of sinnet, with a great variety in the number and arrangement of strands or cords, and I encourage the reader to find them in some of the books noted in the bibliography included at the back of this book. Combinations of differently shaped sinnet are very effective means of transitioning a piece from, say, round to flat and back to round again. Color changes can be easily wrought by introducing a new piece of cord from the center of the round sinnet and then cutting out or hiding the replaced color. In this way it is possible to have a whole rainbow of color along a piece of sinnet for a stunning visual. You might also try using sinnets as a base for a lanyard, enhancing it perhaps with a Turk's Head or a Pineapple Knot to cover the splicing or joining of the ends of the sinnet together. The piece of the lanyard that circles the neck should have a flat cross-section for comfort and, preferably, a breakaway stitching in it someplace to prevent accidental choking or strangulation if it is intended for a child or a person working on or around machinery or any other place it might get caught.

FLAT SINNETS

Flat sinnets are really a type of braid masquerading under a different name. If you have ever braided your sister's hair, watched your mother or aunt braiding hair, or have braided a horse's mane or tail, then you know the beginnings of sinnet work. Braids are usually made with three strands, woven over and through (sometimes under and through) the neighboring strand pair. Because we do not normally start a sinnet piece at a single event, like a head, neck, or tail, we have to start our sinnet with our strings/cords attached together, either in a bundle or clipped together. Of course that means also that we could make a sinnet out of hair attached to a person or animal—it is just much more difficult to remove when it grows out a little—cornrows are a good example of what happens when hair is woven into sinnet or braids. Sinnets are usually made with four or more strands, and unweaving them when made of growing hair can present problems if not done carefully. Because flat sinnets are intended to lie flat, then of course we need to clip or hold them together with a flat clip. If you use a rubber band or a Constrictor Knot you will find that it takes several rows of work to get the sinnet looking flat and not distorted. I have used a clipboard (handy if you want to put a paper pattern under your work as a reminder during the making of the sinnet) and I have used a clip normally used for holding a sheaf of papers together (aka gorilla clip). You may also be lucky and have or be able to find a clamp like the one shown on the previous page.

Some people prefer not to use anything at all to hold the starting strands, but instead knot their strands together with an Overhand Knot, with the Overhand Knot and the first few passes of cord being cut away at the finish of the piece before mounting it—again, be reminded that you will be doing extra work on flat sinnets if you gather the cords together in a bundle instead of keeping the cords flat.

The number of strands to make into a flat sinnet is limited only by what you can physically manage. Making a belt or scarf is possible, although by the time you achieve that width you are looking more at a process of weaving on a loom instead of making a sinnet by hand, which is what is being shown in this chapter. Certainly machine-made sinnet is possible in the form of belts and bags, but we are speaking here of handmade work, so we have not included the various machine-made pieces. Flat sinnets can also be made in a variety of patterns, instead of sticking with a standard over-one, under-one pattern. Here are a few types of flat sinnets for you to try.

THREE-STRAND SINNETS

The first Three-Strand Sinnet is this one from *Graumont & Hensel's Encyclopedia*, made as three strands of Three-Strand Sinnet. This is one of the knot-tyer's favorite things to do with knotting, to form one simple thing using the process itself to make the base from which the finished object is made. Therefore a knot-tyer will count this as a Three-Strand Sinnet rather than a nine-strand. See also the Turk's Head Knot section, where a simple three-lead Turk's Head Knot is itself made into a three-lead Turk's Head Knot, but using one piece of cord. For this sinnet we have used three separate colored pieces of cord so that you can see the pattern clearly when all are used together. It produces a very intriguing piece of decoration when made like this.

STAGE 3 – left over right . . .

STAGE 1 – Form the first three strands of three-strand braid and clamp them together as shown . . .

STAGE 4 – and center over left, for the basic three-strand pattern.

STAGE 2 – right over center . . .

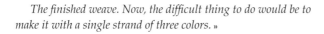

The finished weave. Now, the difficult thing to do would be to make it with a single strand of three colors. »

FOUR-STRAND SINNETS

Four-Strand Sinnets follow the same pattern as one of the Four-Strand Braids illustrated in Chapter 4. The sinnet shown below can be doubled to produce a slightly different appearance. You can also try adding a third strand to each bundle, making twelve strands in all. This more open weave lets you add the sinnet to a frame or a garment when you want to reveal the texture or color of the underlying piece. The round form of this sinnet is shown later in this chapter.

First method

≈ **STAGE 1** – Stretch a pair to each side of center.

≈ **STAGE 2** – Move the center left cord under the center right.

≈ **STAGE 3** – Move the outer right under the center right.

≈ **STAGE 4** – Move outer left over then under, keeping the weave nice and open but evenly taut.

Second method

≈ **STAGE 5** – For a tighter weave, start again with two either side of center and then move outer right under center right and over the left inner strand and then under the left outer strand.

≈ **STAGE 6** – Move outer right again under, over, under.

≈ **STAGE 7** – Repeat Stage 5 and 6 for as long as needed, being sure to tie the sinnet firmly.

≈ *Here is a close-up view of the four-strand flat sinnet by Method 1, an open weave.*

If you make the weave tightly, accidentally or on purpose, here is how it will look: *Method 2 weave made tightly.* ≈

≈ *Here is the same pattern four-Strand Sinnet, Method 1, using four pairs of strands instead, and tied somewhat openly.*

ALTERNATE WEAVES

Four-Strand Emperor Sinnet (aka Snake Band)

As children we played with the plastic lace sometimes known as Gimp® or Rexlace® to form bracelets, lanyards, and other long forms of plastic twists. One of the favorite forms of using this lace was to make the Emperor's Lace, also known as Snake Band, Diamond Braid (a slightly different form) and by various other names. Emperor's Lace is a Four-Strand Sinnet where the center two strands act as a core for the outer two strands. You can also use just a single cord in the center or perhaps alternate the colors, inside to outside and vice versa. The two outer strands are tied so as to form an attractive chevron pattern (if you have different color cords, as here shown) and may also be tied to form a twisted spiral piece. Here is one way of making this popular sinnet:

⌃ STAGE 1 – Middle a core cord (blue) over a cover cord middle (red) and tie an Overhand Knot around the core cord, as here.

⌃ STAGE 2 – Tie the Overhand Knot tight and you should see a small "bump" on one side, as here on the right . . .

⌃ STAGE 3 – Bend an arm of the cover cord that is on the opposite side from the "bump" and tuck its tail behind the core cord, to make a loop on the left . . .

⌃ STAGE 4 – and then tuck the other arm behind the first one . . .

STAGE 5 – and bring it over the core cord, tucking its tail down into the loop you made with the first arm, then pull this overhand knot tight.

STAGE 7 – and then make another overhand knot, just as in Stage 5 above, by tucking the tail down into the loop again. Continue alternate sides until you have finished the length you need.

STAGE 6 – Now you can see that the "bump" has moved over to the other side. Continue to make an arm opposite the bump, putting the tail behind the cover cord . . .

The finished flat form of Emperor Sinnet or Snake Band Sinnet, so called because of the chevron pattern or snakelike wiggle to the finished surface.

Twisted Sinnet

This form of Four-Strand Sinnet is very similar to the Emperor Sinnet, except that you do not change sides at every overhand knot. You make the loop on the same side every time. Take a look:

≈ **STAGE 3** – Bring the left-side cord under the first cord . . .

≈ **STAGE 1** – Start the same as for the Emperor Sinnet in the middle of both cords.

≈ **STAGE 2** – Tuck the right side cord under the core cords.

≈ **STAGE 4** – and tuck the left cord over the core cords and down into the right loop.

» *The right-twisted form of Emperor Sinnet.* Using what we now know about forming the weaves, you can see that other weaves are possible. Here I show two other forms, using a simple designation of over one, under two or over two and under one. Try them and see for yourself!

⚘ **Stage 5** – Repeat Stage 2 through 4 as needed, continuing to use the right cord under first. This twists down to the right. To twist down to the left, tuck the left-side cord under first.

⚘ *Here the method works from right to left, bringing the individual outer cords over one from the left and over two from the right, resulting in the appearance of over one, under two for any individual cord in the finished work.*

⚘ *The opposite working for this weave gives a slightly different effect and one that you may not stop a train to see, but in larger pieces it can be appreciated, particularly when you place one alongside the other!*

EIGHT-STRAND SINNETS

As with all sinnet work, the addition of more strands usually increases the possibilities (some would say complexity!) of the weaves available. Some, though, remain simple in essence, and such is the case here. The first method requires only four separate steps, and the second method follows an over-one, under-one style that we have observed previously.

Method 1

˅ **STAGE 1** – Start five strands to the left and three to the right . . .

˄ **STAGE 2** – outer left under one, over two, under one to the right . . .

˄ **STAGE 3** – outer right under one, over two to the left . . .

˄ **STAGE 4** – outer left over one, under two, over one to the right

˄ **STAGE 5** – outer right over one, under two to the left. Repeat Stages 2 through 5 as needed.

«... and from the back, too!

The resulting tight double chevron weave is a pleasure to see from the front ...»

Method 2

*« **Stage 1 –** Start four left and four right ...*

*« **Stage 2 –** outer right under one, over one, under one to the left ...*

⤐ **Stage 3 –** outer left over one, under one, over one, under one to the right. Repeat Stage 2 and 3 as needed.

The front and back of this sinnet. Notice the pleasing, open-lattice form of this sinnet. When using small cords, the center of this sinnet cannot be closed without taking the edge cords on sharp vertical turns each time, up and down. »

This next sinnet has one side more pronounced than the other. The over-under pattern can be made from either on top (over start) or beneath (under start). First, the over start.

Method 3

» STAGE 2 – Start outer left over three, under one to right . . .

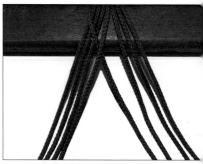

« STAGE 1 – five strands left and three right to start . . .

» STAGE 3 – outer right over two, under one to left. Repeat Stages 2 and 3 as needed.

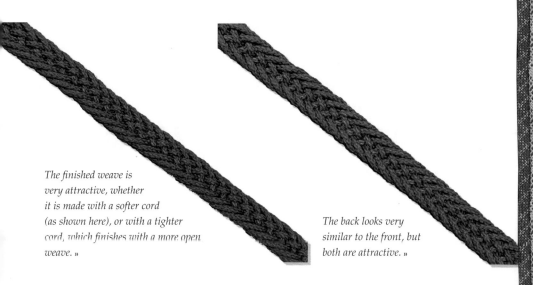

The finished weave is very attractive, whether it is made with a softer cord (as shown here), or with a tighter cord, which finishes with a more open weave. »

The back looks very similar to the front, but both are attractive. »

Method 4

This sinnet has a square cross-section shape and a pleasing chevron finish. The alternative color scheme, using a shift in the starting strand positions, shifts the colors to each corner of the weave instead of appearing as an alternating double chevron. When you master this, try using four separate colors instead of two! The start of "over-unders" is shown first, followed by the normal tying sequence.

⌁ Here is a start with four groups of two colors.

⌁ Tuck the outer left under five to the right.

≈ Take the strand just tucked back to the left over two, rejoining its original four.

Take the outer right behind five to the left.

Take the strand just tucked back to the left over two, rejoining its original four.

≈ Take outer right behind five to the left.

≈ **STAGE 1** – When using two colors, use four strands of each color, two outside and two inside on each pair of four.

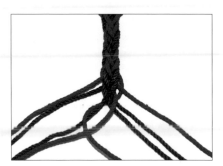

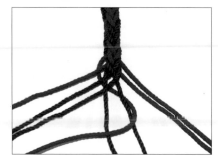

≈ **STAGE 2** – Take the left upper and move it behind the first five strands on the left, then between the two pairs of colors and over two to the left.

≈ **STAGE 3** – Now take the upper right under the first five strands on its left, then over two to the right. Repeat Stages 2 and 3 for as long as needed.

The finished weave has a handsome diagonal setting of pairs of colors, making this great chevron alternate from one face to the other. »

« Take the strand just tucked back to the right over two, rejoining its original four.

≈ *Try starting with four of each color on each side for this corner-colored weave.*

The last weave of Eight-Strand Sinnet here is this English Sinnet, made using a finer cord for a lanyard or other piece where a slender look is desirable. See below for general instructions on making English Sinnet, which applies to all varieties of multi-strand English Sinnet, made with any number of strands.

OTHER NAMED SINNETS

The use of sinnets was very widespread, so much so that some styles have been attributed to specific countries. I am not certain, but I believe that all references to such names were simply the fancy of whoever had tied the sinnet and felt it was worthy of some special name, to be remembered more easily than, say, "fourteen-strand variegated sinnet," which does not trip off the tongue quite as readily.

Sixteen-Strand Russian Sinnet

Russian Sinnet is made with an over-two, under-two weaving method with an even number of strands as a multiple of four e.g. 16, 20, 24, 28, etc., and usually requires at least sixteen strands to look even halfway decent. To make the sinnet, lay all the strands tight and flat together (see photograph of setup below). Start the weave on the left-hand side if you are right-handed (right, if left-handed) and weave over two, under two all the way to the right side. Finish each pass by firmly or moderately tightening the strand you pass (but always the same tension) to the opposite side, while holding the remaining strands tightly with a clamp—you could also use your other hand to clamp, but this becomes difficult to handle. It makes life easier if you use a bamboo skewer (such as is used for kebabs or kabobs) to weave through the flattened strands where the single strand is then going to follow, or you could use a darning needle or a wire loop. Be sure not to confuse the order of the strands—it is so heartbreaking having to go back and undo what you already made! Your temporary second clamp to keep the order of the strands correct can be made by wrapping an elastic band around each end of a pair of popsicle sticks or chopsticks. Remove the elastic band from one side when you need to add a passed strand, then replace that band and remove the other to release a new strand to pass. As you reach the other side of the weaving you will find that you have one strand remaining. Cross this last strand down over the end of the strand woven through where the bamboo skewer was inserted. The sinnet takes some getting used to because it has a tendency to buckle toward your dominant hand. Keeping the tension even in all the vertical strands and the single horizontal strand each time is a challenge! Cut away the first two inches and the last two inches to get rid of the uneven tension that is likely to be present. The largest Russian Sinnet of which I am aware was made by master knotter Skip Hipps, now living in Hawaii, who made one of 40 strands.

« Here is how the setup looks.

Here is how the first pass looks. »

The finished Russian Sinnet »

Nine-Strand English Sinnet

English Sinnet is made with an odd or an even number of strands, starting with the simplest, the Three-Strand Sinnet. All other English Sinnets are made in the same pattern. The pattern is to take the outer strand on the right side over, under, over, under each strand in turn to the left, etc., for the length you need. It is a very simple sinnet and can look quite nice, provided that you do not exceed about ten strands—after that number of strands it starts to become difficult to handle as it is not easy to keep regular tension on too many strands.

Nine-Strand French Sinnet

French Sinnet must be made with an odd number of strands, at least seven strands or it will not look right, and is always made taking the strands five left and four right (if using nine stands—amend to similar split with larger or smaller odd number of strands) moving the left outer over four to center and coming from each side in turn to the center. When you are making a French Sinnet, you must be sure to keep the tension even or the pattern will quickly be lost. With an odd number this will not be a concern. French Sinnet may also be woven loosely. The weave is identical "(left outer over all left cords to center, right outer over all right cords to center)," but looks looser as you might expect. Be aware that some French Sinnet, when made with a large number of strands, may first be woven from a weave of two, three, or more strands into sets of braids that are then woven together to form a more interesting sinnet!

« *The tighter version of Nine-Strand French Sinnet*

a tie or an elastic band. The tie that I prefer to use is the Constrictor Knot. This ensures that my piece does not come undone while I am working on it (though the knot is sometimes hard to remove at the end when you have finished your piece)! If you have not used it before, here is a series of photographs of just one way the Constrictor Knot can be made. I am showing it on white tubing for clarity.

» STAGE 1 – Wrap the line around your strands (shown here as a tube) and cross it over itself to the right (or left).

STAGE 2 – Bring the line around behind your strands, crossing the standing part and then tucking under it. ⨯

ROUND

Round Sinnets start out very similarly to Flat Sinnets, in that the strings/cords are gathered together in one place. There, however, the similarity normally ends. Round Sinnets are normally gathered together using

« **STAGE 3** – Pull through and then pull tight on both ends. Note that the ends come out of the knot in between opposing turns. Use a finer twine than the thickness of your strand bundle for best grip.

The alternative binding knots above have their unique values, particularly when it comes to removing them from where they were placed. A good tug on the standing part (shown below the roll in each case) will release their grip enough to allow you to remove the twine or other small stuff with which you have tied your bundle of string or cords. The Constrictor, Boa and Strangle knots will not necessarily allow you to do that easily, because they tend to grip and not let go! The Boa Knot, invented by master braider Peter Collingwood, and the Strangle Knot, first published as the Eel Knot by Hjalmar Öhrvall, are also useful when gathering a bundle of cords together. I suggest that you try a variety of binding knots and see what is best about each before settling on one or another of them. Now let's take a look at some of the interesting patterns that can be made in round sinnet using a variety of numbers of strings/cords.

FOUR-STRAND ROUND SINNET

The simplest Four-Strand Round Sinnet is the Four-Strand Plait, seen in Chapter 4. It produces a round sinnet when tied tightly and has alternating colors in a spiral or in straight lines along its length, depending on the start used. Some will also tell you that it is a square sinnet—because we only have four strands, it is hard to say who is correct, but I am sticking with round. Here is an alternate weave that produces a different color pattern.

« STAGE 1 – Start two strands left, two right, one of each color . . .

≈ STAGE 2 – upper left under two to the right, then over one to the left.

« STAGE 3 – Upper right under two to the left and over one to the right.

Repeat for length as needed, keeping the cords tight as you go.

Finished Stage: It ends up looking like this when you start with mixed pairs, left and right . . . »

Finished Straight: . . . and like this when you start with matching pairs of colors, left and right. »

Five-Strand Half-Round Sinnet

Here is the next in the round sinnet series—Five-Strand Half-Round Sinnet, very useful when you need a little flexibility or someplace to put the glue when adding it to a picture frame. Compare the method of making it with the Five-Strand Plait, Method 2, for a similar shape with a dimpled face. The method is a little different, but what you achieve is the same.

Stage 1 – Start three strands to the left and two to the right . . . »

⁀ **STAGE 2** – outer left over one, under one . . .

⁀ **STAGE 3** – outer right over one, under one. Repeat as necessary.

« *The view from the back shows the dimpled or flat surface.*

The view from the front shows the half-round surface and a rather nice half-chevron »

Six-Strand Round Sinnet

The Six-Strand Round Sinnet does not require any further amendment beyond what we have already seen in plaiting and braiding, although there are some variations that may prove interesting. The method I have shown below uses one strand at a time.

« Stage 1 – Lay out six strands in a bundle, with three left and three right, numbering them 1 through 6 left to right.

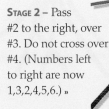

Stage 2 – Pass #2 to the right, over #3. Do not cross over #4. (Numbers left to right are now 1,3,2,4,5,6.) »

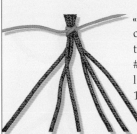

« Stage 3 – Now cross #4 to the right, over #5 (numbers l to r are now 1,3,2,5,4,6).

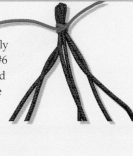

» Stage 4 – The only hard part—take #6 and pass it behind the whole bundle to the left, then cross it to the right over #1 (1,6,3,2,5,4).

« Stage 5 – Now reverse direction so that right passes over left. Pass #3 to the left, over #6 (1,3,6,2,5,4).

« Stage 6 – Pass #5 to the left, over #2 (1,3,6,5,2,4).

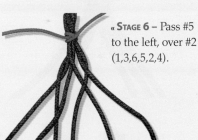

» Stage 7 – Finally, pass #1 to the right behind everything and over #4 (3,6,5,2,1,4). Repeat Stages 2 through 6 until you reach the length you need.

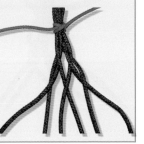

« Here is the finished Six-Strand Round Sinnet. Note that the upper left section has been left a little looser and the lower right section a little tighter on the final fairing.

The next method produces a Half-Round Six-Strand, which looks a little more beefy than the Five-Strand Half-Round sinnet and is also less flexible:

STAGE 2 – Take the upper left behind all to the right, between #5 and #6, then left over #4 and #5. ⸲

« STAGE 1 – Strands are laid out three left and three right.

« STAGE 3 – Take the upper right (#6) behind all to the left, between new #1 and #2, and over two to the right.

STAGE 4 – Repeat Stages 2 and 3 until you reach your desired length. ⸲

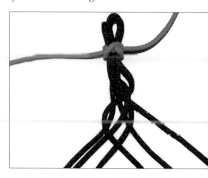

« *A close-up of the shape of Six-Strand Sinnet shows the alternating chevron pattern (half are pointing up the piece and half are pointing down) along its length.*

Seen here from the side, the neat one-way chevron is easily seen. »

» *A long interlocking chevron appears on the back of the piece.*

Other color layouts at the start will produce spiral or alternating chevrons—try some out for yourself!

EIGHT-STRAND ROUND SINNET

The Eight-Strand Round Sinnet is the start of a new adventure—now we need to insert a core under the strands, or our sinnet will collapse on itself. All round sinnets of eight strands or more will require a core. This will remind you of a type of knotting that we have mentioned already in braiding—the covering knot called coachwhipping, which we showed there using six strands. If you want a non-cored structure, then six strands is the maximum. More covering knots are shown in later chapters, as is coachwhipping with considerably more strands. Here is the process for an Eight-Strand Round Sinnet.

« **STAGE 1** – Lay out your eight strands and core, seizing them together with tape or a Constrictor Knot.

≈ **STAGE 2** – Take the upper left behind all, under #8, over #7, under #6, over #5 and back to the new #4 position.

« **STAGE 3** – Do the same with the upper right; behind all, under #1, over #2, under #3, over #4 to the new #5.

≈ **STAGE 4** – Repeat Stage 2 . . .

≈ **STAGE 5** – and Stage 3, as long as needed.

The finished sinnet is exactly like a coachwhipping, over and under alternating strands, but without the multiple strands for each set. The core helps to support the outer covering and may be covered or open, as here.

With round sinnets it is always possible to generate a different over-and-under pattern that is pleasing to look at or to hold. I strongly suggest that, when trying a new method, you write down how you achieved the result, before it slips your mind!

OTHER SHAPES

There is a host of other shapes that can be formed with sinnet. Triangular, half-round, and star-shaped sinnets can be applied to many different surfaces or can be used on their own to form very interesting diversions. If you are intending to cover a picture frame with sinnet, it may be best to use a flat sinnet, though other shapes can also be used on picture frames, particularly those with complex cross-sections, if you place them carefully. In this section we will cover first a triangular cross-section sinnet, then oval-shaped, pentagonal, and star-shaped sinnets (which are one of the most complex, and

should only be attempted by a strong-willed and patient person).

TRIANGULAR SINNETS

Triangular cross-section sinnets are solid sinnets, and so are not difficult to create, but they do need to be organized using a table or bench vise if you are making them for the first time. If you try to start them in your hand you will find that you have more strands in your hand than is comfortable. I have successfully used a table-edge vise to hold a bunch of cords, which, with a marked disk under them, makes for a somewhat easy time of making these splendid sinnets. Here is a simple triangular sinnet, tied in the hand, just to get you started:

STAGE 1 – Shown in progress here: Double each of six strands to make three pairs, knotted or seized together (use different colored cord to hold the strands together) . . . »

« **STAGE 2** – then crown each pair in turn, remembering that to "crown" we make the cords go "down" or away from us, into the page . . .

« **STAGE 4** – Finally, tuck the last pair under the first where you had held your thumb.

« **STAGE 3** – here moving counterclockwise with the next pair.

» **STAGE 5** – When all are in place, tighten each pair. Repeat Stages 1 through 5.

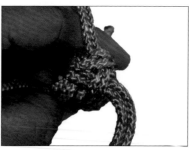

The finished two-over counterclockwise crowning using six strands. Note the rather rounded shape of the sinnet when making all crown tucks in the same direction (counter-clockwise here). ⚅

» *Here the sinnet has been finished by reversing the direction of the crowning on each pass.*

With this latter technique, the Crowns are made first counterclockwise and then clockwise, then again counterclockwise and again clockwise. This reversing action for each "row" gives the sinnet a much more triangular and solid feel than making all Crowns in one direction.

Experiment with other colors if you would like to see some more adventurous sinnets. Jacqui Carey's book, *200 Braids to Twist, Knot, Loop, or Weave*, can be a great source of inspiration. You can also find information on tying triangular sinnets using a fifteenth-century technique called finger-loop braiding that was recently re-examined in a book titled *Tak v Bowes Departed*, by Elizabeth Benns and Gina Barrett.

TRIANGULAR TWO COLOR SINNET

This next shape is a little more difficult to manage, but I found that I could manage it reasonably, once I had the method down pat. If you are going to make the sinnet using the same colors of cords instead of the different colors shown here, I strongly advise you to number the cords with a piece of tape around the working end of each strand, at least initially. It is too easy to lose your place and then get frustrated with having to go back and repeat that which you thought you had finished! In Ashley's reference this sinnet is #3028.

≈ **STAGE 1** – Attach nine strands temporarily to a cork or other base, to separate the cords more than anything else. Here we show two green, one yellow, two green, one yellow, etc., attached around the circumference. As a first step, take the yellow strands and allow them to drop downward in between each pair of green strands. Here the sinnet has been started already, so that you can see the pattern involved.

≈ **STAGE 2** – Each pair of green cords will have one lower and one higher than the other after the initial start. Take the lower one and pass it to its right (counterclockwise) behind its partner and then over the top of the yellow. In the start position only, merely take the left strand of the pair of green strands, instead of the lower one. The word "behind" here means closer to the center of the cork or body on which you are building the sinnet.

STAGE 3 – Now lift up the yellow strand and drop the second green strand down to the left (clockwise) of the yellow. Hold the green strands down with your non-dominant hand—here I am using my left hand.

STAGE 5 – Here is the side view with all three yellow strands raised and all six green strands dropped. Note that the former pairs of green strands, having danced around each other, are now paired up with a strand from the next pair, instead of their former partner—kind of like the valeta waltz, an old-fashioned ballroom dance!

» STAGE 4 – Repeat the action of taking the lower green strand, moving it counterclockwise behind its pair and dropping it over the yellow, then bring the yellow up and drop the second green to the left of the yellow.

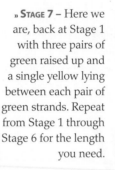

» STAGE 7 – Here we are, back at Stage 1 with three pairs of green raised up and a single yellow lying between each pair of green strands. Repeat from Stage 1 through Stage 6 for the length you need.

» STAGE 8 – Here is a bird's-eye view when the green strands are raised, each having a yellow between each pair of green strands.

« STAGE 6 – Now, raise each pair of green strands pair by pair in the air, and move the yellow strand on the right (c/c) of each pair to its left (c/w) behind the green pair clockwise (to the left) and drop the yellow. Here we show two sets of green strands having been raised up and two yellows dropped down.

« STAGE 9 – And here we show the end result of the green lower strand having moved behind its partner and down over the yellow strand. The upper or higher green strand has been dropped in each case and we are ready to pick up the three yellow strands for Stage 5 above.

ﬔ STAGE 10 – Here is the finished article, seen from one of the faces of the triangle, with that handsome single chevron of yellow striping the center of the face.

« STAGE 11 – Here we have rotated the sinnet by sixty degrees to show one of the corners. The green single chevron is nicely banded by the yellow chevrons on each face.

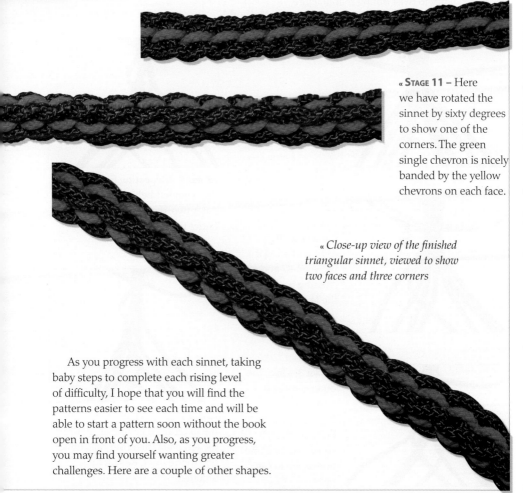

« Close-up view of the finished triangular sinnet, viewed to show two faces and three corners

As you progress with each sinnet, taking baby steps to complete each rising level of difficulty, I hope that you will find the patterns easier to see each time and will be able to start a pattern soon without the book open in front of you. Also, as you progress, you may find yourself wanting greater challenges. Here are a couple of other shapes.

OVAL

I've included three methods for constructing oval sinnets below. The first two methods use eight strands, and the difference between them is very subtle. Oval sinnets feel very good on the hands and are perhaps a little softer or easier on the skin than the round or square sinnets. They do have a tendency to twist during manufacture, as you will see from the photographs below.

This tendency is a result of having more tucks to one side, which causes the structure to be un-balanced. Nevertheless, the finished sinnet still feels good to the hands and is pleasing to the eyes. Try using different colors to emphasize or de-emphasize the shape. For use on fabrics and clothing you should definitely consider using a thinner cord of, say, 0.7mm or thinner.

Method 1

« STAGE 1 – Set up the eight strands with four on either side.

« STAGE 2 – Take the outer left behind the rest to the right and bring it between #7 and #8, crossing back to the left over #7 and under #5 and 6.

« STAGE 3 – Take the outer right and bring it behind the rest, emerging between the left pairs, over one and under one to the right.

« STAGE 4 – Repeating Stage 2, bring the outer left behind, between the outer two, over one to the left and under two to the left.

« STAGE 5 – Repeating Stage 3, bring the outer right behind all, between the left pairs then over one, under one to the right. Repeat for length required.

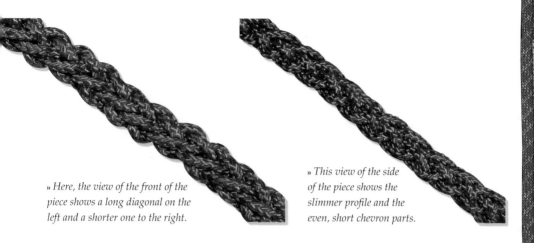

» *Here, the view of the front of the piece shows a long diagonal on the left and a shorter one to the right.*

» *This view of the side of the piece shows the slimmer profile and the even, short chevron parts.*

Method 2

This second method with eight strands makes a different move at Stage 2. Note the difference in the front of the piece. The long diagonal has been replaced with a pair of shorter diagonals. The piece feels firmer to the touch. Again, try using different colors at the start for a whole new experience!

⌃ **STAGE 1** – Start as usual with four strands left and four strands right.

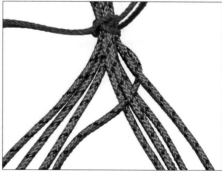

⌃ **STAGE 2** – Bring the outer left strand behind all, tuck it up between #7 and #8, and then move to the left over #7, under #6, and over #5 to sit below its former set.

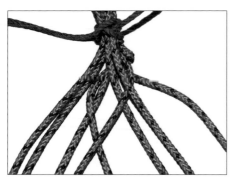

STAGE 4 – Repeat Stage 2, taking the outer left behind, between, then over, under, over to the left.

STAGE 3 – Take the outer right behind all, then between the left pairs, over one, under one to the right, to sit again below its former set.

STAGE 5 – Repeat Stage 3 here, using the outer right. Repeat Stages 2 through 5 until you reach the length you need. »

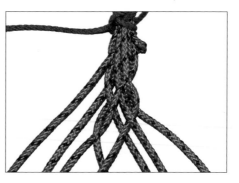

The finished piece, with a different front, although the side remains the same as for Method 1. Note that the piece does not appear to twist along its length in the same manner, which may be preferable. »

Method 3

This method may also be used with eight strands, although using that many cords makes it look chunky and possibly less attractive. Using six strands seems to be the ideal number.

≈ **STAGE 1** – Take six strands and . . .

≈ **STAGE 2** – . . . bring #1 behind all, bringing it out between #5 and #6, and then return it over two to the left.

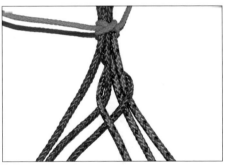

≈ **STAGE 3** – Take the outer right behind and to the left of #2 and return it over two to the right. Repeat as needed.

This last sinnet in this chapter brings more presence to solid sinnets and may perhaps increase your thirst for even more complex sinnets (I highly recommend making a Pentalpha Sinnet (ABOK #3081, 3082) from the *Ashley Book of Knots*—it can try the patience of a saint as the saying goes). Before that, however, here is a regular pentagonal solid sinnet.

« *The finished Oval Cross-Section Sinnet*

Pentagon

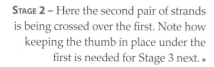

« STAGE 1 – Take ten strands, doubling them to five pairs. Crown each pair to the right (counterclockwise).

STAGE 2 – Here the second pair of strands is being crossed over the first. Note how keeping the thumb in place under the first is needed for Stage 3 next. »

« STAGE 3 – Finish tucking the remaining pairs. Tuck the last pair through where your thumb was (now withdrawn) and start the tightening. Be careful that you lay each pair down flat in the same orientation as they began the crowning, inside on the inside and outside on the outside. Note here that the green pair at the bottom need straightening before tightening to fair them up.

STAGE 4 – Now each pair has been pulled tight and we are ready for the next stage. Be sure that the perimeter looks fair before proceeding. »

« **STAGE 5** – Now crown each pair to the left (clockwise) and tighten each pair . . .

STAGE 6 – then fair up each pair. Repeat Stage 1 and 2 as needed for length desired. »

≈ *The finished pentagonal sinnet (only three faces visible)*

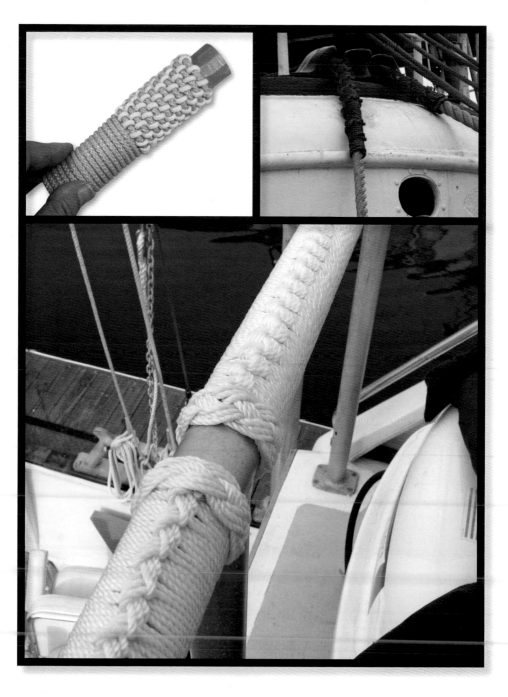

Covering Knots

Covering things with knots is a delight for my eyes, particularly when it is done with knots that are even, tight, and well-laid out. When it comes to covering a surface with knotting it is very necessary that the individual section or piece of the covering should be as simple as possible (because knots are small and surfaces generally are big) and yet the overall effect should be pleasing to the eye. Imagine that you have free rein to decorate something; you could go for simple (such as with a simple color) or complex (such as with a complex pattern) or something with texture. In the world of knotting, you are able to combine the three and have something colorful, textured, and patterned to heighten the viewer's awareness of the covering itself. You can also mute the covering to heighten the appreciation of the object. To add to the sensual experience, why not try using a cord or yarn that has a scent to it also? Tarred hemp, flax, jute—all have an individual and evocative scent to them, which may help the viewer experience something beyond the mere visually decorative effect!

Covering flat, curved, or irregular surfaces is probably one of the simplest and yet most elegant artifices possible with a piece of string, especially colored string, old rope, or perhaps leather lace. The possibilities are almost limitless and all that is required is the ability to tie one or two seemingly simple structures to produce a very charming and beautiful finish to an otherwise utilitarian object. Here are some photographs of some beautiful bottle coverings, made with nothing more than what I have shown in this book.

These coverings to the bottles had a practical use also, in that they prevented the bottles from breaking accidentally if they received a light shock. These bottles were decorated by Ken Elliott, UK.

Using knots to cover the surface of other pieces of line has been a mainstay of nautical work for centuries. The sea is remarkably hard on materials, especially rope. It can be both practical and aesthetically pleasing to cover easily frayed surfaces. If a mariner had a piece of leather or canvas on hand, that would be used, together with a liberal coating of tar or linseed oil, to protect the underlying material, whether it be made of wire, rope, or wood. When no canvas or leather could be found, the true tar (a real sailor) could easily turn to a piece of cord to protect the piece, even if only temporarily.

Soon, the bo'sun's mates and the bo'suns themselves began to realize the effects that cord had on otherwise ordinary objects. A tiller became something even more decorative and very readily handled. A man-rope, when covered, not only looked good but also became more weather-resistant and somewhat easier to hold on to. A regularly handled piece of line, or the end of the hawser that held the anchor, could be covered with pointing to make it not only easier to handle and easier to insert into its required anchor ring, but also a place to show off some fancy work. Grab-rails, mast boots, rub-rails, stanchions, and all manner of tubing or ropes became the target for the eager marlinespike seamanship showoff. Here are some fenders that are used for practical purposes as well as being decorative.

The tipcat fender on a narrowboat on the English canals is one example of the fine ropework found today on these elegant craft. The large round fender is an ancient fender found in a museum in the city of Sevilla, Spain, in the Golden Tower.

Coverings were not only used at sea. Knotting was used to cover the handrails of small house stairways, hiking staves, the handles of coachmen's whips, bedposts in fancier inns, the wearing points on crossbow strings, or the handles of teakettles. Tools and tool handles were of course covered whenever the opportunity arose. Some of the finer sea-chest beckets (the handles with which the ends of the sea-chest are decorated) are covered with coachwhipping, needle-hitching, or some other covering technique. Here are some recent examples by members of the Pacific Americas Branch of the International Guild of Knot Tyers.

Take a look also inside the covers of the earliest editions of *Ashley's Book of Knots* (1944) for some older and still great examples of sea-chest beckets as seen on facing page.

Many of the names for these coverings derive from nautical sources; ample idle time was available on board for eager hands if there were no cleaning or sail-setting to do. Some derive from other, more obvious sources, either by appearance or by usage. St Mary's Hitching probably came from the Scilly Isles off Great Britain, and the term coachwhipping likely came from coachmen's

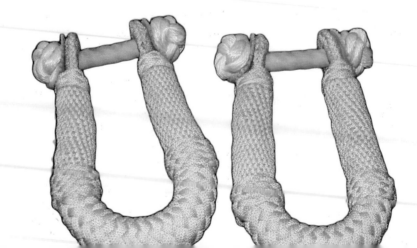

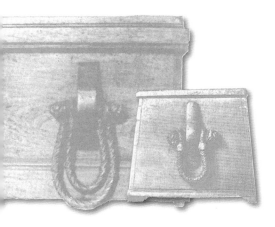

over with rope is also called "keckling" and keeps the end of the cable from being "chafed." The illustration below is from Ashley and shows one right-laid rope laid into the cantline of a plain-laid hawser as worming, to protect the hawser from chafe against sea-bottom rocks or the barnacle-encrusted side of the hull. The wearing piece of the keckling could readily be replaced when worn, rather than having to replace the expensive large hawser.

handle coverings. On the other hand, by conjecture, sinnet work, whose name origins are unknown, may have come from the English expression for a week (the time it took to make some of this at sea) known as a seven-night or a sennite in its original spelling.

≈ The method I have shown here is drawn from another of Ashley's illustrations, # 3604:

≈ **STAGE 1** – Form a Half Hitch.

CACKLING, KACKLING OR KECKLING

Keckling is the process of adding a material to chafing points on a cable (used to tie a ship to a dock) or a hawser (the anchor cable). It was first mentioned in print in about 1627 in Captain Smith's *Seaman's Grammar,* where he noted keckling is "to bind some old clouts [clothes or rags] to keepe it from binding or galling in the Hawse or Ring." Although he does not illustrate the process specifically, Lt. George S. Nares *Seamanship* (1862) notes that when "splicing the eye in a rope cable, long ends are left which are wormed into the lays of the cable; this served

≈ **STAGE 2** – Form another Half Hitch, but in the opposite direction.

The finished work, shown with each half hitch placed over and to the right of its neighbor, so as to give this "ropelike" effect, twisting around the line to the right and following the lay of the line

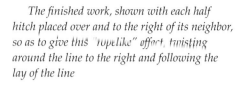

▲ **STAGE 3 –** Form a third Half Hitch, again reversing direction.

Here are some samples of keckling over a dock-line, spotted recently on the *Star of India* in San Diego, California. Here they used the familiar French Spiral, also known as French Hitching, covering, formed by making a Half Hitch for each successive turn. See later in this chapter for instructions on how to make this easy and speedy covering.

▲ **STAGE 4 –** Repeat as necessary, continuing the reversal each time.

Of course, you don't need to apply this covering over a hawser, a dock-line or other stout line—you might find it looks good over a shower-curtain ring, a window-blind pull-ring, or over each corner post of your four-poster bed!

COACHWHIPPING

Coachwhipping is formed over any generally round or cylindrical surface using an even number of cords, each cord or set of cords being laid in opposing directions in an over-under weave. The term may derive from the term "Whip Stich [sic]" used by Edward "Ned" Ward in *The Wooden World* in 1707, according to Ashley. *The Oxford English Dictionary* (OED) refers instead to the noun form "coach whip," which they describe as deriving from a later 1787 publication by Archer (Naval Chronicles, XI) describing the results of a storm, saying ," The Sails began to fly . . . into coach whips," meaning long, thin strips, which are essentially what is used to make coachwhipping. It was formerly used (and may still be used today) to make what the *Oxford Companion to Ships and the Sea* calls "a patterned sinnet to make a ship look smart and tiddley,'" "tiddley" being the sailor's word for shipshape or neat.

Begin by seizing the cords, in this case only four pairs each side so that you can see the pattern develop, to the piece you wish to cover. When you are proficient at this number of cords, increase your handling to six, eight, or any other multiple of two cords, Increase again from there on your next practice project to six separate cords, three in each direction, From there it is but a short step to increase to three sets of two, or three sets of four or . . . who knows how many? If you wish to cover the entire surface with cords having no gaps between, you will have to have an even number of cords, so that you have the same number of cords each side. These may be in one, two, three, four, or more bundles each side—the pattern will be the same, under, over, under, over, under, etc. You will also have to leave a small gap between the individual strands or cords when first attaching them, so that, when angled to cover the piece, they do not overlap each other.

⌐ **Stage 1** – Put the individual pieces in two large bundles on each side of the rail to be covered, holding them in place with tape, an elastic band, or a Constrictor Knot. This holdfast will be covered or removed at the end of the work. Here we are using two sets of eight cords, in four pairs for each side, blue and red.

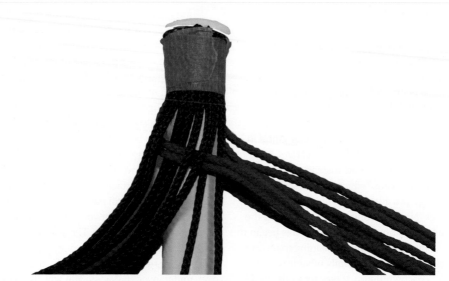

⌃ **STAGE 2** – Bring the outer right-hand pair of cords, in this case a pair of red cords, around behind, under the left outer blue pair, over the next pair, under the next pair, and over the last blue pair to return to the right-hand side.

⌃ **STAGE 3** – Bring the outer left-hand pair of blue cords around behind, under the outer right pair of red cords and then over, under, over, and return to the lower edge of the left-hand sets. Note that the outer red pair we started with is now covered by this blue pair.

≈ **STAGE 4** – Repeat Stage 2 with the right cord . . .

≈ **STAGE 5** – and repeat Stage 3 with the left cord . . .
STAGE 6 – then repeat Stages 2 through 5 until you've covered a desired length.

≈ Note that the coverage of the base rail is not complete, because we are showing how to make it, not a finished article. You may or may not wish to cover the object completely, as you can see from the example pieces below.

≈ This handle on a Cat o' Nine Tails has been almost completely covered, with no large gaps between sets. Note the use of three strands per set and the finishing knot of a Turk's Head of five bights and three leads, tripled.

≈ This pair of rests for a captain's chair on a fishing vessel was covered to provide a wearing surface for the butt-end of the fishing poles. The far end is finished with a seven lead, four bight, tripled Turk's Head and the coachwhipping is made with eight sets of five strands.

The ideal finish on coachwhipping is to have the individual crossings be in a straight line from top to bottom of the finished piece. If your finished piece is not that straight, try twisting it by hand into a neat line. If you have more than two sets, remember to go over, under, over, under, etc., with each set. Note that in this last photograph there are now two sets of three cords each side and the base rod is not completely covered. To cover the base, you need enough cords around the top to fill all available space on the perimeter of the piece you are covering, remembering to leave space for the angle that the cords make with each other to prevent bunching or overlap. You can also start with alternating colors on each side. The great joy of coachwhipping is that you can achieve a covering with fairly minimal effort. You DO have to remember to keep each side separate and to alternate the passing of the set or bundle of cords each side each time. When using multiple strands in each set, remember to keep the individual strands in their same location relative to each other, with no twisting of the set as you progress. Here is a set of coachwhipping I made on one of the vertical rails (I did complete both of them, of

course!) of a companionway stair on a fishing trawler:

The small gaps were deliberately left, so that the owner could check the condition of the underlying aluminum rails from time to time. The ends, which were originally held in place with a Constrictor Knot, are covered with a Turk's Head, worked tight, to hide them. See Chapter 9 for Turk's Head Knots.

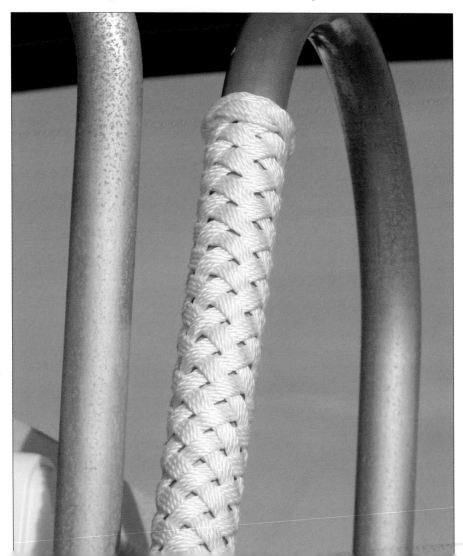

COCKSCOMBING

Any person who has seen one of the more radical or extreme forms of the haircut known as a Mohawk, or perhaps even the crest of a Roman soldier's helmet, will understand the derivation of cockscombing. It is a raised pattern on the top of a curved surface, usually a rail, which stands out in such a fashion that it resembles a cock's comb or wattle (but only if you squint at it really hard!). I find it interesting to note how many terms for nautical elements are so like the farming or agricultural background from which the majority of pressed and indentured sailors came. One of the favorite places where I have seen cockscombing used is on a small ring, used as a pull for a window shade. Several patterns of cockscombing exist and here I have shown just five, including a sample with five strands, instead of three, where three is the more usual number. There is nothing to prevent cockscombing being made with any number of strands, always provided that the basic premise of forming a pattern using half hitches still holds true. Try using two strands to make alternating square knots or to make Carrick Bends on the surface! All the types of cockscombing shown here are made with colored cords for ease of identifying which strand is which. If you are using the same color for all strands, try numbering or lettering the strands for ease of identification.

The cord ends should preferably be made up into small bundles, known as knittles or nettles, which are easier to control. See Chapter 2 for handling techniques and recommended tools. As with all covering knots that are used to cover rails, it is difficult to get full coverage on a curved rail rather than a straight one. A gradual curve will work out OK most of the time, but be very careful when trying to tie a covering around a rail that has a curve of less than twelve units to one, measuring the curve radius and the rail radius for the ratio. A one-inch radius (two-inch diameter) pipe will not be easily or well covered with cockscombing (or coachwhipping) if it bends through a curve that has less than a twelve-inch radius on the inside of the curve.

TYPE 1: THREE-STRAND RUNNING UNDERHAND COCKSCOMBING

This style is known as underhand cockscombing because each of the following Half Hitches is made beneath the previous one. Make sure you keep the individual Half Hitches separate from each other. This means you will be working under another strand from time to time. If you are using the same-colored strands for all parts of the pattern, it is easy to become confused. Remember to practice, practice, and practice again!

« **STAGE 1** – Seize all three strands to the piece and make a Half Hitch under the other strands with the outer right-hand strand . . .

⌃ **STAGE 2** – then make a Half Hitch with the middle strand, again under the remaining strands (here only one remains) . . .

⌃ **STAGE 5** – Repeat Stage 2, to the left, with the middle strand under the remaining one . . .

⌃ **STAGE 3** – and finally make a Half Hitch with the remaining strand.

⌃ **STAGE 6** – and then half hitch the last strand in the same direction as the previous two. Repeat Stages 1 through 6, enough to cover the piece.

⌃ **STAGE 4** – Make a Half Hitch with the first strand, but this time in the opposite direction and still under the other strands.

» *The finished piece looks magnificent in one color and this may take some practice to achieve.*

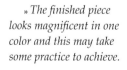

The next type of cockscombing again normally uses three strands, but now they are treated as one strand. Here again, they are made with colored strands to help you see the pattern. To help yourself when making this pattern with the same color strands throughout, you could tape all three together to get the same effect.

TYPE 2: THREE-STRAND SINGLE RUNNING COCKSCOMBING

⚲ **STAGE 3** – Repeat Stages 1 and 2 as needed.

⚲ **STAGE 1** – Seize all three strands together and Half Hitch all to the right.

⚲ **STAGE 2** – Carefully bend all three strands over and Half Hitch them together to the left.

⚲ *The finished simple running cockscombing enables a quick and easy covering of the piece, and can be finished with a Turk's Head or a Spanish Ring Knot.*

Now we return to forming Half Hitches from single strands, but this time alternating directions with each strand instead of having all three go one way and then the next. When making this style of cockscombing the action of making it is one that can be conducted without even looking in close detail at what is being made—you could sit at the table and read a book, or in your favorite backyard lounge chair keeping an eye on the children or grandchildren while covering a piece.

Type 3: Alternating Three-Strand Running Cockscombing (also known as Common Cockscombing)

≈ **Stage 2** – Half Hitch the middle (white) strand to the left . . .

≈ **Stage 3** – Half Hitch the left (red) strand to the right . . .

≈ **Stage 1** – Seize all strands to the piece and Half Hitch the right (blue) strand to the right . . .

≈ **Stage 4** – Half Hitch the next (blue) strand to the left . . .

This next type is a little different, because it is made overhand, with each strand being brought over the others in turn. The difference may only be noticeable to another knot-tyer, but will garner many useful conversation starters when you ask people if they can tell the difference between the two techniques, of which you just happen to have a sample—be sure to carry one with you!

⌐ STAGE 5 – continue Half Hitching left and right until complete.

TYPE 4: THREE-STRAND RUNNING OVERHAND COCKSCOMBING

⌐ STAGE 1 – Seize all three strands together and take the right (blue) strand over the other two and Half Hitch to the left . . .

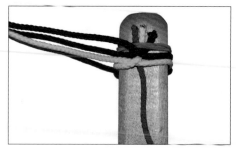

⌐ The finished common cockscombing adds a handsome touch with very little effort.

⌐ STAGE 2 – take the middle (white) strand over the left strand and Half Hitch again to the left

The final type shown, out of many different types, shows that you can really use any number of strands to make the cockscombing, if the piece is wide enough to take the pattern developed with the strands used. The piece used here (a cardboard tube) is just broad enough to show off the pattern of the five strands, so be sure to choose wisely!

≈ **STAGE 3** – take the left (red) strand and half hitch to the left, then take the right strand (blue) over the other two to the right and Half Hitch to the right. Do the same for the white and red cords. Repeat Stages 2 and 3 as needed.

TYPE 5: FIVE-STRAND SINNET COCKSCOMBING

This style of cockscombing requires a slightly wider piece to be covered, because we have so many more strands to use.

≈ **STAGE 1** – Seize all five strands to the piece, three to the left and two to the right . . .

≈ **STAGE 2** – take the leftmost strand and pass it over one (red) and under the other three (white, blue, yellow) to the right, then bring it round behind the piece . . .

≈ *The finished running overhand has a three-dimensional quality, such that the red, white, and blue appear to be standing well above the base rail.*

≈ **STAGE 3** – and Half Hitch it under everything, tail to the right and below the other two.

≈ **STAGE 4** – Now take the right (yellow) strand over the blue and under the green, white, and red to the left . . .

≈ **STAGE 5** – where it is now passed behind the piece and Half Hitched under all and placed below the white strand to form three on the left again.

≈ **STAGE 6** – Repeat Stages 2 through 5 as necessary.

≈ *The appearance of the finished five-strand cockscombing requires a very long piece to fully appreciate the color movement from one end to the other, but this will also look very good with a single color cord*

The use of cockscombing can enhance a simple handrail, a walking cane, an otherwise plain aluminum lawn chair, or perhaps the column of the shift lever on that old clunker or Jeep®. It certainly adds grip and life to an otherwise rather plain surface. A word to the wise, however: If the original rail is painted over after knotting is applied, be prepared to remake the entire covering when it comes time to repaint! Here are some more shots of rail coverings using cockscombing, just to inspire you as to what you may be able to achieve with some fairly straightforward covering techniques.

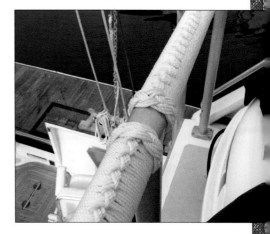

» Common three-strand cockscombing, made with white nylon seine twine

« Running three-strand cockscombing (foreground) and single running cockscombing made with three gathered strands (background), finished with Turk's Heads

HALF HITCHING

Half Hitching is what we have been using to form the cockscombing, but it is not the only thing we can make with Half Hitches. The following Half-Hitch patterns allow full coverage of a piece and are straightforward to make. Remember that Half Hitching is only secure when it is on the piece you are covering or is connected to another base cord or to a prior Half Hitch—it has no intrinsic ability to maintain shape or position otherwise. You may want to attach some Half Hitches to clothing or to a flat surface. The normal way to do this is to sew or glue the Half Hitch in place, so that it is not snagged accidentally. The French Sinnet Single Strand shown here looks complicated when you first see

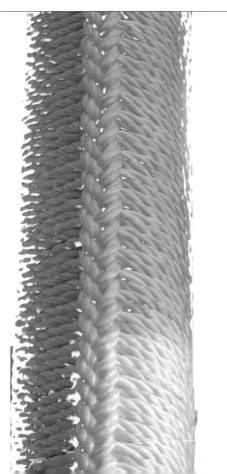

it, but really, once it has been started, it is no more complicated than any others here. As a reminder that a Half Hitch and a marling hitch are not the same structure, I have also included a series of marling hitches over a base rod for you to compare visually, although the marling hitch really has little decorative value because it lies too flat when compared with the Half Hitch. Lastly, needle hitching is mentioned in this section, and some illustrative pieces are included for completeness. More information on needle hitching is given elsewhere in this book. The ends of the Half-Hitched pieces will likely require some kind of covering, like a Turk's Head or a Spanish Ring Knot. If you do not want to add such a covering, the ends may be scattered under the last few turns, as shown near the end of the Half-Hitching section here.

French Sinnet Single Strand

This form of chain sinnet is a little like the bo'sun mentioned earlier, neither fish nor fowl and neither wholly sinnet nor wholly Half Hitching. I have included it here because it is a little light relief from the endless pulling of a whole bundle or knittle of twine each time a Half Hitch is made. Actual French Sinnet is shown in the earlier chapter on sinnets, hence also showing this one here, which vaguely resembles the French Sinnet in appearance although certainly not in manufacture, it being made from but a single strand. It is also not normally a covering knot, but is frequently used as a Bugler's Braid. When wound around or stitched to another object, however, as a covering, it is a thing of beauty!

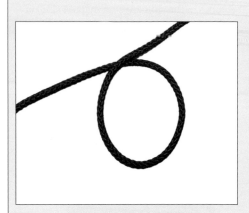

Stage 1 – Make a single overhand clockwise loop . . .

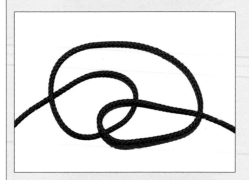

Stage 2 – followed by a second loop, the same direction (clockwise) as the first, but underhand this time. Lay it over the bottom part of the first loop . . .

☆ STAGE 3 – then cross the first loop by tucking the second loop under and over as shown.

☆ STAGE 5 – Repeat Stage 4 with overhand loops inserted under, over, as often as needed for a view from the front like this.

☆ STAGE 4 – Make a new overhand clockwise loop with the standing part as shown and insert under, over as shown.

☆ Here is the back of the finished Single-Strand French Sinnet/Braid, resembling the over-under pattern of regular French Sinnet.

French Whipping (aka French Spiral)

⚓ Here we see the ropelike effect that this type of hitching generates over a rail. The spiral may be either to the right or to the left, as here.

⚓ **Stage 1** – Take a single cord and start with either a Constrictor Knot or a Clove Hitch (used here).

⚓ **Stage 2** – Form a Half Hitch over the rod or rail to the right (or left) and keep half hitching in the same direction until you have covered what you need to cover. Be sure that each Hitch has the same tension as the previous Hitches.

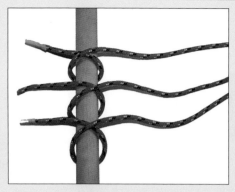

☆ STAGE 1 – Take three strands of line and make a Half Hitch with each one.

☆ STAGE 4 – Tighten the Half Hitch and prepare for the next Half Hitch.

☆ STAGE 2 – Take the nearest strand and pass it up, over and to the right, ready to make a Half Hitch.

☆ STAGE 5 – Make a second half hitch with the next strand in the same manner. Tighten each as you go, forming a "rope" over the pole. Check after each pass that the strand brought up is tightened, in this case first by pulling to the right then by pulling to the left, to bring it tight against the previous pass.

☆ STAGE 3 – Make the Half Hitch by passing the strand behind the base and under itself.

☆ STAGE 6 – Repeat as needed. Here the turns are made to the right, but could equally be made to the left.

⌐ *The finished covering provides a raised decoration on the rail, very handy for gripping!*

Moku Whipping

Again, I am uncertain as to the source of the name of this style—much has been lost in the sources of the names of the knots that should, in my opinion, be recovered, so I may make this the subject of my next task! The word *moku* may have come from the Hawaiian language (*moku* means island) or from the Finnish language (it means a recruit, as in the armed forces). The product of this kind of Hitching is much simpler than the etymology of the word. We start with two cords and rotate our hitches in opposing directions, one at a time, around the rail or rod. This produces a double helix structure and provides a superb gripping surface for holding on to any rail or round surface.

⌐ **STAGE 1** – Tie two pieces of line with an overhand knot around the base material, one to the left and one to the right, one below the other.

⌃ STAGE 2 – Tie a Half Hitch with the first strand, here to the left.

⌃ STAGE 3 – Tie the second strand in the opposite direction, here to the right.

⌃ STAGE 4 – Tie each strand left and right in succession. On reaching the crossing of one strand over the other, pick one to cross over the other before tying it in a Half Hitch.

The Moku Whipping in place, showing the double-helix shape around the base rod or rail. In this situation it is used as a hand-grip. ⌄

Half Hitches and Marling Hitches

Half Hitches are made by tucking the standing part of a cord under itself, whereas a marling hitch is made by tying an overhand knot around the object being hitched. Here they both are applied to the same surface for side-by-side comparison:

⁂ *The center and left-side versions, marling hitches both, lie very flat to the base, whereas the Half Hitching, on the right, stands a little proud of the surface.*

Finishing Half Hitches without a Covering Knot

Half hitches, or any other covering knot, may be finished by tucking the ends under the finished work. If the work is plain, the finishing end may be more visible, but if there is a pattern or a raised surface, then the end may successfully be secured under the turns to make for a secret ending. Here is one way of doing this:

⁂ **Stage 1** – Insert a pen or other thin object along the length of the object you are covering when you near the end.

⁂ **Stage 2** – Continue the wrapping, but incorporate the pen as if it were part of the object (not too tightly!).

⁂ **Stage 3** – When you have completed the length you need, withdraw the pen and insert the end of the cord where the pen used to be.

STAGE 4 – Go back to the point where you inserted the pen and tighten up each turn, one by one . . .

STAGE 5 – until you have nothing left except a loop of line that, when pulled, will disappear under the tightened turns.

STAGE 6 – Pull the end of the loop to make the cord disappear. Cut off the end of the line.

Here are some alternative finishes using square knots and Carrick Bends:

Here the square knots are made in alternating pairs, first to the left, then to the right.

Next, we make use of interlocked Carrick Bends as a covering to one side. I believe this is the first time this has been done like this.

GRAFTING AND POINTING

Rope ends need pointing when used for agricultural, arborist, nautical, and other applications in which a line must be repeatedly passed through a ring or a shackle. Grafting also has a practical use—protecting a line from being frayed early in its life. All rope ends require some finishing in my opinion, whether by burning (not very decorative, but functional), with a stopper knot, or, as shown here, a whipping or a piece of grafting or pointing. A snaked whipping will prevent the end of a line from coming undone regardless of the conditions to which it is exposed, and is also quite beautiful. It is to the decorative aspect that we are drawn in this book.

This example shows a rope end on a dead-eye's lanyard as the finish to a Matthew Walker stopper.

Normally people who wish to use something a little more elegant than simply burning the ends or, worse still, allowing them to fray like cows" tails, will perhaps wish to try this alternative to normal whipping methods when they have some time on their hands and wish to draw admiring glances and discussions from their fellow rope-users. It can be applied equally to braided lines or to laid lines, because it involves taking the yarns out separately and then incorporating them into the finished piece as part of the pattern. The finish can look very elegant on a bellpull, a light pendant, or as an alternative to a tassel end on a curtain tieback.

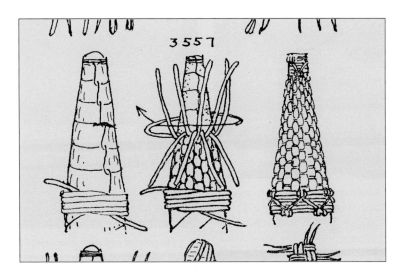

≈ *Ashley's #3557 pointing to the end of a line. Note the snaked whipping top and bottom on the right-most illustration taken from Ashley's famed* Ashley Book of Knots.

POINTING A ROPE END

Many would tell you that you cannot point a rope at anyone because it is too limp, but a rope end CAN be pointed—just using a different meaning for the word! In this alternate meaning, pointing is the wrapping of all alternate layers of the outer covering yarns of each of a rope's basic strands with a wrapping cord, to give some rigidity to the rope end. This helps in being able to "point" the line to where you want it to go. If, for instance, you want to poke the end of the line through a small ring, for keeping some drapes in place, then by applying pointing to the line you will end up with a stiffer and more hard-wearing "end" to your line. Of course, as a decorative finish, a silken rope may be pointed to give it a more elegant appearance. This is often done with curtain tiebacks and the ends of pull cords. To be consistent with

the use of the words in weaving, we describe here the weft threads as those crossing from one side of the line to the other, while the warp cords are those that lie along the piece.

≈ **STAGE 1** – Turn the outer yarns of the rope down out of the way. Be sure to keep an even number of outer yarns, because we will split them, one up and one down, after the next step.

≈ **STAGE 2** – Using a knife, either scrape or cut away only the inner yarns to a taper and cover with canvas or friction tape, as here.

≈ *The pointed end prior to applying the snaked whipping at the base*

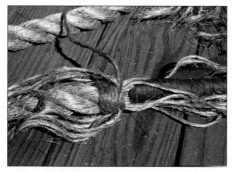

STAGE 3 –Apply three or four turns of marline or other grafting insert cord, then use a half hitch to secure one half of the outer yarns in an upward (or forward-facing) position. These are now your upper yarns. Use another Half Hitch to secure the other half of the outer yarns in the same upward position. Repeat, making sure to alternate the groups of yarns. When you reach the end of the rope, make a snaked whipping around the last fibers to ensure that the end does not fray. If you use an odd number of warp cords you will not need to alternate the upper and lower yarns (warpchords).

Pointing, as can be seen from the first example, is made by "wrapping" the yarns at the end of the line. In that first example the pointing is completed by wrapping the weft over and under the base yarns, the warp. Other patterns of "wrapping" can also be made and the end does not always have to be tapered. Here are two further examples of pointing, first by overhand round turn pointing and then by underhand round-turn pointing. While pointing is normally used to point a line (i.e. ,to put a sharper end to the line as one would to a pencil), it works equally well on tubular shapes.

Overhand Round Turn Pointing

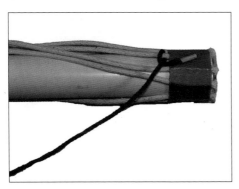

STAGE 1 – Secure the standing end of the pointing cord, here with a half hitch.

STAGE 3 – Continue over two, round turn over one, to cover the cords for overhand round-turn pointing.

This is a started example of overhand pointing. The method requires close attention to tension in the warp cords.

STAGE 2 – Wrap the weft over two cords, tucking under and over (a turn in knotting parlance) the second warp cord.

Underhand Round-Turn Pointing

With this method, we expose a little more of the warp cords, for a slightly different appearance. The verticality it shows helps to heighten the appearance of, say, a long bottle being covered.

☀ **STAGE 3** – Repeat Stage 2 to cover the warp cords.

☀ **STAGE 1** – Again, secure the standing end with the working part facing the desired direction of tying.

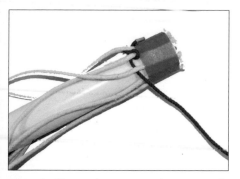

☀ **STAGE 2** – Pass under two, round turn around one.

☀ **STAGE 4** – Continue under two, round turn one for underhand round-turn pointing

The pointing just shown has two important elements that must be kept in mind when making the pieces. First, the ends of all the warp cords (those that lie along the length of the piece) must be secured. Here they have been secured with tape as a temporary measure. This use of tape is expedient if you are going to cover the ends of the cords with something else. If you are not going to cover them with anything of a sufficient size to hide the tape, or if the location is to be an outside or weather-exposed location, you will probably be better off with a Constrictor Knot to hold the cords. The Constrictor will, of course, have to be covered and has the advantage of being much smaller in size than the tape.

The second item to bear in mind is that the warp cords will have to cover exactly half of the circumference of the piece, or there will be gaps in the covering. I find that it is easiest to keep adding cords until at least half of the surface is covered and then make one or two trial wraps with the cords spaced one cord thickness apart to determine whether I have enough or too many cords. The tension applied to each succeeding turn of the weft cord will change the thickness of the warp cords and may leave a slight gap if you are not careful. It does not matter if you use an odd or even number of warp cords unless you want a specific pattern on the surface. The length of the weft cord will depend to some extent on its thickness relative to the warp cord thickness, but a good rule of thumb is to use twice as much weft cord as is needed to singly wrap the piece. Imagine if you will that you are wrapping the whole piece with a single strand of cord. Wrap enough to cover a one-inch length and mark the beginning and end, then measure the length from beginning to end and multiply by two to get the length of your weft. Add to this number about ten percent more to allow for mis-measurement, thickness differences, and handling, and you will have the right length for your weft to be long enough—you wouldn't want to run out before finishing, would you?

GRAFTING

Grafting simply reverses the process used for pointing. Instead of wrapping a weft around the warp cords, spiraling around the cylinder, the warp or long cords are wrapped around the weft cord. Again, it is important to keep the weft cord taught throughout the wrapping process. Notice the slight angle the cords make with the base rod or rail being covered, and use this to your advantage when figuring the final shape.

Overhand Grafting

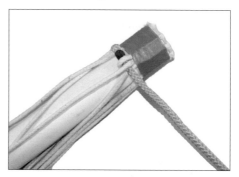

⌢ **STAGE 1** – Secure the weft cord (make sure it's stiffer than the warp cords) and keep it taught.

⌢ **STAGE 2** – Wrap a half hitch over the weft cord with each warp cord in turn.

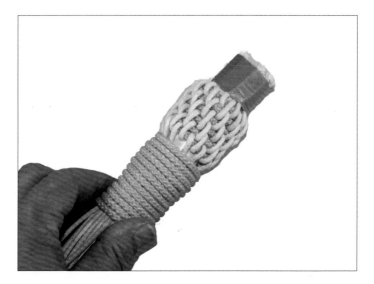

Stage 3 – Continue wrapping half hitches with each warp to cover the piece with overhand round-turn grafting. The end of the weft has here been wrapped around the base of the warp cords, but could equally be immediately started into French Whipping to finish the ends. Alternately, the ends may be covered with a Turk's Head or a variant. Contrasting colors will highlight the warp cords and help to provide a handsome accent, whereas using the same color cord for warp and weft will produce a very interesting textured surface.

Underhand Grafting

Underhand round-turn grafting highlights the color of the weft cord, whereas the overhand round turn grafting highlights more of the warp cords. Here is an example for you to try.

Stage 1 – As before, secure the end of the weft, but with an underhand round turn.

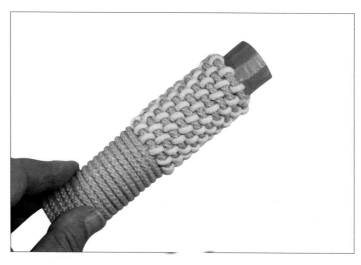

⩰ **STAGE 2** – Continue keeping the weft line taught and taking each warp cord in turn to form underhand round-turn grafting.

Purely Decorative Knots

I really like decorative knots, particularly those where there is no other obvious purpose to them. Purely decorative knots are ideally used wherever there is a need for embellishment. The following selection of decorative knots has no other purpose than this. They do not serve to hide a junction (although they may be used for that purpose), they do not serve to add strength or utility, and they have no other practical purpose. Some would say that the Chinese knots later in this book are purely decorative, but those knots can also tell a story, which is a very practical use indeed. The following are knots I consider to be purely decorative, for which no other purpose exists than to bring beauty.

BO'SUN'S LANYARD KNOT

No collection of decorative knots would be complete without the famed Bo'sun's Lanyard Knot. This is a Carrick Bend that has been modified slightly, so that it can be used to bring two cords together in a decorative manner. It is known by several names; including the Sailor's Knife Lanyard Knot, the Two-Strand Diamond Knot, the Single-Strand Diamond Knot, the Marlingspike Lanyard Knot, and the Bo'sun's Whistle Knot. Names, as I have said before, only serve to place labels—what matters is structure. Here the structure is two underhand loops interlocked and then wrapped by a half turn to bring the ends of the line through the knot. Here is one method of making it.

⌃ **STAGE 1** – Bring two ends of the same piece of cord over the back of your hand to the palm of your hand, as shown here.

⌃ **STAGE 2** – Make a counterclockwise underhand loop with the lower-cord end directly on the palm of your hand.

⌃ **STAGE 3** – Bring the upper-cord end under the first loop, over the top of your lower cord and then under the working part of your lower cord, like this.

⌃ **STAGE 4** – Now cross over, under, over to the top left of your palm. You should now have a Carrick Bend on your palm.

« STAGE 5 – Bring what is now the lower-right cord counterclockwise around your palm, over the top of the upper cord that passes around your index finger (look carefully at the photograph at the tip of the left index finger) and to its left, then pass it up under and through the diamond-shaped hole in the middle of the Carrick Bend, as shown here.

» STAGE 6 – Again, take the cord that exits the upper left of your hand counterclockwise around your palm, over the lower cord and to its right, then up and into the diamond alongside the first end.

« STAGE 7 – Gently pull both cord ends while holding firmly to the cord that was over the back of your hand from Stage 1, and shape the knot gradually, shown here in progress (the two overhand knots are there from a different exercise).

« Here is the finished Bo'sun's Lanyard Knot. It forms a very handy loop in the middle of a cord, perhaps ready for some sinnet work or for attachment to another object.

SPANISH RING KNOTS

Unverified legends say that Spanish Ring Knots were brought to the Americas by Spanish forces in the 1400s, as decorations on horse tack. If this Spanish origin is true, the knots may have been derived from Moorish knots brought to Spain centuries before the discovery of the New World. Today these knots are sometimes referred to as Gaucho Knots for their use in horse tack by the gauchos of the South American plains.

Bruce Grant's magnificent book, *Encyclopedia of Rawhide and Leather Braiding*, shows some wonderful designs of Spanish Ring Knots. The knots shown here are of the one-pass and two-pass varieties, with a nod to the four-pass variety, similar to the ones shown in Grant's book. Other varieties are possible once you have mastered the pattern required. The knot or braid may essentially be thought of a Turk's Head Knot, which has been passed once again, or twice again, with the same cord as is used to make the Turk's Head, giving a very neat chevron pattern to the surface of the knot. The four-pass knot requires a slightly different start, using a series of wraps instead of the Turk's Head Knot. My favorite feature of the Spanish Ring Knot is that it can be made with fine cord into rings or earrings for that special someone in your life. The pattern speaks to the endless cycle of life's ups and downs, but it always stays together!

This knot translates very well into leather, twine, cord, gold wire, or even rope if you treat it carefully. Let's start with a five-bight, three-lead Turk's Head, which forms the basis for the first Spanish Ring Knot.

First, make an "X" by taking the cord once around the tube; the standing part is under my thumb on the left.

⚲ *This pair of braided earrings was made for the author's wife by a very good friend, Barry Brown, UK. Each was made using a single strand of cord and typifies the work of the gauchos, complex and yet from a simple base.*

⚲ **STAGE 1:** – We start with a tube for ease of photographing the subject—you may want to use your fingers or perhaps a paper grid pattern.

« **STAGE 3** – Now turn the tube top toward you (see the letter "B"?) and tuck the working end under the right side wrap. Keep the working end to the left side of the tube and over the left-hand wrap, as shown here. We will continue going under and over, moving from right to left and back from left to right as we progress.

STAGE 2 – Bring the working end around one more time, parallel at the back, to make another "X" in the front.

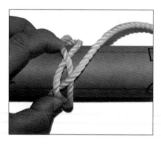

STAGE 5 – Pass the working end from left to right under the left-side wrap and over the right-side wrap. Note that there is now a second "mouth" above the letter "D," by the left index fingertip.

« **STAGE 6** – Pass the working end from right to left under the right wrap and over the left wrap. Note that you have now returned to the origin of the standing part, seen at upper left in the photograph.

STAGE 4 – Rotate the tube toward you again (see the letter "C'?) and pass the left-side cord over the right without doing anything else yet with the working end of the cord, seen here by the left index fingertip. Note that this makes a kind of "mouth," up through which we will next pass the working end.

That completes the three-lead, five-bight Turk's Head, which is the start for this one-pass Spanish Ring Knot. Now for the next part where we pass from left to right and right to left again, but this time we cross **over** the standing part. Here are the photographs, using a different cord.

ONE-PASS SPANISH RING KNOT

« **STAGE 8** – This is the same knot as in Stage 7 above, only in a different cord. Pass the working end from left to right below the standing part as shown here.

» **STAGE 9** – Move the entire working-end cord up and over the standing part, so that the working end is now to the left of the standing part.

« **STAGE 10** – Rotate the tube as shown and bring the working end across the knot, from left to right.

« **STAGE 12** – Cross the working end under one and over two from right to left (working end under left index fingertip).

» **STAGE 13** – Now we are close to the final turn around the knot. Cross once again from left to right, under one and over two.

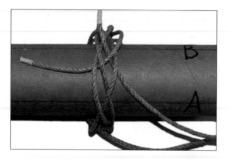

« **STAGE 14** – We must now stabilize the knot. Tuck the working end under two and over two, from right to left.

» **STAGE 15** – At the next bight, pass the working end from left to right, under two and over two ...

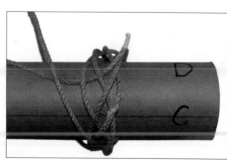

« **Stage 16** – then
from right to left,
under two and
over two.

» **Stage 17** – We have now
successfully returned our
working end to the beginning
part of the standing part. Cut off
the ends and hide them.

≈ *The final view, showing the over-two, under-two structure of this Spanish Ring*

From this start we move on to creating a Spanish Ring Knot of two passes, called so because this is the second time we have gone around the ring, creating more bights and leads.

TWO-PASS SPANISH RING KNOT

« **STAGE 1** – Starting with the single-pass ring knot, we have the working end already passed under two and over two from left to right.

» **STAGE 2** – Lift the most recent bight formed by the working end up and over the standing part.

« **STAGE 3** – Rotate the tube counterclockwise as shown. Pass the working end from right to left, under two and over three, then do the same from left to right.

« **STAGE 4** – We are now back at the beginning of the standing part. Tuck the working end under three and over three, from right to left,

» **STAGE 5** – Repeat at the next bight, from left to right.

« **STAGE 6** – Nearly there! Pass under three and over three, from right to left.

« **Stage 7 –**
Double the
knot or just
tuck under
and secure as
normal.

« *The end result.
Note the double
chevron shape and
compare with the
final stage of the
single pass Spanish
Ring Knot.*

Three-Pass Spanish Ring Knot

Next is the Three-Pass Spanish Ring Knot. As one might expect, this knot follows the same basic pattern as the other Spanish Ring Knots. Note that the more passes we make, the bulkier the knot becomes. You should consider only using thin cord or twine for many passes around one object. When using leather strips, this knot makes a very fine covering knot. Incidentally, you can cover square or otherwise sharp-cornered objects with all Spanish Ring Knots.

The number of bights has increased in the single pass from the initial Turk's Head of five bights to one of eight bights, and now with the two-pass we have increased that number of bights to eleven. The number of leads has also increased from three in the initial Turk's Head, to five in the single pass, to seven in the two-pass. The knot shown here is a doubled two-pass knot, made by adding a "railroad track" alongside the first pass. The three-pass will require that you take the same action of lifting the first pass of the third turn up and over the standing end, so as to add more bights and more leads or parts. When you reach the end either of the single-pass,

double-pass, or the three-pass you can then simply make "railroad tracks" of the standing part to "double" the number of leads. Actually, all you are doing is putting a parallel lead alongside the first lead.

« *A doubled,
two-pass
Spanish Ring
or Gaucho
Knot of eleven
bights and
seven leads*

FOUR-PASS SPANISH RING KNOT

To move from three passes to four we have to make a different pattern. This starts with some wraps, followed by the weaving that we might expect. The knots are normally made over a mandrel or dowel that is marked so that we can recognize where we are with the formation. It is also usually a bit oversized compared to the final size we want, so that we can slip the knot off the mandrel directly into place on our base material. Because the knot will tighten onto its base in ways we may otherwise not want (some slippage may be expected unless controlled), it is better to place a slip-over tube on top of our base mandrel, so that when tightening, we do not upset the rather delicate balance of the bights around the upper and lower edges. If you are making the knot to attach around another object, like a tool handle, it is OK to make it directly on it instead of making it on a base mandrel, but if you are going to attempt to slip it off the mandrel and onto the other object, you would be better off tying the knot over a suitable sleeve that matches the need for your application (say, a thin cardboard tube that will slide over a scarf, or a metal tube that is used to slide over a cane, for example) so that you do not get any unwanted collapse of the finished knot. You could also size, varnish, or clear-coat the knot in its finished form to stiffen its fabric. When using wire, of course, there is little need for any kind of base other than the base tube or mandrel over which you first form the knot. Here we are showing the knot made with a relatively stiff polyester cord, so the need for a separate base is reduced, although you could still use one if need be.

As for the length of cord or wire needed for a Four-Pass Knot, use about nine times the circumference of whatever you are going to make the knot around, so that you have some to work with. If you double the original cord's path, then you will have to double the length needed. When making the knot, I have found no need for pins at each bight, although sometimes this may be preferable if you are making it for the first time. This is particularly beautiful in leather!

« **STAGE 1A** – Starting with a round mandrel or tube, mark a straight line on each of four sides, then make a turn of cord around the tube and pass to the left and then to the right, making a "mouth" over the standing end. Note the letter "A" on each end of the horizontal line for guidance.

« **STAGE 1B** – Pass the cord to the right and then move it toward the left—note the letters on the mandrel!

» **STAGE 1C** – Pass over your first cords to their left and keep to the left of your second pass as you rotate the mandrel, as shown here.

« **STAGE 1D** – Pass over to the right of the second cord—again note the letters on the mandrel as we continue to rotate it and note that we make a bight above the first.

» Stage 1E – Pass over your first cords to their left again.

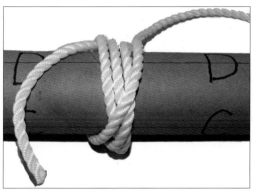

« Stage 1F – Again pass over three cords to their right and notice that we continue to make a bight above the last previous pass.

» Stage 1G – Pass over your first cords, now numbering four cords, to their left once more.

« **STAGE 111** Finally pass over four cords to their right. This completes the setup for the knot and now we start making tucks.

» **STAGE 2** – Tuck under the first strand, from right to left, then pass over four and rotate the tube one half turn.

« **STAGE 3** – Tuck under one from left to right. Pass over the next four and rotate one half turn.

» **Stage 4** – Tuck under TWO from right to left. Pass over the next four and rotate one half turn.

« **Stage 5** – Tuck under two again from left to right. Pass over the next four and rotate one half turn.

» **Stage 6** – Tuck under THREE from right to left. Pass over the next four and rotate one half turn.

« **Stage 7** – Tuck under three from left to right. Pass over the next four and rotate one half turn.

» **Stage 8** – Tuck under FOUR from right to left. Pass over four and rotate one half turn.

« **Stage 9** – Tuck under four alongside the standing part. The knot is finished, so beware that it will be tight to remove from the mandrel and will loosen if not kept on a base.

Here are some examples of other uses of this fine base knot:

≈ *The finished knot of four passes*

≈ *A tool handle decorated with some extra grip*

≈ *A belaying pin trophy with Spanish Ring of Four Passes in cotton cord*

ROSE KNOTS

Rose Knots were derided by some old sailors as being useless embellishments. Some have described as "merely a Star Knot with a Crown" while others see the knot as a style unto itself. Here I have taken the latter tack, because I feel the style deserves greater acknowledgment. The simple Rose Knot itself is indeed a crown finish to a Manrope Knot, or a Wall and Crown, doubled. More than that, however, Rose Knots form a separate classification worthy of more intense examination than is presented in this chapter. Some further examination of the works of Graumont and Hensel, Ashley, and Grainger is appropriate if the reader would like to examine Rose Knots in detail. One of the great knotters now passed, sadly, Mr. Alton C. Beaudoin of Mystic, Connecticut, 1913 -

2003, mastered this Rose Knot craft, among many others, and we give a nod here to his expertise—thank you, Alton!

« *A Rose Knot by Alton C. Beaudoin from the web pages of Vince Brennan, www .frayedknotarts.com*

We will start the path to making Rose Knots with a basic Crown Knot added to a Simple Matthew Walker Knot to make Ashley's #866, a Matthew Walker Rose Knot. Note: When you tie a Rose Knot, tugging hard will ruin the knot. Gentle application of pressure will tease the knot into being. Here, we make a blue rose as a stopper for a small bottle.

BLUE ROSE KNOT

» STAGE 1 – Start with four strands as shown.

« STAGE 2 – Tuck the first strand under two, counterclockwise.

» STAGE 3 – Tuck the second counterclockwise strand the same.

« **STAGE 4** – Tuck the third strand under two and up through the first loop.

» **STAGE 5** – Tuck the remaining strand under two and up through the second loop.

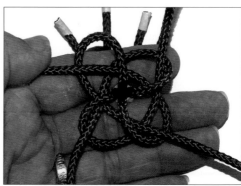

« **STAGE 6** – The Simple Matthew Walker (SMW) when drawn up looks like this.

≈ **STAGE 7** – Here the SMW is opened for you to see where to tuck the first end for crowning, over the counterclockwise strand and down along the starting strands, carefully pulling each strand over its neighbor to tighten the Crown on top of the Matthew Walker Knot base. Maybe think of this like a compass—if it comes up in the NE quadrant, it goes down into the NW quadrant, the NW goes into the SW, the SW goes into the SE, and the SE goes into the NE.

« **STAGE 8** – The SMW drawn up and the four strand ends each crowned down in turn to the starting strands.

The finished Simple Matthew Walker Rose Knot as a bottle stopper

A Rose Knot using a Double Matthew Walker

« Stage 1 – Here, using five strands knotted together with a Constrictor Knot, the first strand is taken counterclockwise under all strands and back up through its own bight to form an overhand knot.

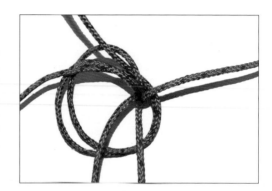

» Stage 2 – The second strand counterclockwise is turned also counterclockwise under all strands and up through the first overhand, then through its own bight to form a second overhand.

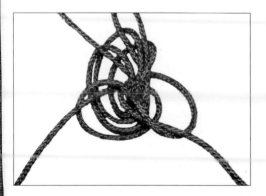

« Stage 3 – Repeat Stages 1 and 2 with the remaining three strands.

↟ STAGE 4 – Take any one of the strand ends and pass it over the next strand and down to the left of it (counterclockwise) through the center of the knot

↧ STAGE 7 – Each of the initial parts of the Double Matthew Walker is now individually and carefully drawn up around the ends of the five strands.

↧ STAGE 8A – Continue drawing up the Double Matthew Walker until all strands are tight around the center—seen here from the side.

↟ STAGE 5 – Repeat Stage 4 with the other strands.

↟ STAGE 6 – Here we see the loops in Stage 5 from the side.

« STAGE 8B – Stage 8, seen from the top, prior to pulling the center down into place—almost seems like it could be left like this, doesn't it?

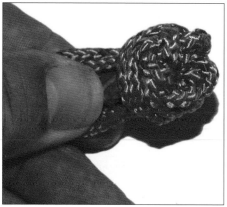

» STAGE 9 – Shown here is the top and side of the final form after drawing the ends of the individual strands down through the Double Matthew Walker and prior to trimming them at the underside.

« A finished Double Matthew Walker Rose Knot

Rose Knots may also be made using the start of a sinnet (for making sinnet, see Chapter 4) and moving through a Rosebud, to a Crown, followed by a Diamond Knot, doubled, and then crowned again. If that all sounds a little daunting, try it in stages, so that we can get each piece one at a time. Let's look at this in sequence with the Sinnet Rose Knot.

Sinnet Rose Knot

« Stage 1 – Make a four-strand sinnet and finish it with a Crown Knot, counterclockwise.

Stage 2A – The Rosebud Knot is then made by inserting each strand in turn over its neighbor (here again counter-clockwise) and up through the center of the Crown. **»**

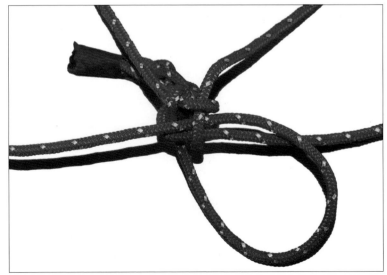

▵ **STAGE 2B** – Here is the completion of the Rosebud.

« **STAGE 3** – Next, crown all four strands.

» **STAGE 4** – Take each strand in turn under the next, counter-clockwise, and wall it just under the Rosebud Knot.

« **STAGE 5A** – Now form a Crown on top of the Rosebud Knot, ready for doubling the Wall, and then follow down.

» **STAGE 5B** – Now we take each of the strands in turn and follow down the Crown and up the Wall . . .

« **STAGE 5C** – and here is the view from the top of the Wall . . .

« STAGE 6 – and from the side it looks like this.

» STAGE 7 – When all strands are pulled up and ready to crown down again, this is what they look like on the doubling down of the Crown.

« STAGE 8A – A side view showing the paralleling of the strands . . .

⌃ **STAGE 8B** – the view from the top.

⌃ **STAGE 8C** – Here the strands have all been passed down, doubling the Crown, ready for the final step.

« **STAGE 9** – Triple up the Wall, ready for the last steps.

» **STAGE 10A** – Insert a wire loop, pricker, or hollow fid to catch the end of each strand and pull it down through next to the starting Four-Strand Sinnet, to exit under the knot.

« **STAGE 10B** – Insert each strand in turn down through the knot to finish by the original sinnet strands, ready to be cut off.

STAGE 11 – Here is a side view of the finished Sinnet Rose Knot. »

« *The completed Sinnet Rose Knot, seen partly from the top and partly from the side, so that you can see the Crown made in Stage 3 (above).*

THE GOLDEN ROSE

Next I show you how to make the Beaudoin Rose (by Alton C. Beaudoin). The Beaudoin Rose is stylized here to show the general form of the knot, rather than the specific form invented by Beaudoin. His knot employed some different Turk's Head combinations but was still built up in a similar fashion. I have named this version of it the Golden Rose. Try it—you may like it and it represents a possible challenge to make it with a single continuous strand instead of three separate strands.

⟰ **STAGE 1** – Form a three-pass Monkey's Fist and leave one end out of the ball, while the other end forms the core.

⟰ **STAGE 2** – Form a five-bight three-strand Turk's Head with three passes with the end from the Monkey's Fist inside.

« **STAGE 3** – Form a three-bight, four-pass tripled or quadrupled Turk's Head with the end of the line from the previous Turk's Head. If you prefer to add some florist's wire covered in green paper as a stalk and perhaps a silk leaf or two, you could go on to make a whole bunch of roses!

TUDOR ROSE KNOT

The Tudor Rose was noted in Issue #100 of the International Guild of Knot Tyers journal *Knotting Matters* as a reprint. It was originally printed in the magazine in April 1993 with instructions from Stuart Grainger. Grainger devised the knot, as far as I can tell, and others have reproduced it since then. I have done so here with a single color cord.

I also wanted to make a knot to give some more color to the Tudor Rose Knot, because the rose is a traditional heraldic emblem of England, the land of my birth. The rose was devised by King Henry VII, otherwise known as Henry Tudor. King Henry won the war against Richard in the Wars of the Roses (only later termed this, being known at the time only as a series of battles) when civil uprisings coalesced under the houses of the Duke of York and the Duke of Lancaster. The Lancastrians took the red rose as part of the symbol of their House and the followers of York took the white rose as part of the house emblem. King Henry melded the two house

roses in what is sometimes known as the Rose of Union by decreeing that the symbol of the winning house of Tudor under Henry would be the Tudor Rose, a combination of the Red Rose and the White Rose. Later Henry VIII, famed for having married six times, had the Round Table painted with the Tudor Rose in the middle to symbolize the unity of the state. Here is my interpretation of the Tudor Rose Knot.

To make this colored knot, first make a White Star Knot and Wall/Crown Rose in the center, leaving the center a little loose. Cast five red strands into the star and tie a Matthew Walker Knot around the center of the star, tucking the ends down into the start of the star. Then cast in five green strands and tie the Lark's Head Knots separately around the outside. All strands may then be gathered in, faired, and the whole tightened and incorporated into further knotting or simply cut off and the whole rose glued to the piece you are decorating. I made this one in less than thirty minutes, so it does not take an enormous amount of your time!

⋆ *The magnificent Tudor Rose Knot—symbol of England*

DAHLIA KNOTS

This particular invention is by Bernard Cutbush, who is from the U.K. He developed his own method of expanding the knot to provide more petals. The original method of making it was recorded by Stuart Grainger in the International Guild of Knot Tyers journal, *Knotting Matters*.

« **STAGE 1** – Starting with eight cords here, although any number divisible by two will also do well, prepare to make Crown Knots with each pair of cords.

» **STAGE 2** – Here, crowned counterclockwise, are the four pairs of cords.

« **STAGE 3** – Now Crown Knot each individual line over its counterclockwise partner.

« **STAGE 4** – The crowned strands from Stage 3 above.

» **STAGE 5** – Take each strand in turn and pass it over two loops then down into the space between the second loop and the center.

« **STAGE 6** – Repeat Stage 5 above for each strand and here is the result.

» STAGE 7 – Now tighten all strands until your knot looks like this.

« STAGE 8 – Turn the knot over and then . . .

» STAGE 9 – start a clockwise over-two Crown (a counterclockwise Wall when seen from above) for each strand.

« **STAGE 10** – The result of your over-two crown when seen from below.

» **STAGE 11** – Tighten the strands into the center around your core.

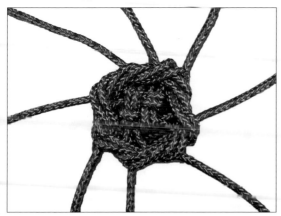

« **STAGE 12** – Turn the knot back to the top again for the next move—your knot should now look like this.

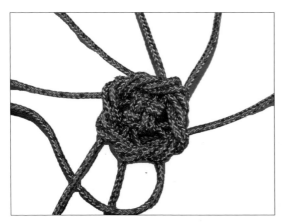

« **Stage 13** – Now we reverse our starting rotation by clockwise crown knotting each strand.

» **Stage 14** – Here all the strands have been crowned over-one.

« **Stage 15** – Turn the knot on its side and pass each strand over the clockwise loop and down into the walled strand as shown.

« STAGE 16 – Here is the Diamond Knot effect from the side, awaiting the next stage.

» STAGE 17 – Back out each part just passed, to form the petals of the Dahlia.

« STAGE 18 – Seen from below, the individual petals are now seen to have the strand of the previous loop coming up through each one. Use some fabric stiffener at this point to make the petals firmer if you are using a silk or rayon cord. The cord used here is polypropylene and quite stiff.

≈ **STAGE 19** – Now form a Half Hitch down to the base of the knot with the end of each strand.

≈ **STAGE 20** – Here, the Half Hitches have been brought down to the "stem" of the Dahlia, and may be wrapped there for security with twine or fixed in place with glue.

The Dahlia Knot— elegant and yet refined also—a knot-tyer's delight! ≈

STAR KNOTS

Star Knots may have been traded for supplies by enterprising sailors who, having nothing else to sell, may have been forced to trade one or two Star Knots, perhaps those made with a single cord instead of the multiple-corded variety usually shown. Both varieties are shown here. Lastly, a yarn about Star Knots. You will notice when you have drawn them up fully that the Star Knots are quite solid and heavy, particularly when made in thicker cords. Take note that some would have you believe that the mates on board ship would visit the shoreside pubs and alehouses at the end of the evening, carrying a handy Star Knot finish to the end of a starter length of cord. When a drunken landlubber (a potential sailor) was hit on the head with such a knot, he would, literally, see "stars" and would find himself perhaps the luckless victim of the press-gang. I do not believe the story, even though I tell it, because who would go to the trouble of making such a splendid knot only to use it as a club? Anyway, here are the purely decorative knots for your enjoyment and to try for yourself.

It has been said that anyone who can make a Star Knot, without looking at the

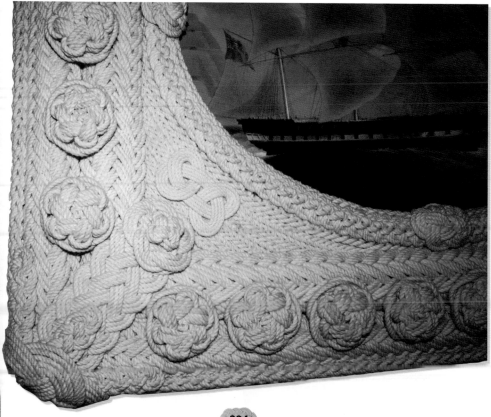

book, has truly arrived in decorative knotting. I sincerely wish this achievement for you. I shall try, through these illustrations, to make the task as easy as possible for you, so that you can not only make a multi-strand Star Knot but also go on to teach others how to make this truly delightful knot. For me, the joy of the knot is the reverse turns that the knot makes as it is formed. I have shown the Single-Strand Star Knot also, so that you can add one to a bellrope, a tassel, or to a stairway adornment of your own. When making the Star Knot with fine cords, my good friend Charlie Bell makes these knots tight right from the start, leaving large loops out of the knot so that the knot can be made firm at the end by closing the loops. I prefer the looser

method, where I can see the rough shape and then fair it into the final form. However, I am more than willing to concede that there are plenty of other ways of making a Star Knot successfully. Normally, the best Star Knots are said to be made with five or six strands, the seven and above sometimes being too "busy" and the four and three-strand too "quiet" to be noticeable. The features that truly make the Star Knot unique are the number of strands to finish the upper or more visible surface—triple strands looking the best, in my opinion, but two strands for the smaller knots and four strands also working quite well on the larger knots. Take a look also at forming a three-strand edge to the Star Knot instead of just the two strands normally present.

MULTIPLE-STRAND STAR KNOT

« **STAGE 1** – Bind five strands together with a Constrictor Knot.

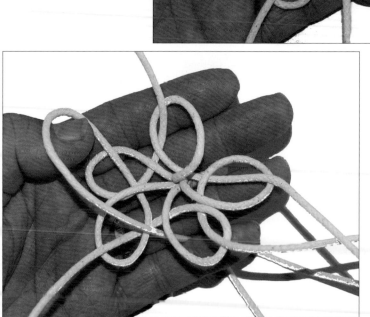

» **STAGE 2** – Form each strand into underhand counterclockwise half hitches and put each half hitch's tail through the loop formed next to it, clockwise.

« **STAGE 3** – Start a one-over Crown, counter-clockwise, started here on the left. Form counterclockwise Crown Knots with each strand, the last one here to be passed, top left, through loop.

« **STAGE 4** – Bring each end clockwise around a strand, aside the next, here shown in lower right.

» **STAGE 5** – Pass the end of each strand down alongside the first tail, shown here the last lower right.

« **STAGE 6** – The view from the top of the Star after passing each of the five strands.

« **Stage 7** – The view from the underside, each strand alongside the first tail.

» **Stage 8** – The top strand in the photo being passed here alongside the first tail, into the top.

« **Stage 9** – After all five strands have been passed from under.

« **STAGE 10** – The view from the top.

» **STAGE 11** – Pass each strand down again alongside the second and back up through the knot to the top.

« **STAGE 12** – Start a two-over Crown (over two and down), passing each strand in turn, lower left starting here.

STAGE 14 – Each strand is now tucked down through the center of the knot, the strands tightened one by one and after tightening, each strand is cut off under the Star Knot.

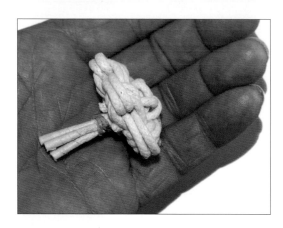

STAGE 13 – Here is the view from the top after all five strands have been crowned.

« *The finished Star Knot with a Double, Crowned Rose finish. If you start with the Half Hitches to the right instead of to the left, the "rotation" of the star will be reversed from the counter-clockwise "rotation" shown here, to clockwise.*

The insertion of a Star Knot into any kind of decorative work is a mark of true accomplishment, as you can probably tell from the above instructions! However, not all Star Knots can be made in the process of making another element. For instance, what if it looks right to have a red Star Knot in the middle of a pole or rail that is already covered with white Half Hitching or square knots? Seem impossible? Here are a couple of methods that a Star Knot of any number of "points" may be made and inserted into a piece of work without disrupting the flow of the base work, or may even be inserted after all the other work is complete. It is known as a Single-Strand Star Knot and is, indeed, made from a single strand of cord. If it is likely that the Star will be poked, prodded, or pulled (people seem to want to pull on knots for some reason), then you might want to insert the start of your strand into the underlying cords or, if there is no underlying cord, glued into a small hole drilled in the base piece specifically wide enough to receive the starting end of the cord you are working with.

The first method shown here was introduced by Thomas Solly in *Knotting Matters*, Spring 1985:11.

« *Single Strand Star Knot, made according to Solly's "recipe" given in IGKT Knotting Matters, Spring 1985. Single Strand Star Knot, side view. Note slope of doubled strands entering each loop.*

CLARIFIED SINGLE-STRAND STAR KNOT

The Single-Strand Star Knot is a superficially similar knot to the regular Star Knot of several strands, but it is not the same knot. An excellent explanation of the Single-Strand Star Knot is given in *Harrison's Book of Knots*, and the venerable Geoffrey Budworth[IGKT] shows, in his *Complete Book of Decorative Knots* [1998], an original solution to the method offered by Solly as an improvement over Harrison's method. Solly does not like the jointing in Harrison's knot, and offers his own solution in the form of an extension to the method of the Double-Chain Braid, shown above. Although the method offered by Harrison is less than clear from his text, it may appear easier when seen in photographs, which I cannot find anywhere else in the literature available to me. That having been said, it would seem appropriate then to offer this slight improvement in the literature through the addition of clear photographs, at least as it applies to Harrison's finish. Stages 13 through 25 below show the finishing of the knot, with the basic formation found in the first twelve stages—recall that we are trying to make something complex in easier steps.

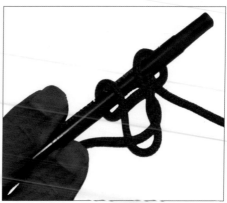

▲ **STAGE 2** – Bring the left cord under and over, to tuck down alongside the standing part. This is the first upward tuck and first bight.

▲ **STAGE 1** – We will start by making a fourteen-point Single-Strand Star Knot. Make a Lark's Head near the end of the cord over a pen, pencil, or other rod-shaped object. Wrap the right cord (standing part) over the left and hold it with a finger.

« **STAGE 3** – Keeping the right cord still, bring the working end around and up by the first upward tuck.

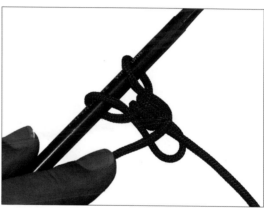

» **STAGE 4** – Tuck the working end down under the standing part and the wrap.

« **STAGE 5** – After repeating this process we see the second upward tuck near the end.

« **STAGE 6** – The downward tuck. Note it passes under three parts.

» **STAGE 7** – The second downward tuck completed and faired.

« **STAGE 8** – Here the process is re-started, making an upward first tuck under one part, leaving the bight.

« **STAGE 9** –
Tucking down
for the first
tuck under
two, end to the
right.

» **STAGE 10** –
Follow the
bight around
clockwise and
come up under
two parts . . .

« **STAGE 11** –
over the same
two parts and
under three,
then repeat
from Stage 7.

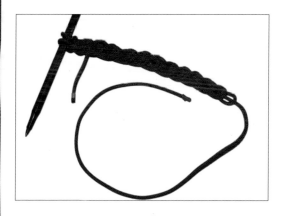

« **STAGE 12** – Here the thirteen points are ready to wrap, one less than the fourteen points we needed for this project.

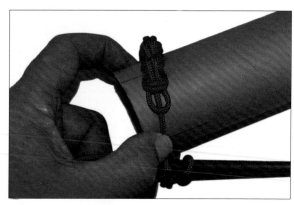

» **STAGE 13** – Wrap the strand around the tube, with pen still in place and the points facing outward.

« **STAGE 14** – With the pen still in place, pass the working end through beside it from left to right. Remove the pen.

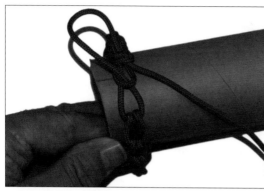

« **STAGE 15** – Pass working end up through last bight, over two parts and down.

» **STAGE 16** – Bring the working end around the bight and under two parts.

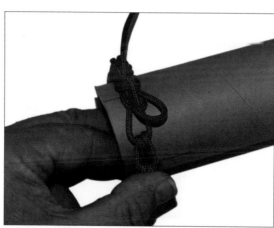

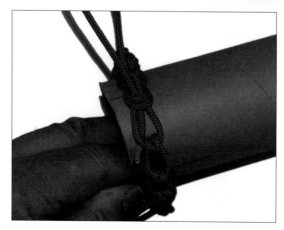

« **STAGE 17** – Tuck over two parts and under three to alongside where pen was.

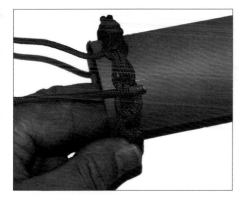

STAGE 18 – Pass through where pen was, left to right.

STAGE 20 – Pass over last two parts and down to the right.

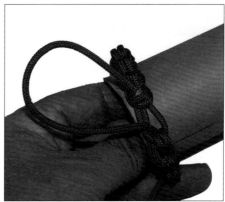

STAGE 19 – Pass up into last bight that was formed through the pen loops.

STAGE 21 – Using a fid or pricker as here, open the pen loops.

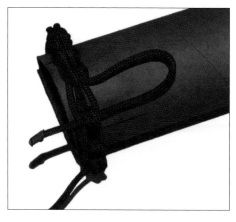

≈ **Stage 22** – Pass the working end right to left through the loops.

▴ **Stage 23** – Pass up under last two parts.

⇝ **Stage 25** – Seen from the side, the working end is now ready to be tucked alongside the standing part to finish.

≈ **Stage 24** – Pass over last two parts and down into last bight.

⌇ **Stage 26A** – The completed knot awaiting tucking and trimming of the ends, seen from the top.

⌇ **Stage 26B** – The completed knot seen from the side, ends waiting to be trimmed.

⌇ *A view of the fourteen-point Single-Strand Knot neatly finished, requiring only the placement of the star in its permanent location*

Turk's Head Knots

The Turk's Head Knot is what truly embodies a decorative knot for many people, and—oh, what magic that term "Turk's Head Knot" evokes! The would-be knot-tyer wants to know its mysteries, the novice wants to practice it once again just to solidify their new knowledge, the practiced knot-tyer wants to know how to expand a Turk's Head, and there are those who profess to be able to tie any Turk's Head Knot in any fiber all done in hand! The dreams and wonders that this knot tells! One could easily fill a book or several books on the subject but we have limited ourselves to just this chapter. With that in mind, I am going to show you how to make many types of this one-strand Turk's Head

Knot (TH Knot). We will do this by expanding on some simple basic structures—not all TH Knots perhaps, but close enough that you can add decorative TH Knotwork covering to almost any piece with panache. I will also show you how to add to a simple Single-Strand TH by inserting a second or third strand, as a different color, to enhance the appearance. Lastly, I will show you how to make Flat and Globe-Shaped TH Knots to allow for a more varied use. Be aware that this work is not for the faint of heart, but also that, unless you try it, you may never know the joys of achieving a perfect Turk's Head Knot, in mat, cylinder, sphere, cruciform, or any other solid or flat object shape!

Here is what we have included in this chapter:
Cylindrical Turk's Head Knots
Flat Turk's Head Knots
Globe-Shaped Turk's Head Knots

INTRODUCTORY NOTES

We will focus on the first type of TH Knot for most of the chapter, particularly looking at ways in which we can "grow" or expand one Knot into another. Expanding one TH Knot into another involves some pattern recognition. I suggest you look carefully at the photographs and read the accompanying instructions to give yourself an opportunity to see what is happening for each one. If you are still unsure, don't lose hope, but instead try again. It is a simple weave, going over and under, but made such that it returns to its starting point, just like wrapping a cord around something but deliberately

moving over and under one pass after another as well as remembering to move from one "side" to the other. If neither the photographs nor the written explanations work for you, perhaps try creating a string pattern to follow, something like connect the dots, but with the lines drawn in for you. I show a tool to help you do this toward the end of this chapter.

Turk's Head Knots as flat mats are made on the basis of two circles, one inside the other, that are made with a single strand. Those two circles form the inner and outer edges of the TH weave. The TH weave moves between the two circles, first one circle and then the other, inside to outside and back again, ever repeating itself until it completes the entire woven round, like the mythological Ouroboros that swallows its own tail. Woven circles can then also readily be formed into a cylinder if the outer edge or circumference of the circle is matched in size with the interior ring of the TH weave to make the weave go around the face of the cylinder instead of lying flat. Beyond the circle and the cylinder, the TH can then further be manipulated into a sphere, with care being taken to form a small enough number of bights and a large enough series of crossings and by adding some interior bights within the weave to enable the surface of the sphere to be covered. We will describe more of that later in the chapter. Our first attempts will be made using a cylinder. Many people use the center cardboard tube from the center of a roll of kitchen paper or foil for this purpose. In most cases in this chapter we will be making our TH Knots with single strands, except for a few instances in which we parallel a strand with another strand of a different color or texture.

First, let's take a look at the single strand TH Knot. We have to start with a couple of brief definitions:

Bight: The "bump" around the perimeter circles or the one in the center circle of a TH Knot, whether in flat, cylindrical, or spherical form.

Lead: The crossing of one strand by another strand between bights—leads are sometimes also referred to as "parts."

Pass: The number of times that a single cord or strand travels around the TH Knot from start to finish; once from start to finish is a single pass, twice and the TH Knot is doubled, three times around and the TH Knot is doubled and doubled again or, for most of us, tripled. When making a Single-Strand TH there is one golden rule to follow: The number of bights and leads must not be divisible by the same number, except when dividing leads or bights by the number one.

Let's try a few examples. If a TH has four bights it cannot have an even number of leads, because even numbers are divisible by two, just as four is divisible by two. Another example: If a TH has six bights it cannot have three leads, four leads, six leads, eight leads, nine leads, ten leads, twelve leads, fourteen leads, fifteen leads, etc., because six and the other numbers are divisible by both two and three.

SINGLE-STRAND TH KNOTS

Fortunately, someone (Clifford W. Ashley) has worked out a handy table that shows which TH Single-Strand Knots can and cannot be made. The ones that can be made are labeled with an X in the following table.

Table of possible Turk's Head Knots that may be tied with one strand »

L \ B	1	2	3	4	5	6	7	8	9	10	11	12	13	14	15	16	17	18	19	20	21	22	23	24	25
1	S																								
2	X		X		X		X		X		X		X		X		X		X		X		X		X
3	X	X		X	X		X	X		X	X		X	X		X	X		X	X		X	X		X
4	X		X		X		X		X		X		X		X		X		X		X		X		X
5	X	X	X	X		X	X	X	X		X	X	X	X		X	X	X	X		X	X	X	X	
6	X				X		X				X		X				X		X				X		X
7	X	X	X	X	X	X		X	X	X	X	X	X		X	X	X	X	X	X		X	X	X	X
8	X		X		X		X		X		X		X		X		X		X		X		X		X
9	X	X		X	X		X	X		X	X		X	X		X	X		X	X		X	X		X
10	X		X				X		X		X		X				X		X		X		X		
11	X	X	X	X	X	X	X	X	X	X		X	X	X	X	X	X	X	X	X	X		X	X	X
12	X				X		X				X		X				X		X				X		X
13	X	X	X	X	X	X	X	X	X	X	X	X		X	X	X	X	X	X	X	X	X	X	X	X
14	X		X		X				X		X		X		X		X		X				X		X
15	X	X		X			X	X			X		X	X		X	X		X			X	X		
16	X		X		X		X		X		X		X		X		X		X		X		X		X
17	X	X	X	X	X	X	X	X	X	X	X	X	X	X	X	X		X	X	X	X	X	X	X	X
18	X				X		X				X		X				X		X				X		X
19	X	X	X	X	X	X	X	X	X	X	X	X	X	X	X	X	X	X		X	X	X	X	X	X
20	X		X				X		X		X		X				X		X		X		X		
21	X	X		X	X			X		X	X		X			X	X		X	X		X	X		X
22	X		X		X		X		X				X		X		X		X		X		X		X
23	X	X	X	X	X	X	X	X	X	X	X	X	X	X	X	X	X	X	X	X	X	X		X	X
24	X				X		X				X		X				X		X				X		X
25	X	X	X	X		X	X	X	X		X	X	X	X		X	X	X	X		X	X	X	X	

Every X represents a *possible* TH of *one* strand. The number of bights is read across the top row, the number of leads is read down the left column. The "S" is a special case; one lead and one bight is a grommet, or circle. I have left in the obvious case of the single bight with any number of leads, which results in a double helix and does not seem to me to follow the "spirit" of the TH Knot, even if it is technically true!

Obviously, the table does not show all possible combinations of leads and bights to infinity, but there is enough information in it to make the determination that not all combinations are possible and that those which are possible are the ones to master and to master well.

As a last element of understanding the making of a TH Knot, the basic structure is to take a cord from one side or edge of the knot (which edge is called a bight) across to the other side, weaving over and under as one does so. Then the cord is taken back again to the starting side or edge, again weaving over and under, running from bight to bight. This action of moving the cord first to one edge and then back again is another inalienable

element of making the TH Knot of one cord. The cord normally will pass over one cord then under one cord, but may also go over two cords and then under two cords, or over three cords and then under three cords (these are more advanced patterns and are not included in this chapter). The pattern thus developed is the final appearance only and again, NOT the method of making the knot. In fact the cord may well have an odd sequence, such as over one, under two, as part of its makeup in deriving the final knot. It may also skip one tuck under or a pass over altogether during the making of the TH Knot. The final appearance is really what matters and is what we will focus on, not the method of achieving it—we will leave a discussion of the method of making any TH Knot until later. This final appearance has been likened to a continuous weave or braiding, but the obsessive among knot-tyers will deny its existence as a braid. No matter—to the untrained and yet still-appreciative eye, it does look like a continuous braid, but one where the braid has neither any discernible start nor any discernible finish, unlike a braid that has both start and finish.

⁀ A sample of Turk's Head Knots, each of a different number of leads.
Note the over-one, under-one pattern of each of the leads, which are shown here in pairs.

Let's look at how to count the number of leads in a TH Knot, as this seems to present the greatest confusion for the beginning knot-tyer.

Here, on the previous page, is one sample each of a TH Knot with three leads, four leads, five leads, and six leads. Don't concern yourself with the number of bights for now. The leads are all doubled (a second part of the original cord length is run continuously from the beginning, parallel and to the same side of the original lead), in this case only so that they can be seen more readily against the background. Note the horizontal line on the tube and imagine cutting through the threads along that line. In doing so you would cut through three pairs, four pairs, five pairs, and six pairs, left to right, as you proceeded. Those pairs are the leads and that is how they are counted and labeled, whether the leads (parts) are in pairs as here, or singly, tripled, quadrupled, or whatever.

The number of bights present is not independent of the number of leads, but is in accordance with the table previously shown, if each TH Knot is made with one cord.

CYLINDRICAL TURK'S HEAD KNOTS

With that universal explanation out of the way, at least for the moment (we will come back to this later), let's start by making a TH Knot of three leads and four bights (also labeled here as 3L4B), a so-called Square TH Knot. It is called this because the number of leads and bights differ only by one in number; hence, a 3L4B, a 4L5B, a 5L4B, or a 6L5B are all Square TH Knots, or as near as TH Knots of one strand can come to an equal number of bights and leads. Its other common name among knot-tyers is a Casa TH Knot (used when created for horse tack or when worked in leather or ribbon). We will start by making one as a cylindrical knot using a transparent tube in place of our hand, so that we can see the other side of the knot as we build it. If you prefer to use your hand, don't forget to turn your hand over once in a while to see the other side.

The 3L2B TH Knot

« STAGE 1 – Start by passing the cord from lower left completely around the object, bringing the cord upward on the right side of the first pass and crossing over itself. This makes one round turn crossing left to make an "X." Note that the working end is under the left index finger and will need to be pulled through further to complete the knot.

« **Stage 2** – From the upper left we now pass behind the object and bring the line up to cross to the right over the first part to make an "X" below the first "X." Again, note that the working end has been paused here and will need to be pulled through further to continue.

» **Stage 3** – Cross under the first part, over the second to the left, and tuck back to the start. You are now ready to double the knot [strongly suggested!] or simply secure the ends and finish your knot.

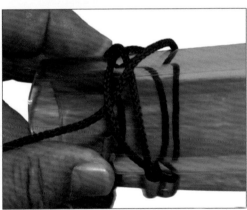

« *The 3L2B TH Knot, doubled—the simplest form of this, start "A'*

THE 3L4B TH KNOT

» **STAGE 1** – Wrap a round turn, crossing with an "X" in front, continuing to the back . . .

« **STAGE 2** – and to the left of our start point, then crossing over the strand above the first "X" . . .

» **STAGE 3** – again moving from left to right, we cross under our first pass.

« **STAGE 4** – Now pick up the entire left-side turn and cross it over the right-side turn to make a "mouth" (by left index finger) . . .

» **STAGE 5** – crossing the cord now, right to left, pass down into the "mouth" and out on the left . . .

« **STAGE 6** – round behind to meet up with our start cord.

⌐ **STAGE 7** – Start to lay parallel "tracks" following the original lead and, staying always to one side (here we stay to the right, but we could have stayed to the left), follow the entire lead to double it . . .

⌐ **STAGE 8** – continuing until the lead is doubled.

« *The Three-Lead, Four-Bight Turk's Head, doubled*

Practice the above structure until you can do it without thinking, if you are serious about "getting it." Remember the three most important words in knot-tying: perseverance, patience, and practice.

Once you have this structure underneath your fingers it's time to try the 4L3B TH Knot, so that you can see the difference between it and the last one. Remember, this one will be different because it has one more lead and one less bight.

THE 4L3B TH KNOT

STAGE 1 – Tie an Overhand Knot around the cylinder or tube. »

« STAGE 2 – Bring the working end around the tube and up through the "mouth" of the Overhand Knot. Exit on the upper left.

» STAGE 3 – Bring the end around on the left, cross just below the "mouth" and tuck under . . .

« **Stage 4** – and behind, over one, under one to exit on the right. Note the "over-over" cord to the left of the working end here.

» **Stage 5** – Cross over the "over-over" cord, then under the next ('under-under') and then over the next to exit on the left.

« **Stage 6** – Bring the cord around behind again to the start to begin doubling.

⋧ *The Four-Lead, Three-Bight Turk's Head, doubled*

We will go on now to describe how to make several other TH Knots, up to seven leads.

THE 5L4B TH KNOT

» **STAGE 1** – Start as you did for the 3L4B TH, crossing in front with an "X".

STAGE 2 – Now cross to the right of the "X," forming a second "X" beneath the first. »

« **STAGE 3** – Bring the end of the cord round on the right to cross under the right-side cord above the first "X".

STAGE 4 – Bring the cord around on the left, parallel to the start for a 3L2B TH. »

« **STAGE 5 –** Cross over the start cord, instead of making it parallel, passing under then over the next cord . . .

» **STAGE 6 –** and bringing the cord round again on the left. You should now have two "over-over" cords and one "under-under" cord as a "ladder." Pass over the first, under the second and over the third cord . . .

« **STAGE 7A –** where you will now see another "ladder" but this time of two "under-under" cords and one "over-over" cord. Again go under, over, under.

« STAGE 7B – The view here is turned slightly so that you can see the end as it moves through the "ladder" and works around to the start.

» STAGE 8A – Finish up at the beginning again (projecting left), and proceed with the doubling, paralleling the original lead all the way round.

« STAGE 8B – Shown starting here in a slightly rotated view.

« The Five-Lead, Four-Bight Turk's Head, doubled

THE 4L5B TH KNOT

STAGE 1 –
Start with an Overhand Knot as for the 4L3B TH, but cross behind . . . »

« **STAGE 2** – and bring the end around and under the start and to the left.

» **STAGE 3** – Cross up into the "mouth."

« **STAGE 4** – Now cross over the first exit cord from the Overhand Knot . . .

« **STAGE 5 –**
crossing to the
left (see the
"over-over"
cord above the
start cord?).

» **STAGE 6 –**
Cross and trap
the start cord,
then under,
over, under to
the right . . .

« **STAGE 7 –** to
where you can
see the two "over-
over" cords, which
you go over . . .

Stage 8 – then under and over to the left . . .

Stage 9 – where you meet up with the start cord again. Parallel the start cord all around for the first doubling. Make a tuck under the next cord in this photograph before you meet with the standing end!

The Four-Lead, Five-Bight Turk's Head, doubled

I mentioned in the text above the notion of the "first doubling." Knot-tyers call repeating the original lead of a pattern "doubling" it. For some knot-tyers, "doubling again" means to parallel the second lead again, making three passes; the original, its double, and the second pass or "doubling again" of that second double. So a pattern that has been doubled and doubled again is one that has been followed around three times—confusing, isn't it?

The 6L5B TH Knot

» **Stage 1** – We start with the 4L3B TH and begin doubling it parallel with the first lead . . .

« **Stage 2** – and then we tuck under the first lead of the standing part (here the working end is passing under and then to the left of the first standing part).

» **Stage 3** – Take a complete turn around the base to arrive back at the paired standing part . . .

» STAGE 4 – where we start to split the pair, over, under, over, under, passing now to the right of the original standing part.

« STAGE 5 – Now, turning the base toward us at the top, we see a "ladder" ready to pass over, under, over, under, over . . .

» STAGE 6 – allowing us to complete our first pass by bringing the end back around to the starting end.

« *The Six-Lead, Five-Bight Turk's Head, doubled*

THE 5L6B TH KNOT

» **STAGE 1** – We start with a 3L2B TH, which we make as for our 3L4B, but pass to the left and don't make a "mouth."

« **Stage 2** – Pass the working end over the standing end, to its left, passing over, under, over to the right, making a "ladder," then around behind, under one, over one.

» **Stage 3** – Pass to the right of the standing part in our first lead, over, under, over, making a second "ladder."

« **Stage 4** – Returning to the start, we pass between the start and our first left-side doubling "ladder," over, under, over, under . . .

⚹ **STAGE 5 –** and then pass back to the left over, under, over, under . . .

⚹ **STAGE 6 –** where we meet the start again.

⚹ *The Five-Lead, Six-Bight Turk's Head, doubled*

THE 6L7B TH KNOT

» **STAGE 1** – Form a 4L5B TH and bring the working end (under thumb) under the standing part. Leave plenty of space.

« **STAGE 2** – Parallel the standing part to its *left*, under, over, under then over itself, forming a "ladder." This will be used later for weaving.

» **STAGE 3** – Move the working end to the right of the original standing part, weaving over, under, over, under to form another "ladder."

« **STAGE 4** – Pass under the start of the first "ladder," weaving over, under, over, under the rungs.

» **STAGE 5** – Weave the cord from right to left over, under, over, under, and over the second "ladder."

« **STAGE 6** – The completed single-pass Turk's Head.

⌇ *The Six-Lead, Seven-Bight Turk's Head, doubled in red onto a plastic core*

THE 7L6B TH KNOT

The 3L2B Turk's Head is the start for this one, which also formed the beginning of the 5L4B Turk's Head. We start this one, therefore, with the 5L4B Turk's Head. Take note of this pattern of expansion, called "Laddering"—we will use it again for other TH Knots.

« STAGE 1 – Start with a 5L4B.

» STAGE 2 – Parallel the standing part to the right to form a "ladder." Note the side parts are the cords and the rungs are the previous passes.

» STAGE 3 – Parallel the standing part to the left to form another "ladder."

« STAGE 4 – Split the first ladder over, under, over, under, over.

« **STAGE 5** – Split the second ladder under, over three times.

» **STAGE 6** – Back to the start and begin doubling.

« *The Seven-Lead, Six-Bight Turk's Head, doubled*

THE 7L.8B TH KNOT

« **STAGE 1** – Start with the 5L6B.

» **STAGE 2** – Pass to the left of the standing part and parallel left to right.

« **STAGE 3** – Pass to the right of the standing part, crossing it, and parallel right to left.

⌃ **STAGE 4** – Pass between parallel parts ("ladder") over, under, over, under, over, under

⌃ **STAGE 5** – then over and under three times . . .

« **STAGE 6** – back to the start and double it.

« *The Seven-Lead, Eight-Bight Turk's Head, doubled*

THE 8L7B TH KNOT

The last knot in the Square TH Knot series in this book represents what is probably the physical limit for making Square Turk's Head Knots "in the hand" without having some sort of paper pattern or pin-mold to work with if making this for the first time. There are many people in the world who use both pin and paper/grid methods and you can make a paper pattern of your own or with a knot-making tool. If not, there are other resources to use. Patterns and molds will be discussed later, but for now, let's go through the sequence for this latest Square Turk's Head.

« **STAGE 1** –
Start with
6L5B from
a 4L3B.

» **STAGE 2** –
Parallel on
the right
of the start
to make a
ladder left to
right.

<< **STAGE 3** –
Then make
a ladder
right to left.

>> **STAGE 4** – Split
the ladder over
and under three
times.

<< **STAGE 5** – Split
the ladder
again, over and
under three
times and then
over. Double
the lead.

« The Eight-Lead, Seven-Bight Turk's Head, doubled, made with Chinese silk cord

You may by now have seen—and could recognize if you saw them again—some similarities about each of the Square TH Knots presented. Let's remind ourselves of what we have done and learned so far.

NUMBER OF LEADS AND BIGHTS

It is certain that the number of leads and bights in a Square TH Knot differ by one in number, whether greater by one or lesser by one, because that was the rule by which we determined to show these particular knots. It is also apparent that there is a progression from one to another and that it is neither a simple progression nor yet perhaps even a readily discernible one. I will later show you what that progression is and also what it is not, and introduce to you a similar table of progression as the table of unique TH Knots.

Types of Starts

If you look back over the TH Knots we have shown thus far you will see that there are really only four starts to Square TH Knots. They are:

Make an "X" on the front, then a round turn and cross below the "X."

Make an "X" on the front, then a round turn and cross above the "X."

Make an Overhand Knot and cross to the left, then up into the "mouth."

Make an Overhand Knot and cross to the right, then up into the "mouth."

Here is a table, as promised, of the starts and progression from one start to the next in the series:

Start	'X'	Cross above	Cross below	Overhand Knot	Wrap and tuck left	Wrap and tuck right
Start A: 3L2B	☺		☺			
Start B: 3L4B	☺	☺				
Start C: 4L3B				☺		☺
Start D: 4L5B				☺	☺	

TYPES OF EXPANSION

The next part of the tables that I discussed above is this one, where you can see the manner in which a particular Square TH Knot may be expanded from one to another. Not all TH Knots are square, as we shall see directly, but these will be good to start the ball rolling. The idea of the table is to help you in understanding the progression from one type of TH Knot to the next.

The 2L3B is technically a starter for the 4L5B, but I find it easier, visually, to progress the way I have it in the table—it seems to be a more "natural" fit—but for those who want to see the 2L3B, tie the Overhand Knot and continue the line around to meet the beginning, and there you have it! Here is a photograph:

	2L	3L	4L	5L	6L	7L	8L
2B	N.A.	Starter A	N.A.		N.A.		N.A.
3B		N.A.	Starter C		N.A.		
4B	N.A.	Starter B	N.A.	Starter A	N.A.		N.A.
5B			Starter D	N.A.	Starter C		
6B	N.A.	N.A.	N.A.	Starter B	N.A.	Starter A	N.A.
7B					Starter D	N.A.	Starter C
8B	N.A.		N.A.		N.A.	Starter B	N.A.

« *The Two-Lead, Three-Bight Turk's Head, doubled three times*

I will now discuss TH Knots that are not square, but that have either a larger (or much larger) number of leads than bights, or have a larger number of bights than leads. Those TH Knots that have a larger number of bights than leads are known as Narrow TH Knots, while those with a larger number of leads than bights are known as Wide TH Knots. Looking back at our table of possible knots, we see that in the table we could have the following table of Non Square TH Knots:

L \ B	B	1	2	3	4	5	6	7	8	9	10	11	12	13	14	15	16	17	18	19	20	21	22	23	24	25
1	S																									
2	X	X		X		X		X		X		X		X		X		X		X		X		X		X
3	X	X	X		X	X		X	X		X	X		X	X		X	X		X	X		X	X		X
4	X	X		X		X		X		X		X		X		X		X		X		X		X		X
5	X	X	X	X	X		X	X	X	X		X	X	X	X		X	X	X	X		X	X	X	X	
6	X	X				X		X				X		X				X		X				X		X
7	X	X	X	X	X	X	X		X	X	X	X	X	X		X	X	X	X	X	X		X	X	X	X
8	X	X		X		X		X		X		X		X		X		X		X		X		X		X
9	X	X	X		X	X		X	X		X	X		X	X		X	X		X	X		X	X		X
10	X	X		X				X		X		X		X				X		X		X		X		
11	X	X	X	X	X	X	X	X	X	X	X		X	X	X	X	X	X	X	X	X	X		X	X	X
12	X	X				X		X				X		X				X		X				X		X
13	X	X	X	X	X	X	X	X	X	X	X	X	X		X	X	X	X	X	X	X	X	X	X	X	X
14	X	X		X		X				X		X		X		X		X		X				X		X
15	X	X	X		X			X	X			X		X	X		X	X		X			X	X		
16	X	X		X		X		X		X		X		X		X		X		X		X		X		X
17	X	X	X	X	X	X	X	X	X	X	X	X	X	X	X	X	X		X	X	X	X	X	X	X	X
18	X	X				X		X				X		X				X		X				X		X
19	X	X	X	X	X	X	X	X	X	X	X	X	X	X	X	X	X	X	X		X	X	X	X	X	X
20	X	X		X				X		X		X		X				X		X		X		X		
21	X	X	X		X	X			X		X	X		X			X	X		X	X		X	X		X
22	X	X		X		X		X		X				X		X		X		X		X		X		X
23	X	X	X	X	X	X	X	X	X	X	X	X	X	X	X	X	X	X	X	X	X	X	X		X	X
24	X	X				X		X				X		X				X		X				X		X
25	X	X	X	X	X		X	X	X	X		X	X	X	X		X	X	X	X		X	X	X	X	

Table of possible Non-Square Single-Strand TH Knots—Boxes with yellow shading are Square TH Knots, those with red shading are Wide TH Knots, and those with blue shading are Narrow TH Knots.

Expanding the Number of Bights in Three-Lead, Four-Lead, and Five-Lead TH Knots

Let's start with the progression that takes Three-Lead TH Knots from 3L5B to 3L8B, then 3L11B, etc. You can see that the number of bights is increased by three for each successive expansion. Here is how to make the expansion or progression from one to the next in the series.

» **STAGE 1 –** Start with a 3L5B TH as the base.

« **STAGE 2 –** Tuck from left to right, following the standing part.

« **STAGE 3** – Cross the right part over the left part.

» **STAGE 4** – Tuck back up from right to left for the first expansion to 3L8B. Repeat the process as many times as you can for an increase of three bights each time the tuck goes from left to right and back again (3L8B to 3L11B to 3L14B and so on).

« *The Three-Lead, Eleven-Bight Turk's Head, single pass*

Starting with the 3L4B TH, we can expand it by the same process to 3L7B, 3L10B, 3L13B, etc. By so doing we can create almost any Three-Lead TH Knots we wish, just by having the right start configuration. I wish it were that easy for all the TH Knot progressions! This brings us next to the expansion/progression of the Start D TH Knots.

The process for a 4-Lead TH Knot start is to expand an Overhand Knot. Because the 4-Lead has no even-numbered bights (the number four and any even number are divisible by the number two and therefore impossible with one strand, according to the law of the common divisor), so we must expand the knot *before* we have formed the final start. What this means is that we have no way of forming the expanded knot after forming the base knot as we did for the three-Lead knots, where we could add more Bights. To increase (expand) the bights of knots built on Start D, we instead simply add another Overhand Knot tuck *at the start*, as shown below.

4L7B TH Knot Increasing from 4L3B

« **Stage 1 –**
Start with an Overhand Knot.

» **Stage 2 –** Make another turn, left to right.

« **STAGE 3** – Bring the working end around to the right and tuck up to the left.

» **STAGE 4** – Tuck down to the right, being sure to keep the tucks a little loose.

« **STAGE 5** – Tuck up to the left.

« **STAGE 6 –**
Parallel the
standing part,
but passing
over, under
instead.

» **STAGE 7 –**
Open the
ladder and . . .

« **STAGE 8 –**
pass over,
under, over . . .

« STAGE 9 –
opening the next
"ladder"...

» STAGE 10 –
and passing
under, over,
under ...

« STAGE 11 –
opening the
third "ladder"...

« STAGE 12 – over, under, over, to finish one pass.

≈ *The Four-Lead, Seven-Bight Turk's Head, doubled twice in red Chinese silk cord*

Thus, we have expanded the bights from a 4L3B to a 4L7B by adding one twist to our starting Overhand Knot. Incidentally, if you tie your Overhand Knot left-handed, you end up with a mirror image of the right-handed version. Try it out! If you want to expand the number of bights on a 4L5B to a 4L9B, start as above with two Overhand Knot tucks instead of one (Start D is a One-Tuck Overhand Knot), and then pass to the left instead of passing on the right like the one above. Then follow the same procedure as above in terms of tucking up and tucking down into the "mouth" of the knot. Therefore the start for the 4L11B is the 4L7B (three tucks instead of one or two) and for the 4L13B it is the 4L9B (again three tucks instead of one or two), and so on in pairs of expansions. These expansions and their original starts are shown later in a table. Then, from what we have discussed earlier, by "laddering" the 4L7B, we get a 6L11B, increasing the number of bights by four and leads by two.

Five-Lead TH Knot expansions are a little different than either the Three-Lead or Four-Lead TH Knots. The 5L4B will expand by laying down a "ladder," first to the right of the standing part, then crossing over it

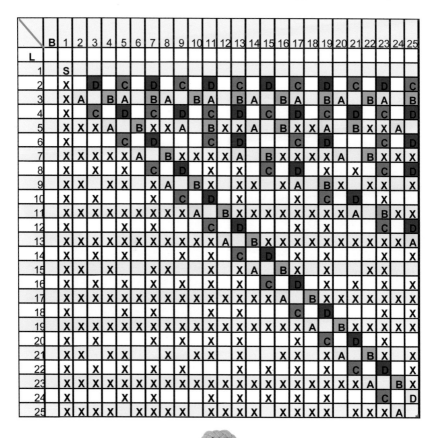

to the left and passing through on the left of the standing part, right to left, to form a second "ladder." This expansion then forms a Seven-Lead, Six-Bight TH Knot. Expanding this 7L6B by the same "laddering" process will give you a 9L8B TH Knot.

Therefore, we can see from our brief foray into expansions of TH Knots that expansions or progressions are not necessarily easy to work from first principles. However, to help you get past that, I have devised this next intermediate table (see page 285) showing the expansions from TH Knots of 2L3B and

3L2B, passing either to the left or to the right, to form a TH Knot of one cord.

Starts A, B, C, and D are as shown on the previous Tables. To give you an example, take the 8L17B TH Knot. It starts as Start D (4L5B), a single Overhand Knot passed to the right, then doubled, and is then tucked and laddered three times (4L5B to 4L9B to 6L13B to 8L17B) to make the 8L17B TH Knot.

Here is the laddering process for expanding from the 4L5B to the 4L9B, so that you get some idea of what is involved.

4L5B to 4L9B Expansion

Stage 1 – Make an Overhand Knot around the tubing.

Stage 2 – Make a second Overhand Knot by making one more twist of the working end.

« **STAGE 3** – Pass the working of the line around to meet the standing end and then pass it on the left, as shown here, under the standing end.

» **STAGE 4** – Make a pass into each of the double Overhand Knot crossings. The first one looks like this, crossing left to right, paralleling the standing end on the left and then passing over it.

« **STAGE 5** – The next one looks like this, crossing from right to left, again paralleling the standing end but now on the right and passing under the standing end.

« **STAGE 6 –** Cross again from left to right, like this . . .

» STAGE 7 – then like this from right to left, being sure to cross over, parallel, then under and lastly over the standing end where we started. Now we are ready to cross the ladders we made in the last four passes.

« **STAGE 8 –** The first ladder is between the standing end and the parallel track, so we pass under, over, under from left to right . . .

« **STAGE 9** – and then find the next ladder and pass over, under, over from right to left.

» **STAGE 10** – Returning to the right, pass through the next ladder under, over, under. You can now see the next ladder for Stage 11.

« **STAGE 11** – Make the last pass before re-joining the standing end, from right to left over, under, over.

≈ *Here is the finished 4L9B Turk's Head Knot, passed three times over a napkin ring.*

What then should we make of the unshaded boxes above of possible TH Knots that are still marked with an "X"? Cyrus Day suggests that these must be made directly, while Ashley gives but a few hints, other than to say they must be drawn out on a grid and followed from there. Ashley does, however, discuss the division of TH Knots into three classes as we did earlier, so that we may classify and understand or speak of them a little better:

Square TH Knots
Narrow TH Knots
Wide TH Knots

As we said before, a Wide TH Knot has more leads than bights and a Narrow TH Knot has more bights than leads. Of the 375 possible Single-Strand TH Knots that are shown in this 25-by-25 table (25 leads and 25 bights), we have looked at only 111 of them; our Square TH Knots and three, four, and Five Load Narrow TH Knots. Wide TH Knots are covered below.

WIDE TH KNOTS

Wide TH Knots are, generally speaking, those below the diagonal line of Square TH Knots in the table given on page 285. To define the methods for making the Wide TH Knots, we need a different system of starts. (We also need something to describe the starts for the remaining TH Knots above the line—that description will come later).

When making Wide TH Knots we usually start with a tube to which pins are attached at the ends to represent the number of Bights we need. There are some fantastic tools on the market now, one of which is the KnotTool by Don Burrhus (www.knottool.com). I highly recommend it to those who want to just make a Wide or Narrow TH Knot. Unfortunately, it is difficult to use when you need to put the Wide TH Knot in place on an existing tube or railing if you do not have access to the end of it. For projects like that, you may find that you need a simpler method. Instead of using pins (which are not much use for stainless steel railings!) try using loops of cord held in place by a Constrictor Knot or pieces of adhesive tape such as drafting tape. Try not to use duct tape, which will leave marks that are hard to remove from the base rail and from the cord, and may disturb your knotting when you remove it. When using loops, each loop is temporary and represents a pin location and that loop can be cut when the project is in place on the rail, making for an easier transition.

Wide TH Knots are split into two essential groups. Each of these groups is itself split down into an even number of leads or an odd number of leads. Do you recall that when we were looking at the Square TH Knots there were four types of start? Perhaps there is something here that we can formulate into a more general rule that we will look at again later. For now, remember again the Golden Rule that no combination of leads and bights can have the same divisor, and all should go well.

Here is Start A, a 5L3B TH Knot, shown in photographs below, for an odd number of leads and an odd number of bights.

Place your loops at each end of the piece you are going to cover. Wrap a piece of tape around the piece and write the number of each loop on the tape next to where the loop is placed. Make the numbers sequential for ease of use. This series of photographs does not use loops, because it is very straightforward. This, by the way, is the smallest Wide TH Knot for this start, Start A – 5L3B (odd leads, odd bights).

STAGE 1 – Start at top right and make a turn down and to the left, crossing the first lead over to the right . . .

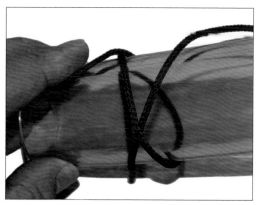

« **STAGE 2** – behind again, and crossing itself to the upper left.

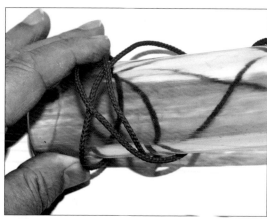

» **STAGE 3** – Cross down over the first lead and over the second lead, to finish at bottom right.

« **STAGE 4** – Bring the cord behind again, crossing over two leads and then under one to the lower left. Notice that you now have two bights on each end.

« **STAGE 5** – Now pass over, under, over, under from top left to bottom right, making a third bight (held together here).

» **STAGE 6** – Notice that with the work turned a little, there are now three bights on the left and two on the right.

« **STAGE 7** – Forming the last bight on the right alongside the standing part.

The completed Five Lead, Three Bight TH Knot, tripled

The next Wide TH Knot with three bights has Start B – 7L3B (again, odd leads, odd bights):

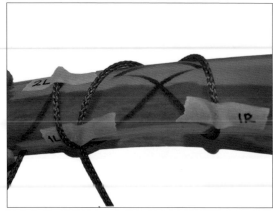

» **STAGE 1** – Start winding from front left, bight #1 L, behind and up toward you in front (nearest you) to bight #1 R, and return over itself to the left, passing under the start of the cord past bight #1 L (see near end of index finger) to make bight #2 L.

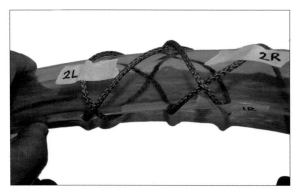

« **STAGE 2** – Stay to the left of the start cord and parallel it to the right side of the knot, passing under the first cord to make the second bight on the right, bight #2 R . . .

» **STAGE 3** – then pass under the first cord, over the second cord to the left side of the knot, and over the first and under the second, finishing at bight #3 L.

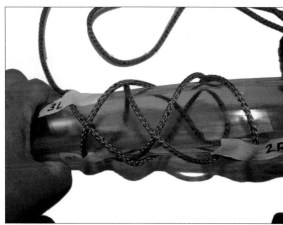

« **STAGE 4** – Now parallel the right side of the first cord, under, over, over, under, to bight #3 R . . .

« **STAGE 5** – and return to the left, over, under, over, under . . .

» **STAGE 6** – over, under to bight #1 L to complete the circuit.

« *Wide TH Knot with seven leads and three bights, passed twice*

Notice that with the last two starts, there was a round turn or more than one round turn to begin the knot. Then there followed a series of over-under moves to form the knot, including some over, over passes to form the typical "railroad tracks," or ladders, that we have seen before. Despite the fact that both knots are odd bights, odd leads, there is no consistency between them as to how they

may be formed! Adding another turn or half turn does nothing for us because it alters the pattern of over, under that follows. Let us pursue some other Wide TH Knots.

Continuing the starts for Wide Three-Bight TH Knots, the 10L3B has Start C (this time an even number of leads, and an odd number of bights).

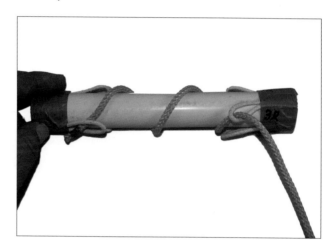

» **STAGE 1 –** Start at 3L, make two round turns to 3R.

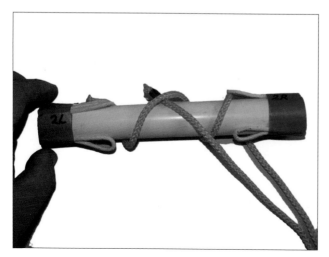

« **STAGE 2 –** From 3R go over one, under one . . .

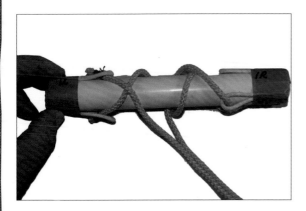

« **Stage 3** – and over one to 1L.

» **Stage 4** – Parallel the first round turn on its right to make a ladder . . .

« **Stage 5** – continuing around toward 1R . . .

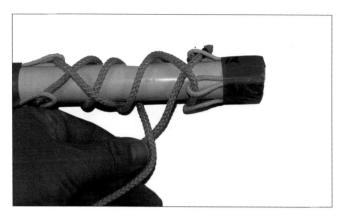

« **STAGE 6** – where it is tucked under the cord out of 3R to pass to 1R.

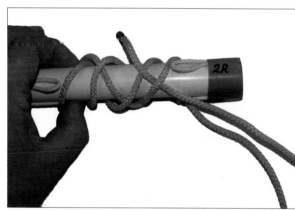

» **STAGE 7** – Tuck under, over . . .

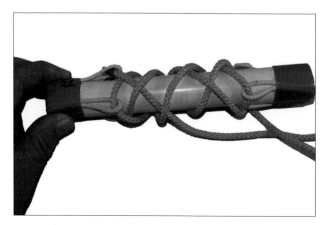

« **STAGE 8** – under, under, over to make a ladder to 2L.

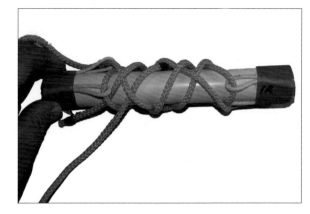

» STAGE 9 – Then over, under, under . . .

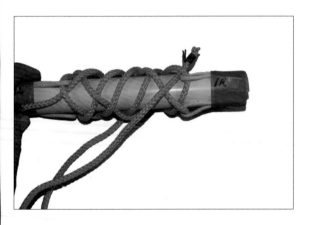

« STAGE 10 – over, over, under to 2R.

» STAGE 11 – From 2R thread the ladder over, under, over, under . . .

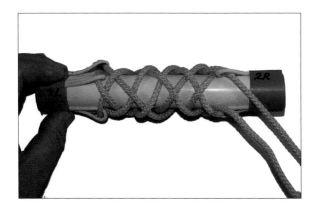

« **STAGE 12 –**
over, under,
over, under,
over . . .

« **LAST STAGE –**
and back to
the beginning.

« *The Ten-Lead,*
Three-Bight Turk's
Head, doubled

The 17L3B TH Knot (odd leads, odd bights, page 302)

NOTE: *From the above starts you can by now see that there is no way to increase the parts (leads) of a Wide TH Knot once you have started it, other than by over-wrapping. However, you can expand a Wide TH Knot once you have formed it by adding to the number of bights, rather than adding to the number of leads.*

So, now we have covered three starts—the odd leads and odd bights, the odd leads and even bights, and the even leads and odd bights. But what about even leads and even bights? You should know already why we cannot start One-Strand TH Knots this way; two even numbers can each be divided by the number two, and thus are clearly not following the Golden Rule.

So we now know that we have only three types (notice I did not say "starts") in the Wide TH Knot family. Similarly, we have only three types in the Narrow TH Knot family.

This is a pivotal moment for those who have been learning as we go. This brings TH Knots more readily within our reach, making them easier to start and reproduce without having pattern pieces of paper or grids laid out for us to follow around. We have now mastered the basics of TH Knots, by remembering the starts, remembering the progression of wide, square, and narrow TH Knots and their expansions that are key to being able to easily impress any knotting master with your skills—well done!

Just for a break while we let that seep in, here are some sequential photographs of a couple of odd TH Knots that I cannot find specifically detailed in any other book of knots, decorative or otherwise. To start with, here is the 5L7B TH Knot. This knot cannot be readily made in hand, because it involves leaving many open turns. I have found that using tape on a cylindrical form really helps. You could also try using the loops I mentioned previously. This kind of separation of bights and leads will help to keep the structure open, and keep you from confusing the leads with each other. Don't be too concerned with the makeshift look of the form that we are using here—whatever comes to hand is the most useful!

5L7B TH Knot

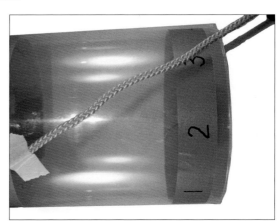

» **STAGE 1** – Mark the number of bights you intend to make on a cylinder.

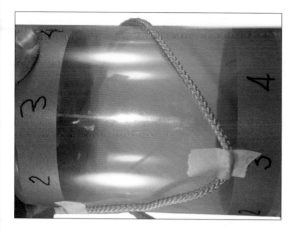

« **STAGE 2** – Starting at position #1, run down to position #3, then up to position #6.

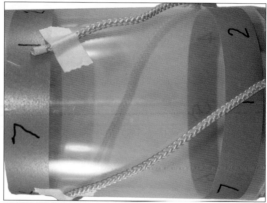

» **STAGE 3** – From position #6, move down to position #1. Note that you have no crossings yet.

« **STAGE 4** – From position #1, cross over the first pass to position #4.

« **STAGE 5** – From #4, cross the second part to position #6.

« **STAGE 6** – From position #6, cross over two leads to position #2 at the top (here the left).

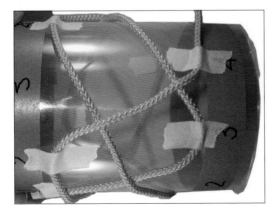

« **STAGE 7** – Again cross two leads from #2 down to position #4.

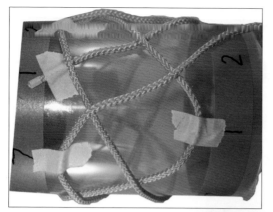

« **STAGE 8** – Not shown here, cross over two leads from #4 to #7, then from #7 down to #2.

» **STAGE 9** – Cross under the lead between #1 and #3, then over two leads to position #5.

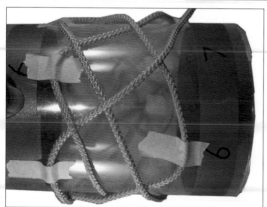

« **STAGE 10** – Again, go under the first lead then over two leads from #5 to #7.

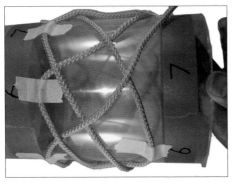

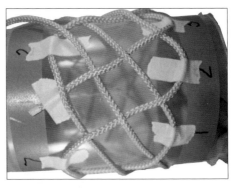

⌕ **STAGE 11** – From #7 pass under one, over one, under one, over one to #3.

⌕ **STAGE 12** – From 3L pass again under one, over one, under one, over one to position 5R, shown ready but not passed yet here.

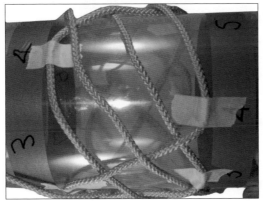

« **STAGE 13** – Again shown ready here, pass from 5R under one, over one, under one, over one along the ladder to position #1, where we began.

» **STAGE 14** – Shown passed here from #5 up to #1, ready to make the second and subsequent passes

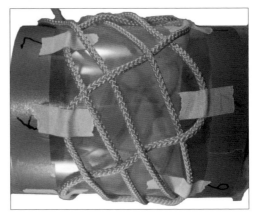

≈ The finished article in a handsome blue cord, applied over a wooden beaker

The 5L8B TH Knot

Again, it is difficult to make this knot "in hand" and so I have shown it wrapped around a see-through cylinder. Once more we start with a tape around the top and bottom of the cylinder. This time we have also added a tape around the middle to help with viewing the knot as it progresses. Mark the positions of the eight bights on the top

and bottom tapes. Notice that the lower row of numbers sits "between" the upper row of numbers, i.e., the top row "1" lies between the bottom row "1" and "2." After you get the idea of how to approach this kind of knot, I will introduce you to a kind of shorthand to enable tying these knots using a similar tubular arrangement.

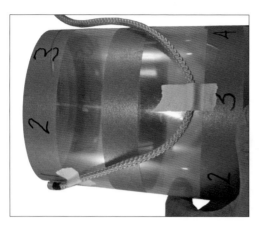

« **STAGE 1** – Begin at station #1, pass to #3 . . .

» **STAGE 2** – station #3 to #6 . . .

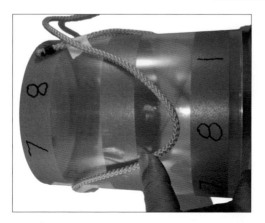

« **STAGE 3** – station #6 to #8, then over 1 cord to #3 . . .

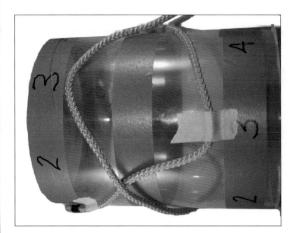

« **STAGE 4** –
from station
#3, over 1
cord . . .

» **STAGE 5** –
to station
#5 . . .

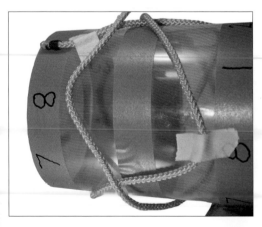

« **STAGE 6** –
then over
1 cord to
station #8.

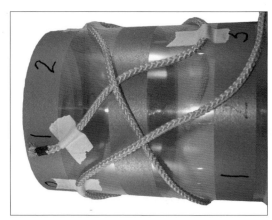

» **STAGE 7** –
Pass from
station #8
over 1 cord
to #2.

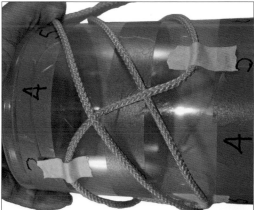

« **STAGE 8** –
From there
over two
cords to
#5.

» **STAGE 9** –
From station
#5, over 2
cords to
station #7.

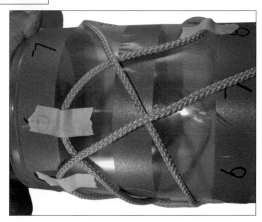

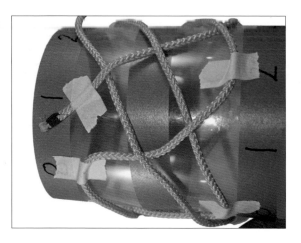

« STAGE 10 –
From #7, over
2 and under 1
to #2 . . .

» STAGE 11 –
from #2, over
2 and under
1 to #4 . . .

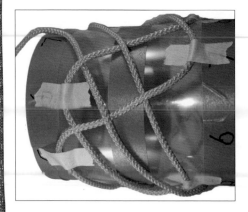

« STAGE 12 –
pass over 2
and under
1 from #4 to
#7.

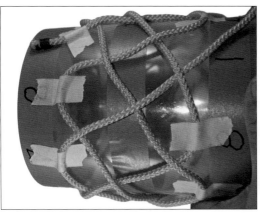

« STAGE **13** –
Over 2 and
under 1 to
station #1 . . .

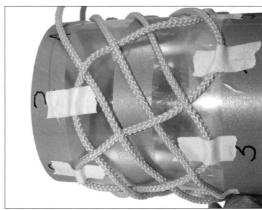

» STAGE **14** –
and now over,
under, over,
under to #4 . . .

« STAGE **15** –
over, under,
over, under
to #6.

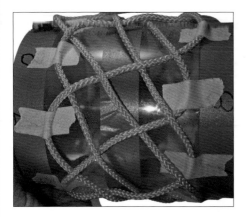

⚞ **STAGE 16** – Finish up the first pass with an over, under, over, under and back to #1.

⚞ *The shape stands out quite nicely against a white background.*

⚞ *Here is the pair, so that you can see the difference. Note that the 5L8B Turk's Head has only been passed twice, whereas the 5L/B has been passed three times.*

Looking back over the directions for each of the last two knots you can see that there are two sequences.

First Sequence: Over one, then over two, then under one, over two, then over, under, over, under.

Second Sequence: Over one, then over two, and then over two and under one, then over, under, over, under.

A shorter way of writing this is to write down the station numbers in bold, and the pass between as O for over and U for under when moving past another cord or strand that has been passed previously. Here are the first two knots in such a shorthand form:

1L, **3R**, **6L**, **1R**-O1-**4L**, **4L**-O1-**6R**, **6R**-O2-**2L**, **2L**-O2-**4R**, **4R**-O2-**7L**, **7L**-O2-**2R**, **2R**-U1-O2-**5L**, **5L**-U1-O2-**7R**, **7R**-U1-O1-U1-O1-**3L**, **3L**-U1-O1-U1-O1-**5R**, **5R**-U1-O1-U1-O1-**1L**. Start again to double.

1L, **3R**, **6L**, **8L**, **8R**-O1-**3L**, **3L**-O1-**5R**, **5R**-O1-**8L**, **8L**-O1-**2R**, **2R**-O2-**5L**, **5L**-O2-**7R**, **7R**-O2-U1-**2L**, **2L**-O2-U1-**4R**, **4R**-O2-U1-**7L**, **7L**-O2-U1-**1R**, **1R**-O1-U1-O1-U1-**4L**, **4L**-O1-U1-O1-U1-**6R**, **6R**-O1-U1-O1-U1-**1L**.

This formulaic approach works if you're using pins or tapes or loops to hold the bights in place as you progress. But what about making these knots using easy-to-remember methods instead of complicated formulas? Sadly, there is no Grand Unifying Theory of how to tie every single type of TH Knot! The methods already explained for tying Square TH Knots are an indication that this is a challenge that should be met by most. When considering the Wide TH Knots, you need to bear in mind the number of leads or parts of which the TH Knot you want is made— this generally can not be expanded without having a different start configuration of making an extra turn or passing the original lead to the right instead of the left. For Narrow TH Knots, the methods of making a greater number of bights, while keeping the number of leads or parts the same, shows that there are yet more complexities, none of which are unique to all expansions or to all TH Knots, except, of course, the Golden Rule!

« *The 7B5L TH Knot (lower left) with the 8B5L TH Knot (lower right), the 12B5L (upper left) and finally the 13B5L (upper right), not one of which is commonly shown in decorative knot books, but each looks very handsome in my opinion.*

Good news! There may not be a Grand Unifying Theory of tying all 111 Knots, but there is a way you can tie any size of single-cord simple TH Knot; recall if you will that we spoke at the beginning of a method of forming any TH Knot? We will use a grid of diagonal lines, marked off to denote the number of leads and bights.

For example, assume that you want to tie a TH Knot with thirteen bights and seven leads. We know that this TH Knot is possible because neither number is divisible by a common denominator (other than one). You can set up a universal grid showing how to tie this (and any other) single-strand TH Knot. In it, "overs" are shown as thicker lines and "unders" as thinner lines (on a sepia background for easier viewing).

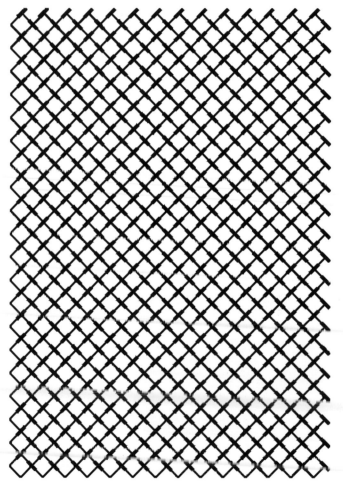

« *Universal TH Knot grid—pick the number of bights across the lower edge and the number of leads up the left side.*

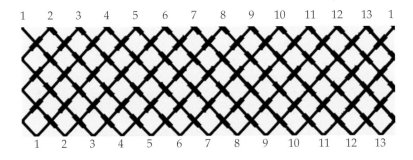

Select the Single-Strand TH Knot you want to tie and count off the number of bights along the bottom or lower edge of the figure. Then, carefully, count the leads up from the lower-left corner, with each diagonal line counting as one lead. Here is an example of a 7L13B TH Knot grid.

Notice the numbered nodes, top and bottom, forming the bights, and that the upper-right corner shows a line exiting upward and to the right at Node 1, and that there is a similar Node 1 at upper left showing a line entering from the upper corner. These two lines and nodes are one and the same, forming the thirteenth (or the first) upper bight. Ignore all the thickened lines at the top edge, which are simply the result of cropping the grid, and treat each one as a bight, just like the lower edge. On the right-hand edge, take particular note of the thickened lines and follow them horizontally to the left edge to find the continuation. To tie the knot from the grid, simply attach your line at any point on the grid and follow along a line—if the line is thick you are going to go over at the crossing, whether there is another

line there at that time or not. If the line is thin, you are going under at the crossing.

Remember the notation we used to show a sequence when tying from left to right? Here we are moving from top to bottom and back to the top, reversing as we go, so the sequence will be, using T for top and B for bottom:

1T, 4B, 8T, 11B, O1 2T, O1 5B, O1 9T, O1 12B, U1O1 3T, U1O1 6B, U1O1 10T, U1O1 13B, O1U1O1 4T, O1U1O1 7B, O1U1O1 11TO1U1O1 1B, U1O1U1O1 5T, U1O1U1O1 8B, U1O1U1O1 12T, U1O1U1O1 2B, O1U1O1U1O1 6T, O1U1O1U1O1 9B, O1U1O1U1O1 131, O1U1O1U1O1 3B, U1O1U1O1U1O1 7T, U1O1U1O1U1O1 10B, U1O1U1O1U1O1 Finish at 1T. Repeat as necessary.

NOTE: If you are adept at using a spreadsheet program, you can make a grid of your own.

As I noted earlier, this method of counting pegs (or pins or pieces of tape or loops of string) works very well using a Universal TH Knot Grid, and does not require too much thought. Do try it—you never know, it may turn out to be just what you needed!

FLAT TURK'S HEAD KNOTS

Well, so far, so good! Each of the preceding knots is shown here as a cylindrical knot. So how do we make a flat knot? The process involves some mind-bending turns that may surprise you. Let's start with the 3L4B TH Knot, beginning as a cylinder, and then make it into a flat knot, with a neat trick to help you through the change of going from cylinder to flat! Take special note that the number of bights inside and outside the knot should be the same. This is a useful thing to check if you want to see whether or not your knots are coming together as they should.

3L4B TH Flat Knot

We start with the cylindrical shape.

« **STAGE 1** – Look at the beginning of this chapter for instructions on how to make this base knot.

» **STAGE 2** – Turn the knot on its end, with the bights facing you, to make a cylinder.

« **STAGE 3** – Grasp the bights on the end of the cylinder farthest from you, pulling them upward and outward. At the same time, flatten down the upper Bights into the center, making the knot flatter. Notice that the strands now start to go out of shape.

» **STAGE 4** – With the knot now looking a little flatter, start to pull on any strand that appears to be most out of shape until it lies flat with the other strands, remembering that, in this case, the knot was made starting clockwise, so pull all strands in a clockwise direction.

« **STAGE 5** – Keep pulling each strand around the flat mat until you reach its end.

« **Stage 6** – Keep going in the same clockwise (or counterclockwise, if you made it that way) direction from the center.

» **Stage 7** – The flat mat is gradually taking shape.

« **Stage 8** – Stop when all bights around the perimeter are even and the strands all lie close together. Cut off the ends and stitch, glue, or tape them in place on the underside of the mat, so that they cannot be seen from the top and so that the number of strands visible is the same all the way around, as shown in the next two photographs.

« A completed flat mat TH Knot of three leads and four bights, the symbol of the International Guild of Knot Tyers, made with braided hemp

» Another 3L4B flat TH Knot, made with a more open center. This mat is made from twisted polished hemp, made in Belgium, a very natural cord, slubs and all.

Using the same technique of "turning" the top of the cylindrical knot inward to the center of a flat mat and "pulling" the lower edge of the bights outward, we can then dress the knot by adjusting the size of the space in the center and the appearance of the bights around the outside. Here are a few more "regular" TH Knots made from cylindrical knots into flat knots.

≈ At left, a tripled 4L3B TH Knot. At right, a tripled 5L4B TH Knot.

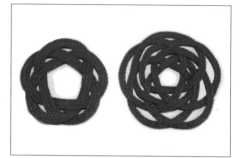

≈ At left, a 3L5B TH Knot as a flat knot. At right, a 6L5B TH Knot as a flat knot. Notice the pentagon in the center.

Notice that the inside of the knot, when made as a flat mat, tends to get more crushed or crumpled as the number of bights increases—the bights have to ride up over each other, producing a bumpy effect that is often undesirable in a flat mat. To overcome this tendency it is necessary to open the center so that there is room for the bights to lay flat. Take a look at the 3L5B and the 6L5B above. One has an open center, the other is a little more closed off. Conversely, you can see in the photographs of the 4L3B and the 5L4B above that three or four bights will nest together nicely to close off the center of the

mat, while still leaving it relatively flat. Take a look back also at the chapter on flat mats, where we show the Thump Mat, and compare the number of bights inside and outside that mat to the flattened TH knots in this chapter. One last thing about flat TH Knot mats—you can always start them flat and make your "overs" and "unders" in accordance with your Universal TH Knot Grid maker. However, it does take some patience to work them out this way—forewarned is forearmed!

Adding Color as a Feature

By adding a second strand of a different color into the open form of the weave, we get some really stunning effects of color and even texture, as seen here.

Note that the second color is inserted between the two passes of the first color. All four ends are then glued, sealed, taped, or sewn to the back of the knot. Be sure to tighten the first color only after inserting the second color. For small knots, use tweezers to pull the inner strands in tightening.

Adding Texture as a Feature

Here we have taken the 5L8B TH Knot as a cylinder, made it flat in one color, doubled the knot, and then inserted a new strand adding a second color and texture between the two parts of the doubled primary color.

Next, here is a photograph of a 14B5L TH Flat Knot made as a wreath for hanging on a front door.

≈ A 5L8B TH Knot, tied as a cylinder, then flattened and shaped, with a second color added and then the whole knot faired. Notice the change of texture from the shiny braided yellow polypropylene to the more subtle tan braided hemp in between. Notice also the long, graceful curve from the outer bight to the center, and the sharp return from the center.

≈ *See the door knocker? Note also the florist's wire frame, used for placing the knot (sewn in place to the wire) and keeping its shape, both of which are essential. Note that the outer bights have been extended away from the others—a nice feature!*

325

Spherical Single-Strand TH Knots

A TH Knot that was first formed as a cylinder can be shaped into a sphere instead of a flat mat. As with forming the flat knot, bring the top row of bights closer together (gathering the top), but instead of spreading the bottom bights, bring them together as well to form the sphere. Do you recall that we spoke of the effect of gathering several bights together and the crowding that can occur with those multiple crossings of cord? This is especially true of spherical TH Knots, where the "ends" of the cylindrical knot have three, four, or at the most five bights only. Without that restriction, the TH Knot as a sphere can become very bulky and "bumpy" at its poles. You should also be aware that if you use too few leads, the knot's center or equator will be insufficient to cover the core of the sphere.

Here are a few spherical TH Knots with few bights at the top and bottom but lots of "belly" leads that help cover the sphere.

NOTE: Although many think of this style of TH Knot as a Globe Knot, I think of it a little differently. For me, the pattern of the TH Knot is different than the Globe Knot, which comprises a series of circles, rather than the weave that is visible and ever-present in the TH Knot.

The following single-cord, spherical TH Knot has four bights at top and bottom, and four additional interior bights to thicken up the middle. Each of those inside and outside sets of four bights have three leads each; hence a 3L4B (or 6L8B). The knot ends up having 24 facets, which are hard to count unless you mark them with tape or something else you can later remove from your finished piece. Here is the knot.

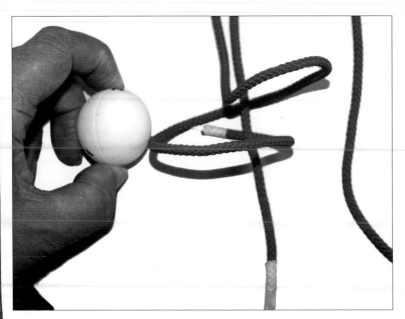

« Stage 1 – Wrap the spherical center twice.

« **STAGE 2** – Insert the long end of the line down through the turns.

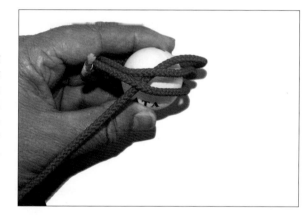

» **STAGE 3** – Bring the working end to the left (if you started counterclockwise, stick the end to the right).

« **STAGE 4** – Cross the starting tail up over the first two turns and pass the working end under, over, under the turns.

« **STAGE 5** – Now bring the working end through and pass the starting tail over and down to the right.

» **STAGE 6** – Pass the working end down to the left under the top turn and over two, then slide the top turn under the lower one to make a "mouth."

« **STAGE 7** – Pass the working end up to the left over, under, over.

« **STAGE 8** – Now pass the working end over, under, over, under, trapping the tail as you do so.

» **STAGE 9** – Pass the working end over, under, over, under up to the left through the "mouth" from Stage 6 . . .

« **STAGE 10** – to meet the starting tail again.

⚓ **STAGE 11** – Start doubling the line from the first pass.

⚓ **STAGE 12** – The doubling is completed. Note the four bights at north and south poles with the four center equator bights.

Here is another spherical TH Knot, this time with forty facets, AKA Ashley's #2217, with the same number of bights, adding two leads to bring each TH Knot to a 5L4B Knot, making it a 10L8B.

» **STAGE 1** – Start winding the cord from pin #1UU down to the right to pin #3ML.

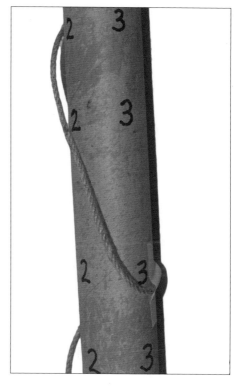

« **STAGE 2** – Continue round the mandrel to pin #1MU . . .

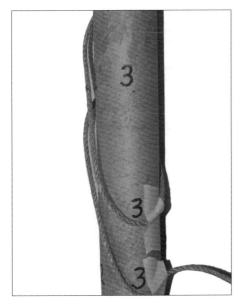

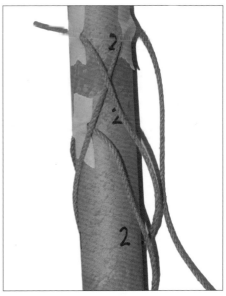

≏ Stage 3 – then down to the right again to pin #3LL . . .

≏ Stage 4 – to the first crossing, over, under, and up to pin #2UU . . .

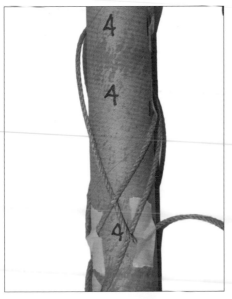

« Stage 5 – then down to the right to pass under, over to pin #4ML.

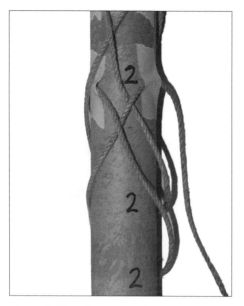

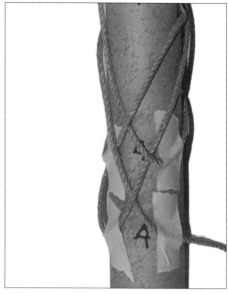

⌅ **STAGE 6** – From here, go under, over to pin #2MU . . .

⌅ **STAGE 7** – then over, under, and down to pin #4LL . . .

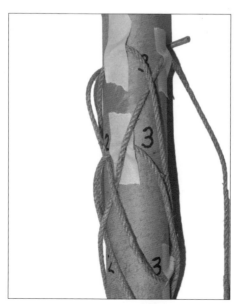

« **STAGE 8** – over, under, over, under to pin #4UU . . .

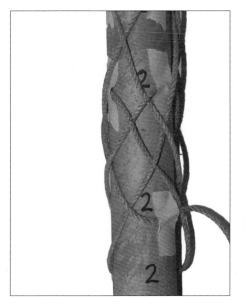

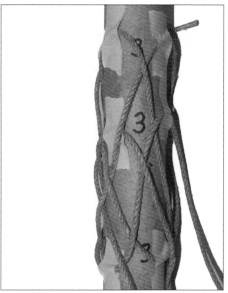

⌃ **STAGE 9** – over, under, over to pin #2ML . . .

⌃ **STAGE 10** – under, over, under, over to pin #3MU . . .

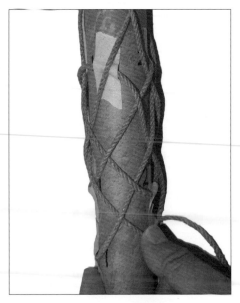

« **STAGE 11** – over, under, over, under to pin #2LL

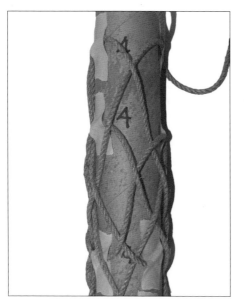

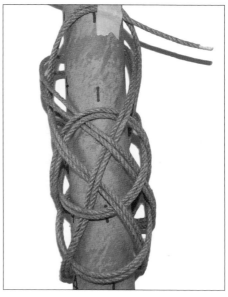

⌃ STAGE 12 – Then under, over, under, over, under to pin #1UU, where we started.

⌃ STAGE 13 – The first doubling, made loosely . . .

« STAGE 14 – and now faired and tightened a little, ready for transfer to a sphere.

≋ *Here is the hemp cord on a sphere, Ashley's #2217 or a forty-faceted spherical TH Knot*

≋ *Here we have another 40 faceted spherical TH Knot, this time tied with six passes of 0.6mm cord over a nineteen mm sphere.*

Now for our last spherical TH Knot. This one has far more facets than the others and so I have not shown it in stages, just the finished article, which is very similar to Ashley's #2218, but has more faces and a prolate spheroid (egg-shaped) cross-section.

When showing someone a finished spherical TH Knot, I am often asked, "What would you use it for?" to which I readily respond, "Why, to look at of course!" The better answer is that you can use it for the covering of a gear shift, your favorite drawer pull-knobs (assuming they are spherical), a door handle covering for arthritic hands, a light pull-knob covering, a cane-top covering, a covering for an artist's maul-stick (from the Dutch word *maalstok*, for "painter's stick"), a knob on the end of your fireside tongs, etc.

A word of caution; not all spherical knots can be formed from cylindrical TH Knots. In fact, some spherical knots have nothing to do with TH Knots, as we shall see in the chapter on spherical or Globe Knots.

THE PINEAPPLE KNOT

The Pineapple Knot is one that also fascinates people, probably just because of the name. Because the pineapple comes from Asia as well as South America, perhaps the Chinese as well as the gauchos had a hand in naming this knot. The *vaqueros* of the plains of Argentina know pineapples as a wonderful fruit exemplified in Guayaquil, Venezuela, as the best fruit in South America. Meanwhile, in Asia, they are celebrated by the Chinese as the symbol of prosperity. Pineapple leaves in themselves are used to make a fiber so fine that it is used, in South America where the wild variety of pineapple grows, to string beads. Red pineapples, knotted from silk cords, are symbols of prosperity and as such are very welcome in Chinese culture. The pineapple knot is a variant of the TH Knot, formed by weaving another TH Knot inside the first one—as if the first one was not difficult enough! The Pineapple Knot (hereafter PK) is normally made using a regular TH Knot with any odd number of leads as its base. For example—if you tie a 5L7B TH Knot, you could conceivably weave a 3L7B TH Knot inside the first TH Knot to make a PK. However, the PK still has to obey the Common Divisor rule, because it, too, is a TH Knot. This means that one cannot start out with a 5L6B TH Knot and add a PK of 3L6B, because the 3L6B has a common divisor and can therefore not be made with one strand. As for the 5L7B and the 3L7B— yes it can! The PK then is a knot within a knot or a nest of knots. The two (or more) knots usually share the same number of bights top and bottom. The leads or passes can vary,

however. We could conceivably begin with one PK of two Turk's Heads and add a third Turk's Head to it to make yet another type of PK! Let's stick with the simple ones for now.

The following table shows the possible PKs that can be made from a regular TH Knot.

From this we can see that, for example, a 13L5B TH Knot can include within it a TH Knot of 11L5B without either of the TH Knots violating the Common Divisor or Golden Rule. Another example of a possible PK is the 5L23B, which will accommodate a 3L23B, again with neither knot violating the Common Divisor rule. So where do we go from there? Knowing that a PK is possible is one thing, but how do we go about making it? The first thing to do is to make the base TH Knot, so that we can build the next TH Knot into it to make a PK. Let's select a 7L6B TH Knot and then build into it a 5L6B TH Knot.

Let's also make a start by addressing some terms like "coding" and as-yet unfamiliar terms like "sobre" and "casa" in relation to Pineapple Knotting.

First, the subject of "coding," which is a subject near and dear to the hearts of leather-braiders. The coding is simply the method of expressing the number of "overs" and "unders" in any particular turn of the line around the knot. What we have seen so far is all referred to as "O1, U1," which stands for "over one, under one" or the coding for how we make the finished passes through our knot. We could equally have spoken of "O1, U3, O1" coding, which would again refer to the number of cords passed over or under. It is simply the pattern of "overs and unders" that we make with each successive move of the cord around the perimeter of the finished knot.

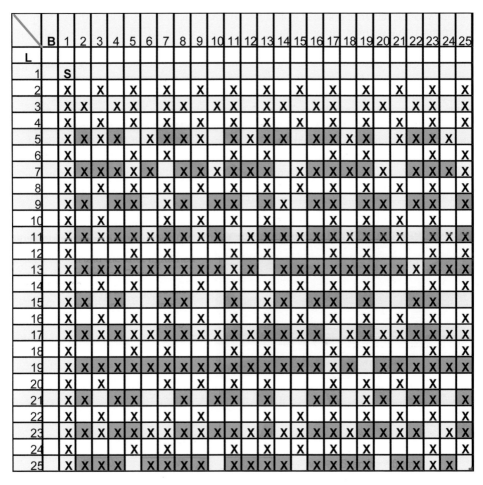

≈ *Table showing (in green shading) the possible odd-lead start TH Knots that could also be a PK with an odd-lead TH Knot inside it*

Now, what do we mean by "sobre" and "casa" when referring to the coding? Sobre finishes by tucking up under a part adjacent to the standing end at the finish of the knot. The Sobre Knot also progresses by one bight each time we make a turn around the base.

We will use the sobre coding here, which is to say "upon" the manner in which the original Turk's Head is built. The other common expression we see in Pineapple Knots is "casa" coding, which means literally "in the house of" or "within." Casa coding, when referring to simple Turk's Head Knots, means that it has an over-one, under-one style of making the knot and that we may skip one or more bights each time we make a pass around the knot, until we complete the knot. For this first Pineapple Knot, I have shown the sobre coding, or manner, of making the crossings. Later, in Chapter 10 on Knob Knots, I show the casa coding form, which is perhaps a little more difficult in cord, because the cord moves, whereas when made in leather strips the leather does not move as much. Here is

a *sobre* coded 7L6B Turk's Head into which is woven a 5L6B Turk's Head. This version is more stable in cord, because the cord is trapped by the interweave. Note the hollow blue threading needle in the photographs below, which is very useful for making knots of this and many other over-under weaves with fine threads. You can purchase them ready-made at craft stores or on the Internet, or make one yourself from an empty ball-pen ink reservoir or some fine copper or steel tubing.

« **STAGE 1** – Form the base knot, a 7L6B TH Knot doubled and viewed sideways.

« **STAGE 2** – Apply tape and number the upper and lower bights, even on top and odd below, right to left. Because we have six bights on each end, our numbers progress from 1 through 12.

« **Stage 3** – Starting under bight #6, trace pairs of the existing knot, to the left in this photograph, over, under, over, under, down to bight #5.

» **Stage 4** – From bight #5, where the original cord tucks under #5, again trace pairs to the left over, under, over, under to bight #4, but follow the one that tucked under #5 in the original knot.

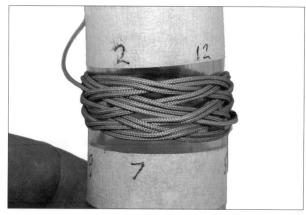

« **Stage 5** – From bight #4 to bight #3, again over, under, over, under.

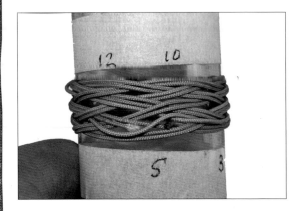

« **Stage 6** – From #3 we move under our new first color pass to again pass the pairs under, over, under to bight #2.

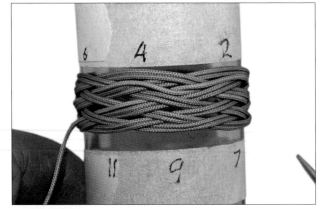

» **Stage 7** – From #2 we move over then under its own color, then under, over, under to #1.

« **Stage 8** – Now we have two of our own color to cross, under the first and over the second to bight #12.

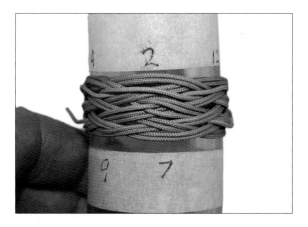

« **Stage 9** – From #12 we move down to the left under our new color and over our new color to #11, again passing pairs of the base knot over, under, over, under.

» **Stage 10** – Take the cord now from #11 up to the left to #10, under, over, under our new color and over, under, over, under the pairs.

« **Stage 11** – Here, from #10 we go under, over, under our new color to #9, moving past pairs over, under, over, under.

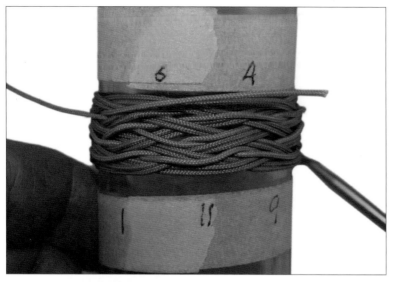

⋩ **STAGE 12** – Now from #9 we move under, over, under, over the new color and over, under, over, under the first set of pairs to #8.

⋩ **STAGE 13** – From #8 we move under, over, under, over and over, under, over, under the pairs to get to #7.

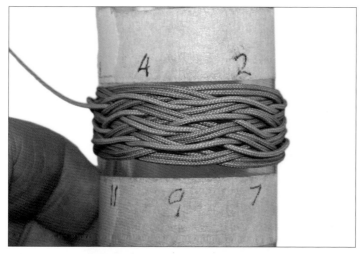

⚡ **STAGE 14 –** From #7 to #6 we start doubling the new color and follow it around.

⚡ **STAGE 15 –** Having passed the doubling all the way around, we just have to fair the knot by gradually tightening it all the way around, being careful not to over-tighten on the first color. Recall that we started at #6? We also finished at #6, which is encouraging to think that we did it right!

≈ *A Pineapple Knot made on the end of my hiking staff, in red and green, the red being a 5L4B and the green being a 3L4B. Note the over-two, under-three pattern or coding made by the red and the under two, over three by the green, giving a great pattern with both knots.*

There are many, many more variations of the Pineapple Knot to try—so many that I would encourage you to try making them for yourself, based on following the central idea of making the number of bights the same and the number of leads two less than the starting TH Knot. Look in Tom Hall's book *Turk's Head Workbook* and Bruce Grant's *Encyclopedia of Rawhide and Leather Braiding* or perhaps online. From that simple introduction to Pineapple Knots you should try to add two colors or more and to incorporate patterns inside the weaves. I wish you well as you try your own variations on them. Many friends and fellow knot-tyers have shown that patterns that can be made include zigzag, lightning bolt, "W," "X," and even "O" shapes, by using two or three additional strands in the second and third weave. Those efforts are beyond the scope of this book.

Knob Knots

*A ball of sea-grass string, (opposite, lower)
with not quite as much "pattern" as one
might otherwise wish, although some do prefer
the rather unstructured look of this kind of
knotting.*

*An assorted collection of knotted ball knots in a
variety of colors and weaves, something that can
be copied or modified to suit (opposite, upper).*

Of the many forms of decorative knot, the
Knob Knot may be one of those most feared
or yet most revered by knot-tyers. This form of
knot is an excellent introduction to thinking
in three dimensions. Many find doing so
maddening. Because of this they revert to
recipes and two-dimensional plots instead,
just so that they can start and finish their knot.
There is, of course, nothing wrong with a little
help from wherever one can get it.

Why would you want to make a Knob Knot?
There are some obvious applications; a finial
on a decorative lamp, a decanter stopper, the
handle of a tool, perhaps a readily found knob

for your keychain, or just a chew toy for your dog or perhaps a chase toy for your cat. You also may come up with some different applications, such as covering your cuff-link ends, the end of your favorite pencil, a stir-stick for your favorite cocktail glass, the end of your hiking staff, or the brass knobs on the end of your bed frame. This chapter starts with some relatively simple globe knots, such as the Monkey Fist and the Double Monkey Fist, so that you can learn how Globe Knots cover things that are spherical instead of cylindrical or flat. Then we cover things that are at the end of a piece of plain or decorative rope, like a tassel, or round-raised lumps on leather work for horse tack. Find a ball or spherical end like the knob on your gear shifter and you will be able to cover it.

MONKEY FIST

SINGLE MONKEY FIST

This rather ubiquitous knob knot is also used today as a decoration, although it was originally a fully functional knot. It is named in part because it looks like a small, closed fist, with cords for fingers. However, "monkey" was also a slang term used aboard sailing ships to refer to something diminutive (e.g., monkey jacket, monkey engine, monkey block, monkey forecastle), and the term "Monkey's Fist" was adopted as being somewhat easier to remember. The knot's principal function is as weight at the end of a light line to help with heaving (tossing to another ship, dock, or other mooring). The weight of the line combined with the core of the Monkey Fist will carry for a considerable

distance, depending on the type of line and the mass of the core. That is not to say that a heavy core is always a good idea—if you try heaving a line from ship to shore, for instance, it is better to use a Monkey Fist with a light, floating core so that it will float if your toss is off and lands in the water. A heavy cored Monkey Fist will sink and could snag on a rocky sea-bed. In an arborist's work, a heavy core is an advantage for getting the ball and line through heavy twigs and leaf cover in a tree of perhaps fifty or more feet in height. A Monkey Fist may also be useful in rock-climbing to get a top rope over a projection above to use when assisting another climber.

There are seldom any Scouts with whom I have met, be they Boy, Cub, Sea, or Girl, who have not at least heard of the Monkey Fist, and many of them have learned how to tie more than one. I made matching-sized Monkey Fist earrings, one red and one green (for Port and Starboard), in light cotton thread for my wife, many years ago. She wears them

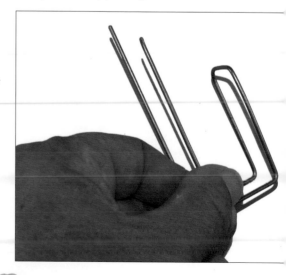

to this day! You may find it helpful, if you are going to make many Monkey Fist knots, to devise a formwork skeleton on which you make them, such as the one shown in the photographs, which was made from simple dry-cleaning hanger wire. Forms can also help if you are making just one Monkey Fist, although your fingers will work well for most small projects. Ultra-small projects may need a smaller and thinner wire frame, shaped similarly to the one shown here.

The second method of making the Monkey Fist used here is the British Admiralty method, useful for making the ends of the single cord come out of the knot at the same place. The normal method shown in many other books of knotting is to have the two ends exit the knob knot at each side of the turns, instead of together like the second one. Take a look at Hervey Garrett Smith's illustration of the Monkey Fist in his book *The Marlinespike Sailor.* His description is very well done and very well worth getting your own copy!

« **STAGE 1** – Wrap enough turns so that there are the same number on each face and enough turns to cover at least three-fourths of the sphere.

« **STAGE 2** – Turn the cord only (not the frame) to wrap the same number of turns at 90 degrees to the first set of turns. Note that the first wrap from the bottom appears loose, so hold it with your thumb and build upward on it.

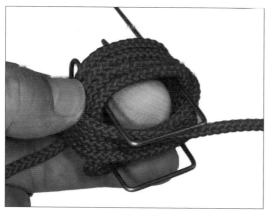

« **STAGE 3** – Slip a ball or other core inside the first two sets of turns.

» **STAGE 4** – Make the third and final set of turns at 90 degrees to both of the first two sets of turns, completing the x, y, and z axes of the sphere.

« **STAGE 5** – Here the turns have been slightly tightened before pulling the frame out to the right in this photograph.

« **STAGE 6** – Now all the turns are tightened along each axis so that the core is well and truly set in place and the ends are even, so that you can finish them with a loop, a True Lover's Knot or perhaps a Two-Strand Matthew Walker Knot.

The finished Monkey Fist »

The finished article, fit for use as a key fob, a zipper toggle, or simply to add to your thumb drive or cell phone.

STAGE 1 The alternative Admiralty pattern Monkey Fist start is the same as previously. »

« STAGE 2 – Now the cord is carried to the top end of the wraps instead of starting around the bottom end, and the wraps are carried down instead of being carried up (compare with Stage 2 of the first Monkey Fist).

STAGE 3 – Now make one crossing diagonally, to exit on the far lower side as here. »

≈ **Stage 4** – Now insert the core to fill the center . . .

≈ **Stage 5** – and complete the passes to bring the end alongside the starting cord. This finish enables a neat splice to be made with no chance of anything being able to foul inside the splice eye.

The finished Admiralty Pattern Monkey Fist, as seen in the Manual of Seamanship, vol. 2 (HMSO London 1952) ≈

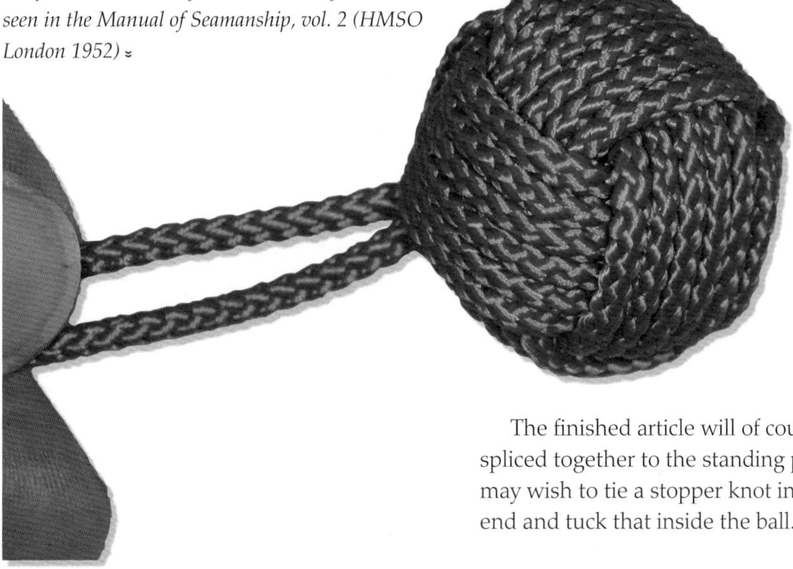

The finished article will of course be spliced together to the standing part or you may wish to tie a stopper knot in the working end and tuck that inside the ball.

DOUBLE MONKEY FIST

If a single Monkey Fist has six faces (the number of faces of a cube) then a cuboctahedron may be said to be a cube whose corners have been modified to form a Double Monkey Fist with fourteen faces (cube = six faces; octahedron = eight faces; total = 14 faces).

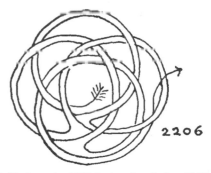

» Ashley's version (#2206) of a cuboctahedron (C/W, CC/W, C/W, CC/W)

» A cuboctahedron is a polyhedron (a solid object having poly- or many faces) with eight triangular faces and six square faces—fourteen in all

Each corner (junction of three square faces) is therefore a triangle, and the former upright square face has become diagonally the same height as the original cube face, oriented now so that its corners are upper and lower, rather than northwest, northeast and so on. For us knot-tyers, this means we have eight places (triangular faces) where there is a meeting of three cords (eight corners of the original cube) and six places (square faces) where there is a meeting of four cords, as in the original six faces of the cube. The colored diagram above from Wikipedia may help you visualize it. The dictionary definition also helps in visualizing the shape:

A cuboctahedron therefore has 12 identical axes (aka vertices) originating at a singularity or a single point of origin, with two triangles

and two squares meeting at each axis. It also has twenty-four identical-length edges, each separating a triangle from a square as you can see in the diagram.

However, here is the knot as it is tied when pinned to a board, and as shown in Ashley's Book of Knots, #2206, which he states is a cuboctahedron. If you count the number of faces where there are cords meeting each other (not the spaces between) then I only count twelve, making this knot what I think of as a true Double Monkey Fist or dodecahedron, having twice the number of faces that a regular Monkey Fist has. Note that, because the ends do not meet in

« Burrhus's version of a cuboctahedron having fourteen faces, built as a 3B5L modified TH knot

this first version of a Globe Knot, you must determine the number of circles you will need for complete covering before you start. There is no easy way out of this. If you are covering a sphere of one inch using a 3/32-inch cord (approximately 25-mm diameter sphere and 3 mm thick cord) you will need to use five or six passes to get the right coverage, depending on how fuzzy your line and how tight you pull the individual parts. It is too difficult for beginners to tie in the hand. Alternatively, a second method of tying a real fourteen-faced Globe Knot (a cuboctahedron) is also shown, one by Don Burrhus as a modified TH Knot and the third one as a modified version of Ashley's #2206.

STAGE 2 – Continue counterclockwise over, over, then under, over, under to the right side, ready for the last two turns.

Modified #2206

This knot has been modified to include all fourteen facets, but with an added counterclockwise turn thrown in to Ashley's #2206 to produce this third covering.

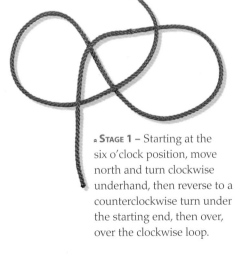

STAGE 1 – Starting at the six o'clock position, move north and turn clockwise underhand, then reverse to a counterclockwise turn under the starting end, then over, over the clockwise loop.

STAGE 3 – Now pass the cord clockwise under, over, under to the inside of the NW loop and pass finally over, under counterclockwise to rejoin the starting cord. Mold the loops into a sphere and be sure to include a solid sphere inside for support.

The finished amended #2206, with a second color added between the outer two passes of the base cord, for a touch of pizzazz! ≈

The third version, scanned as a flat knot. Note the turns (C/W, CC/W twice, C/W, and CC/W) as a modified form of Ashley's #2206. ≈

The second version by Don Burrhus incorporates a modified 3B5L TH Knot. Look carefully at the diagram to see the added bight inside the leads at the six o'clock position. Yet a third way is to put an additional partial clockwise turn to Ashley's #2206, so as to finish alongside the start, and to create the added two faces, making fourteen in all. The added bonus with the third version is that the end cord meets the start cord, allowing you to make all passes separately instead of having to work out the number of passes in each direction first. The actual knots in cord, when

tied either as a four-pass or six-pass knot, are not immediately that different from each other, as you can see here:

» *Ashley's #2206, finished with six passes and twelve facets*

≈ *Burrhus's Fourteen-Facet Globe Knot, finished with four passes*

≈ *The third cuboctahedron, finished with four passes*

However, the skill required to tie these three knots varies considerably, so do try them all for your own enjoyment! Trace the pattern, so that you can then follow around to make your own.

A second type of Double Monkey Fist has twenty-four faces instead of six, twelve, or fourteen. To my mind this is not a true double, because the number of faces is quadrupled, although each face of the cube does have a bi-directional weave. I therefore will call it a

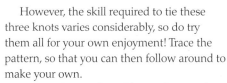

Double Monkey Fist (not Ashley's name for it—he calls it a two-ply knot) because the weave is doubled on each of the six faces. However, let my point of view not get in the way of your enjoyment! Here is the twenty-four-faced Double Monkey Fist. It is shown as Ashley's #2207, where it is illustrated beautifully to show its woven, three-dimensional structure. It takes a little while to get used to it, but it is a very handsome knot.

In the Ashley Book of Knots this knot is tied on a board, but with a little practice and some not-too-small measure of dexterity, I tied it in hand. You may also like to try a wire form to tie the knot around. It is a handsome knot, no doubt! An additional single pass will still satisfy the over-under pattern, so you will be able to expand the number of passes from four to six, eight, ten, or more in order to achieve full coverage. Note that the form of the knot is a series of circles around the sphere, two circles in each of the three principal axes, exactly like the regular Monkey Fist, but using a weave instead. This first photograph below, just before the

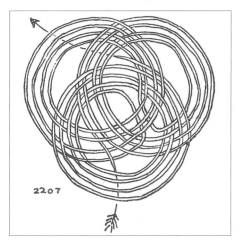

tying sequence, shows the basic structure, shown open so that you can see how it develops. The series of photographs after that shows how to make the knot on a wire frame, using a wooden ball as the core. If you use a wire frame for your Globe Knot, be sure you can remove the wire frame easily, without having to resort to scissors or wire cutters! You can make an easy and inexpensive frame using two U-shaped wires (four legs), inserted up through a poly-foam or corrugated cardboard base.

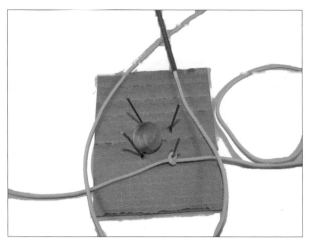

▲ *Ashley's #2207, tied in 3-mm cord around a 25-mm core. The coverage is deliberately sparse, and shows the 3D-structure clearly!*

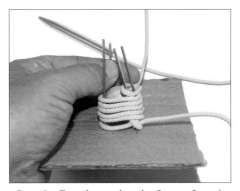

« **STAGE 1** – Make six wraps around the sphere, more for a larger ball and smaller cord and less for a smaller ball and larger cord. Here, 3-mm cord is used on a 25-mm sphere and approximately two thirds of the cord is used for the first clockwise wraps.

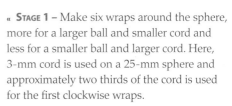

» **STAGE 2** – Pass the cord under 3, over 3, under 3, over 3 for the first three wraps, and then change to wrap over 3, under 3, over 3, under 3, as shown here and next, finishing at the taped end as shown.

« **STAGE 3A** – The final passes for the second round of building.

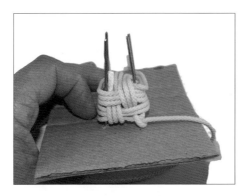

STAGE 3B – Here is an oblique view of the sphere to show the wraps so far. »

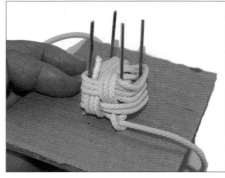

« **STAGE 4** – The completion of the passes, making over-under passes as before for the first half and then switching to under-over passes.

Thus far, as you may have already seen, the idea of the spherical covering has a central theme. Go back over the patterns shown to see the meeting at each face of three or four separate faces in those examples to bring about a covering on a spherical object. So it is with the patterns of Globe Knot coverings we have looked at so far—they form panels with three, four, five, or six sides to them, so that the meetings of the cords at each panel junction point are not overcrowding the face of the panel.

LITTLE LUMP KNOT

Strictly speaking, this knot is not a Globe or Sphere Knot all to itself—it

requires some lower end base or support work of perhaps over two crowning and a Matthew Walker, to act as a support to the knot. First, here is the Matthew Walker Knot in stages, followed by the Crown and the Wall, so that you have a reminder of how each is formed. Essentially, the Matthew Walker is a series of Overhand Knots tied through the previous knot. The knots are stacked, one on top of the other, to form a winding of sorts around the base cord. When tied in the individual strands of a three-strand or four-strand rope, with the strands re-laid after tying the knot, the knot is impossible to remove without first unlaying the line back to the top of the knot.

« **STAGE 1** – Lay out all the strands you intend to use, made here with eight strands.

STAGE 2 – Pass the end of your first strand under all other strands and then tuck the end up into its own loop, to make an Overhand Knot around the bundle. Note that the knots are tied counterclockwise here and that we work on them one-by-one in the same direction. »

« **Stage 3** – Take the next counterclockwise strand and tuck it under all other strands, then up through its own loop AFTER passing through the previous loop. Try to keep the strands as shown, rolling them under the prior strand.

Stage 4 – Here the last of the eight strands has been passed up through the preceding seven loops and then up through its own loop. »

« **Stage 5** – Starting with the last strand tied, tighten up each strand little by little, pushing the overlying strands around the knot counterclockwise so that the strands all lie next to the preceding and following strand that was tied.

STAGE 6 – Keep working the knots tighter, little by little. Here we see that the left-most strand has been tightened (see also that it comes up through its own bight on top) and that the bundle, yet to be tightened, requires shifting one of the strands over its neighbor, to keep the order correct.

» *The finished Matthew Walker Knot, with each strand appearing at the top coming out of its own loop.*

CROWN KNOTTING

Crown Knotting may be over one, over-two or, for the ambitious knot-tyer, over-three. The process may be made clockwise or counterclockwise or may be alternated, one layer clockwise, the next counterclockwise, then clockwise again, etc. Crown Knotting

may also be enhanced by using alternating different-colored cords. Crown Knotting forms the basis of many other knots and is used here, in Globe Knots, as much as anywhere else. It is a technique that should be easy to remember and easy to reproduce, and I have presented it here in step-by-step photographs to show the start and end of the process.

« **STAGE 1** – Lay out all the strands radiating from a central point, as here.

STAGE 2 – Working either clockwise or counterclockwise (here working counterclockwise), pass one of the strands over the strand next to it in the chosen direction and allow it to hang down, or hold it down. »

« **STAGE 3** – Take the strand that was just crossed over and cross it over the next strand in its turn. Repeat this with each strand until you have no more strands sticking out to cross over.

STAGE 4 – To complete the Crown, pass the last strand over and down into the loop formed by your first crossing in stage 2, to complete the circle. »

« **STAGE 5** – Because this set of strands was laid over counterclockwise, they are now tightened clockwise against the preceding strand and loop to get the ring of strands as tight as desired. You can see from this photograph that a core inside the passes would help to stabilize the structure. You will likely need a core on over-one crowning any time you exceed approximately five strands.

« **STAGE 6** – Here two passes of Crown Knotting have been completed and are viewed from the side, above the Matthew Walker Knot.

Crown Knotting on a Bellrope, to form the major part of the handle. This Crown Knotting is over-two knotting, where each line is taken over the next two instead of just over one. »

The technique of over-two crowning is just what it sounds like—you pass the strands one at a time over the two adjacent strands instead of over just one strand. Here in the technique in photographs.

« **STAGE 1** – Starting as you did for over-one Crown Knotting, pass one strand over two adjacent strands instead of one. Try to keep your thumb in the loop formed with that strand if needed.

STAGE 2 – Take the next strand in turn, moving counterclockwise here again. »

« STAGE 3 – The second-to-last strand is inserted into the first loop formed above in Stage 1.

STAGE 4 – The last strand is now inserted into the first loop *and* the second loop. Check to be sure that you have one strand exiting from each loop. »

« STAGE 5 – The strands are all pulled tighter here, ready for the next layer to go on top. Notice the tighter center for this style of Crown Knotting and that each strand is passing under two loops around the Crown.

« The view from the side of over-two Crown Knotting, with the single Crown Knotting directly below it, for comparison.

WALL KNOTTING

Remember that crown rhymes with down, which is the principal direction in which the cords are laid, and that walls are built up, which is the principal direction the cords lie when making the Wall Knot. Again, over-two or over-three may be used in making Wall Knotting—or should that be under-two or under-three? No matter, if you turn the page upside down you will see that Crown Knotting and Wall Knotting are the same but their direction of laying the cord is reversed from down to up. Look a little closer and you will also see that clockwise Crown Knotting is counterclockwise Wall Knotting!

▲ **STAGE 1** – Lay out your strands as usual, then pass one strand up between its neighbor and the strand next to that one, as shown here.

« **STAGE 2** – Here the second strand has been passed and is being held against the first strand to steady the process.

STAGE 3 – Each strand has now been passed in turn and the knot tightened around the underlying Crown Knotting core. Without that core the knot will require more tightening or possibly need under-two Walling instead. »

« **STAGE 4** – Seen here from the side, the first round of Wall Knots has been applied.

⁂ The Wall Knot is difficult to discern from the Crown Knot, unless they are side-by-side. The structure is the same, only it is made in a different direction for each type. Note that, in this photograph, the Wall Knotting has been laid over the base Crown Knotting, making the joints seem farther open, and revealing the passes of the Wall Knots.

Back to the Little Lump Knot! One person in the United States, Dan Callahan, can probably tell you more about the Little Lump Knot than almost anyone else, except perhaps the inventor of the knot, Pieter van De Griend of Holland. Dan Callahan (RIP) was from Alaska, and he developed the Little Lump Knot into a Lighthouse Knot finish. Others around the world, including Vince Brennan, Andre van der Salm, and Don Wright (to name but three), also show you how to make this Knob Knot through their online tutorials. What I have done here is to bring together the shoulders of the giants who came before me to assemble several different weaves.

The Little Lump Knot (LLK for short) is a great way to finish the end of a bellrope or key fob with a sphere. The difficult part of the LLK is getting the final crossings to go across the end of the knot and to take a slight detour along the way. One look at the photographs should explain this a little better than mere words can do.

The LLK can be made with any even number of cords from as few as eight up to as many as twenty-four or more. The number of cords used should, when divided by two, result in an even number. For example, 8/2=4; 12/2=6; 16/2=8; 20/2=10; 24/2=12, and so on.

This is necessary to produce a balanced knot. This is not to say, of course, that you cannot make any even number of strands into a LLK, like a ten-strand, fourteen-strand or eighteen-strand LLK. You can, but the end result is a little different, as you will see from the attached photographs.

The basic premise of the LLK is to make a Footrope Knot and then finish off the top of the knot with a cover of over-under passes, some of which will cross in a "pass-and-tuck" pattern. For LLKs with more strands, it will be necessary to provide some padding under the final passes, to bring the surface up and provide the "rounded" look to the finished knot. This padding is most readily provided by tucking the ends of the strands into the knot, much as is done with some two-sided Chinese Knots, to give them some "body" as needed. Here are the instructions:

Make a Matthew Walker Knot and tighten it. Add an over-one crowning on top of this knot, tighten it, add another over-one crowning on top of that, and tighten it as well. Next, add a doubled over-one crowning—doubling here means to take each successive pair of cords and crown them over between the next pair of pairs, tighten it, then take the second pair between the next two pairs and so on, finishing with a tuck of the last pair under the first pair's loop. Now tighten it all. On top of this, add another doubled over-one crowning. You have now built up four layers of tight knotting on top of the MWK and are ready to start the edge work of the LLK itself. The layers provide the "padding" of which I spoke earlier. Using the four pairs of strands (assuming you are making an eight-strand LLK) you will now make a Doubled Wall Knot. So far we have Crown, Crown, Doubled Crown, Doubled Crown and Doubled Wall, all on top of the MWK at the end of your bellrope or whatever you are adding the LLK onto.

Now that you have the Doubled Wall Knot on top (I strongly suggest you make this with the ends upward!) make another Wall Knot, but this time with each single cord as an over-one Wall Knot. Let the ends of these single Wall Knot cords hang down over the MWK you built this up from, to help cover the crowning you did earlier—yes, you are now going to cover the fine tight work you just did! For each cord of your Wall Knot hanging down, here assuming you are clockwise walling, cross over the cord to its immediate left and then tuck under the next cord above that. The last part of this knot is easier explained in photographs, so take a look at Stages 1 through 10 below:

LOOK AT THE 8-STRAND LLK:

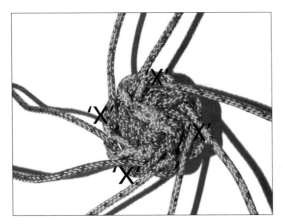

« STAGE 1 – After following the instructions above, we next make the top crossings. This photo shows the start after you have made the side walling. Notice the doubled cord marked "X" on the photograph at the start of the Wall Knot.

STAGE 2 – Now we pick out alternating strands to cross at right angles by crowning. Look for the cords that exit to the left (for clockwise crowning) of the double cord marked "X" in Stage 1 above. »

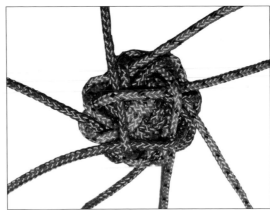

« STAGE 3A – Tuck the ends of these crowned strands down out of the way for the moment.

STAGE 3B – The side view of the prior stages. »

« **STAGE 4A –** North cord goes under, over, then left of the south cord; south cord goes over, under, over, then tucks right under the north cord.

STAGE 4B – Here north and south are tucked and in place, leaving the grid ready for east-west. »

« **STAGE 5** – East goes under, over, under, over and then above, while west goes over east, then under, over, under, over and tucks below east to the right. This now leaves us with all eight cords hanging down.

STAGE 6 – Next we double up the wall on the side with each of the eight cords, shown here with a pink alongside the blue for clarity of the doubling. »

« **STAGE 7** – All cords that were hanging down are now walled up by their respective partners, ready to cross the top again for the final doubling.

« STAGE 8 – Here is the top immediately prior to fairing the knot by tightening the cords in turn.

The pattern for the Little Lump Knot seems to be the greatest problem. Review it in the drawings below, which may be enlarged and then followed. The overall pattern is to find the center-crossing arcs and make those first. Outside of those arcs will then be the outer arcs. The pattern across the top has arcs that cross to the other side, exiting in a consistent direction. With the notable exception of the twelve-strand, all patterns shown here are clockwise exits, which means that the tails point clockwise around the top of the knot. They could equally all be counterclockwise exits.

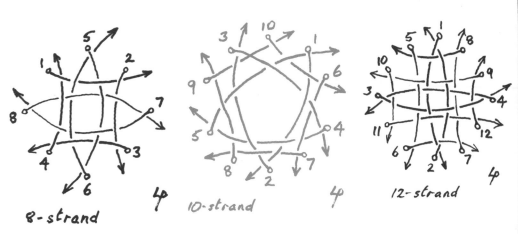

8-strand

10-strand

12-strand

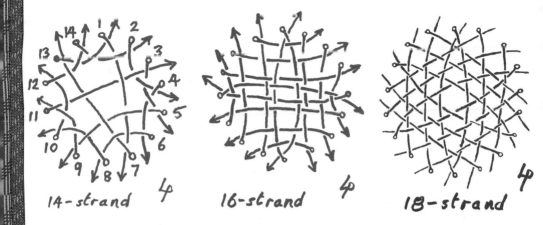

14-strand 4   16-strand 4   18-strand 4

After exiting across the top, the strands are then doubled to follow down the hanging Wall Knot and up the Crown Knot, then doubled again across the top. Finish by tucking the ends inside the outer Footrope

Knot finish. Here are some more explanatory photographs of the finished eight-strand LLK, and then some others to show how to make the ten-strand LLK.

≈ *The side and top view of the tightened LLK, sitting nicely atop the Matthew Walker as the end of your new bellrope!*

« **STAGE 1** – After the doubled Wall Knot, we go to the singled Wall Knot with each end hanging down over the MWK.

STAGE 2 – Here, in purple, we go over one, under one . . . »

« **STAGE 3** – completing the pass (over, under) for each of the strands.

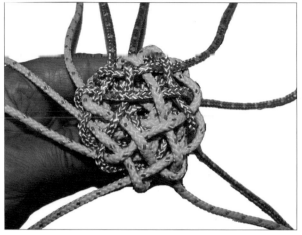

« STAGE 4 – Use every other cord to make a pentagon in the center. Start with the cords not next to a doubled cord, then use the in-between cords by the double cords to complete the ring around the center. Exit beside each cord's right at the perimeter.

STAGE 5 – Here is the side view with each cord alongside and below its mate prior to following the Wall Knot up. The green cord goes up first here. **»**

« STAGE 6 – Now we have all the cords alongside and ready to go below their mates.

STAGE 7 – Turn up alongside the mate, cross the top and disappear on the other side behind the Wall Knot, to appear beneath it by the MWK. »

« STAGE 8 – A pre-tightened knot . . .

STAGE 9 – and the final tightened knot from on top . . . »

STAGE **10** – and from the side, with the ends removed. Voilà! »

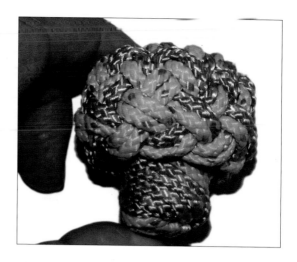

MANROPE KNOT

This knot was used (and is still, if I am not mistaken), at the end of a rope used to help people board ships up ramps, stairways, or attic access ladders. It forms a handsome knob that helps prevent the boarder's hand from slipping off the end of the rope, thus preventing an accident or an accidental soaking! There are many fine examples of this Knob Knot on rope handrails used on stairways and staircases in small, exclusive bed and breakfasts throughout the European/American world, and no doubt in other parts of the world. The Knob Knot was also used on the end of a cat-o'-nine-tails, to prevent a bo-sun's hand from slipping off the end of the grip. Making a cat o"nine-tails is not covered here—there are plenty of illustrations to be found elsewhere—but the idea of the handle being unable to slip from the grasp of the person applying the lashes is something to keep in mind! To construct a Manrope Knot you simply wall, crown, wall, crown, and then fair and cut off. Here is the process shown in several steps:

≊ STAGE **1** – Take four strands of line and seize them together, here with a Constrictor Knot. You may also make a Manrope Knot with each of the three strands of a three-strand line, but you will still need to seize the strands at the point you want the Manrope Knot to start.

STAGE 2 – Wall each of the strands. The photo shows one strand started.

STAGE 3 – Here all four strands are walled counterclockwise (with right-laid line you need to wall counterclockwise). »

STAGE 4 – Now crown each strand over the next strand counterclockwise from it, remembering that crowning goes down.

« **STAGE 5** – Here all four strands have been crowned down. Note that the crown sits atop the knot.

« **STAGE 6** – Now we double the knot by making a complete turn with each strand under and alongside the first wall strand and staying below it to tuck up as shown. East goes around the compass to exit north, north goes around the compass to exit west, and so on. Be careful not to mix the strands. It may help you to number them so that you do not tuck the same strand twice.

« **STAGE 7A** – Here all the wall strands are doubled and we have tightened up all strands a little, to give a more spherical shape.

Stage 7B – Stage seven, seen from the side. »

« Stage 8 – Here we have started tucking the south-facing strand down into the space that exists on its left side from the earlier crowned strand.

Stage 9 – And here we see all four strands tucked down, completing the doubling of the crowned strands into the center, where they are drawn below the knot. »

« **STAGE 10** – The finished Manrope Knot, with its seizing still in place. You may want to tighten yours further still or leave it like this and add another Manrope Knot at the other end of your strands.

« *A Double Manrope Knot, doubled by adding a second Manrope Knot at the other end of the strands.*

FOOTROPE KNOT

The Footrope Knot is a three-strand Turk's Head-style knot. It was used to prevent slippage of a sailor's feet on the footrope, which was slung under the yard on a square-rigged ship so that the sailors could have something to stand on when furling or setting the sail. The advantage of using this construction is that it is impossible for the knot to move along the line once tied and tightened, a fact greatly appreciated by sailors swinging about a hundred feet or so in the air and looking to find something firm to hold onto with their bare toes! Of course, you don't have to stick this through a footrope to enjoy the attributes of the Footrope Knot—just follow the general pattern of crown, wall, tuck up, and finish (or double with crown, wall, and tuck again if you like to finish in the center). For those who study such things, this is the opposite of the Manrope Knot, and yet, because the Wall and Crown are simply the inverse of each others" structure, they could both be viewed as one and the same! By adding a Footrope Knot right after a Manrope Knot you could easily fool someone into thinking it was the same knot, as a nice finish to, or a part of, for example, a Bo'sun's Lanyard. Here are the details of how to tie both the Single and the Double Footrope Knot.

Single Footrope Knot

« **STAGE 1** – First, seize (join) three pieces of line together, using a Constrictor Knot.

STAGE 2 – Next, crown all three strands. The first strand is started here. »

« **STAGE 3** – Here, all three strands have been crowned.

« **STAGE 4** – Next comes the Wall. Here the first strand is started.

« **STAGE 5** – And here the other two are complete, ending part two of the Footrope Knot.

⌃ **STAGE 6** – Tuck the strands up into the center of the Crown Knot, taking each up through on the left of the crown strand.

« *The finished Single Footrope Knot. Note the strands finishing on the inside of the Crown Knot, from alongside the crown strands.*

Double Footrope Knot

« **STAGE 1–**
Start with
a Single
Footrope
Knot (above)
but without
the ends
tucked
through.
Instead, stop
them at the
outside edge,
as shown
here.

« **STAGE 2 –**
At the left
of the top
Crown, tuck
the end that
was brought
up on the
left of the
start of that
Crown.

« **STAGE 3** – Here is what the Crowning looks like after all strands are tucked.

STAGE 4 – Seen here from the side, the strand end is now tucked alongside the wall into the center, as it was in the Single Footrope finish. »

« **STAGE 5** – Here is the finished knot, with the strands all tucked above the Wall and through the center. If you started with a three-strand manila rope you could now, of course, re-lay the strands to form a different kind of Matthew Walker Knot, which cannot be undone!

The finished Double Footrope Knot, with the strands at the end ready for the next part of the decorative work ❧

Here, the Footrope Knot is tied through a piece of line, exactly as originally intended (except for the choice of blue line)! ❧

KNOB COVERINGS

Knob coverings vary greatly by both complexity and the number of places where they may be applied. Whether it is to the shifter knob on your favorite vintage car or the tip of a gentleman's cane, or just a covering to a round stone ball to be used as a door stop, the spherical covering has much to offer. Geoffrey Budworth, in his *Book of Decorative Knots*, shows some excellent globe or ball coverings. He has named them, rather prosaically I think, for some of the planets of our solar system, including our own Earth. He has also included the famous ten-strand knot that was noted in Susan Patron's book

The Higher Power of Lucky, noted at the end of this chapter. I have included those here, together with some other Globe Knots for you to try out. In *Ashley's Book of Knots*, numbers 2216 and 2217 are spherical knots that allow you to cover a knot with a single cord. Number 2218 is also a spherical knot, but in it, one pass is all that a single cord can make, according to Ashley. Any more passes than that, and you will have to add a second (or third) cord alongside for a more decorative flourish, but I have a surprise in store! Ashley points out that the size and shape of the object you wish to cover, as well as the size of the object to which it is attached, will have a strong bearing on which knot you choose. If you have a thick staff or cane, with a small sphere on top, you will likely need a spherical covering with a large number of bights to its circumference. On the other hand, a relatively thin rod, like a gear-shifter, can accept as few as three bights around its circumference. Take a look at these three knots, which each have three or four bights to their circumference, making triangular and square facets through which the support may be inserted.

Ashley's Knot #2216 (Budworth's Earth Knot)

This knot is quite handsome and can be constructed in less than an hour. Because it starts and finishes at the same point in the crossings, it can be made using multiple passes with one cord, (you can also introduce a contrasting color between

the first two passes). The knot has twenty-six facets, of which eight are triangular. The knot makes a wonderful cat toy. Cover a light plastic core with this and watch your pet have hours of fun chasing it.

⇗ **Stage 1** – Start with overhand clockwise turns, crossing over two parts.

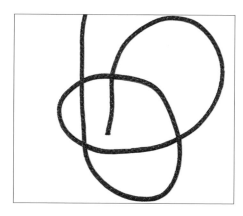

⇗ **Stage 2** – Follow with two more overs, again continuing clockwise.

⌃ **Stage 3** – Add four more.

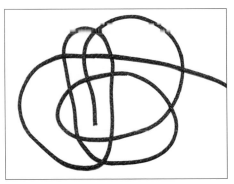

⌃ **Stage 4** – Add one more over, go under the start, then over, and then a false over (we will re-direct the working end in the next move) . . .

⌃ **Stage 5** – over, over, over, under, over to arrive at the top left . . .

⌃ **Stage 6** – over, under, over . . .

« **Stage 7A** – and then again under, over, under, over to get back to the start.

<< **STAGE 7B** – Start forming the weave into a sphere. Don't forget to take up whatever small slack you may find.

STAGE 7C – Compress the sphere into a more recognizable shape. >>

<< **STAGE 8** – Fit in a wooden ball or other core of your choosing.

▲ **STAGE 9** – Now tighten, fair, and then make a second pass (or a third or fourth) to complete the covering, left slightly gappy here.

« *Here is the view of the finished knot, viewed from the equator, where you can see the mix of triangular and square meeting facets.*

ASHLEY'S KNOT #2217 (BUDWORTH'S URANUS KNOT)

Uranus takes eighty-four Earth-years to orbit the sun. Knot #2217 in Ashley's book (Budworth's Uranus Knot) takes about eighty-four Earth-minutes to make, fully faired. Note that the final pattern shows four sets of two concentric rings, with eight triangular facets and the rest of the facets square, formed by making, alternately, the inner and outer rings. The planet Uranus is mostly icy hydrogen and helium with an atmosphere of methane. Methane has four hydrogen atoms to every carbon atom, which may be the reason for the name Budworth gave it (four rings and one center). It makes

for a grand spherical covering that is not too time-consuming to make. In the instructions below, I have used compass bearings to denote a direction or location.

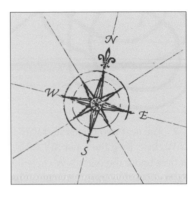

≈ *The Compass Rose, with labeled points around the perimeter, to give an idea of direction in the instructions following. You are assumed to be standing at the center of the rose.*

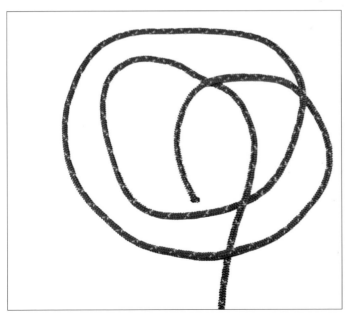

« **STAGE 1** – Start by making two concentric circles, clockwise here, although this may also be made counterclockwise. These are the inner NE and the outer NW circles respectively. The crossings are over, then under, over, under.

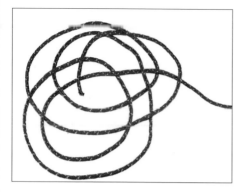

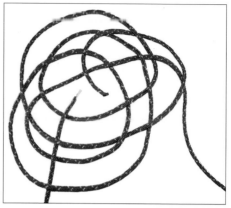

≈ **STAGE 2** – The next two circles start with the outer SW circle, then the inner SW circle. The cord moves under the outer NW circle then over five cords to the inner NW circle, then under, under, over, under, over, under to start the outer SE circle.

≈ **STAGE 3** – Now move under, over, under, and over the western circles and head toward the east to begin the outer SE circle.

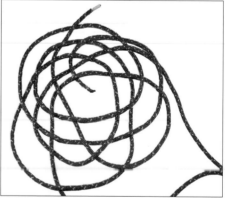

≈ **STAGE 4** – Move the end of the cord over, under, over, under, over to start the inner SE circle. You can see in the photograph that the outer SE circle has not yet been pulled in.

≈ **STAGE 5A** – Completing the inner SE circle we now move past four pairs over, under, finishing by passing over the outer NW circle, ready to make the outer NE circle.

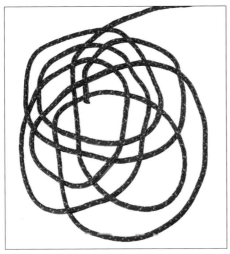

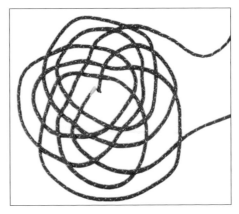

≈ **STAGE 5B –** Here the outer SE circle is pulled in a little to give you a better view.

≈ **STAGE 6 –** Lastly, the outer NE circle is turned, with the working end passing under, over three times to reach the starting point, ready for doubling. After starting the doubling, squeeze the sphere roughly into shape, pulling through any excess cord and then fitting a spherical support (in this case a practice golf ball) inside. Tighten and fair the finished sphere.

Budworth's Uranus Knot, Ashley's #2217, finished by tripling the passes »

Ashley's Knot #2218 (Budworth's Jupiter Knot)

This knot is a really splendid knot for covering a sphere. At first blush it seems an impossible task to make, but be not of faint heart, for if I can make it, so can you! I have made it here with a cord that reflects light at night. I found the cord at a camping goods store, where they use it to help prevent people tripping over guy-ropes. The knot has fifty-one facets. You can make this covering starting with the outer circles, followed by the inner circles. The outer circles are made in a counterclockwise direction (SW, SE, NE, NW) and the inner circles in a clockwise direction (NW, NE, SE, SW). The cord travels along its paths in a counterclockwise direction and does not meet itself again in the center according to Ashley. Take a look. However, I have amended Ashley diagram (see stage 8 hereof) so that it does meet the start cordage and may be doubled or tripled readily.

« **Stage 1** – Form a counterclockwise underhand loop and pass the end under itself. Here I show the knot pinned to a board under the background.

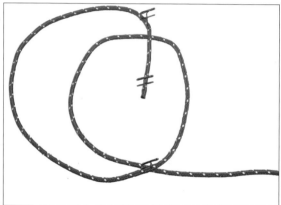

Stage 2 – Form the next counterclockwise overhand loop, over, over, and then tuck under, over to make the inner NE loop. »

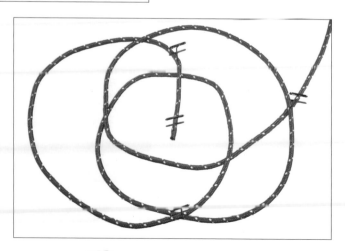

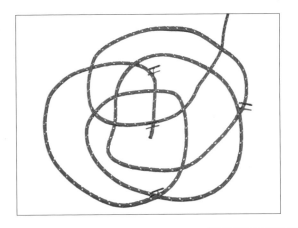

« **Stage 3** – Now form the outer NE loop. Pass the cord counterclockwise over three strands, then under four strands to the NE.

Stage 4 – Now start moving the working end toward the NW. »

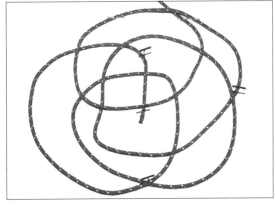

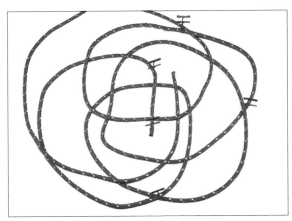

« **Stage 5** – Pass the cord over, over, over, under, over. This forms the NW outer loop and starts toward the NW inner circle.

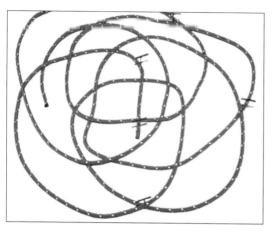

« Stage 6 – Pass over, over, under to start the inner NW circle . . .

Stage 7 – and continue under, under to work toward the inner NE circle. »

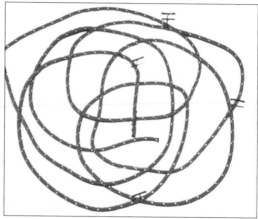

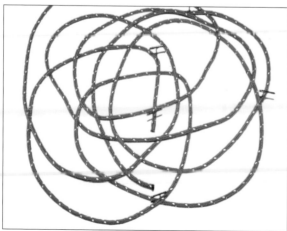

« **Stage 8** – Pass over three strands, then under, over the NW circles, then under, under the SW circles, and over, under, over a ladder. Take note that we next amend the starting cord to make it start under, over instead of over, over. Reading the Ashley instruction, I see that this gives the impression that the end does not meet the start. The end here DOES meet the start by changing this starting position.

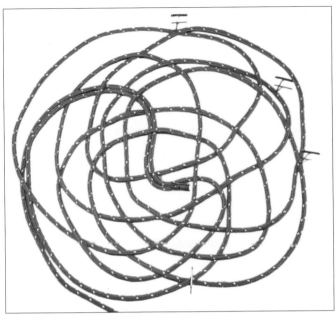

« **STAGE 9** – Pass the working end over, under eight pairs of laddered strands to rejoin the amended starting end (see last stage).

STAGE 10 The compressed globe about to be drawn up and faired into a spherical covering.

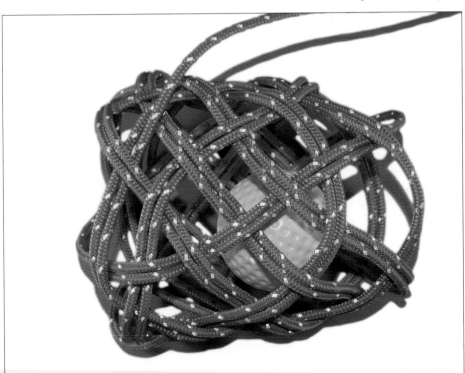

≈ *The finished Jupiter Knot – enough said!*

FIADOR KNOT

A Fiador Knot is the name given to a knot made with rope or with leather thongs or strips to form part of the horse's headstall or hackamore on Southwestern or *vaquero*-style riding tack. It is designed to balance the Bosal Knot, a heavy band around the horse's nose and under its chin, ending in a decorative knot (see next section). The Fiador's ends run from the bosal, up behind the ears and over the poll (the cervical joint behind the top of the skull, usually quite sensitive and therefore useful in controlling the horse) and finishes alongside the jaw in a sheet bend. The method of tying the ends of the assembly in this fashion prevents the bosal

and headstall from falling off the horse's face. The knot itself is under the lower jaw and may be a true Fiador (also known as a Diamond Knot), used originally in South America and previously Spain, or else a Matthew Walker Knot, a Spanish Ring Knot, or another, more decorative, knot. Ashley calls this a "Theodore Knot," saying it was rumored to have been named in honor of President Theodore Roosevelt. The knot may be found by searching the Internet for either name or by looking in Bruce Grant's Encyclopedia or any other competent horse-tack tying book. The shape changes from one place to another and can be quite decorative just by itself. Here are a couple of examples for you to try.

Fiador (Traditional Style)

» **Stage 1** – If you are making a headstall, you will need a couple of Overhand Knots in the center of about twenty feet of line. These two are about ten inches apart, but you could adjust yours to the size of your horse's head (or mule's, or donkey's, etc.).

» **Stage 2** – Make an overhand counterclockwise turn with one end of the line, for our first loop.

« **Stage 3** – Continue it around on the left in a counterclockwise overhand loop, which is our second loop.

STAGE 4 – Wrap a clockwise underhand loop through the first loop. »

⁀ **STAGE 5** – Turning our attention now to the other end of the line, pass it over then under the second loop, counterclockwise, passing under three parts and up out of the third loop we made with the first end of the line.

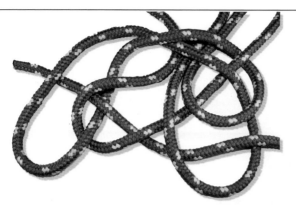

« **STAGE 6** – Pass from right to left down into the first loop, then under, under, over, under, under to the left side. The first and second loops you made are the double loop hanging below the Fiador Knot.

» STAGE 7 – Lastly, turn the end of the second line over and under both parts of the second loop. Pull gently but firmly upward on those two exiting lines to form the knot, shown below, and adjust the size of the loops and the headstall by tracing the lines around the knot.

» *The finished Fiador Knot as part of the headstall. For the remainder, please see your local horse tackle shop or tackle dealer.*

Fiador Knot (Another Way)

» **STAGE 1** – Form two clockwise loops and arrange as shown, noting that one loop is superimposed over the other and that there is a crossing of the lines.

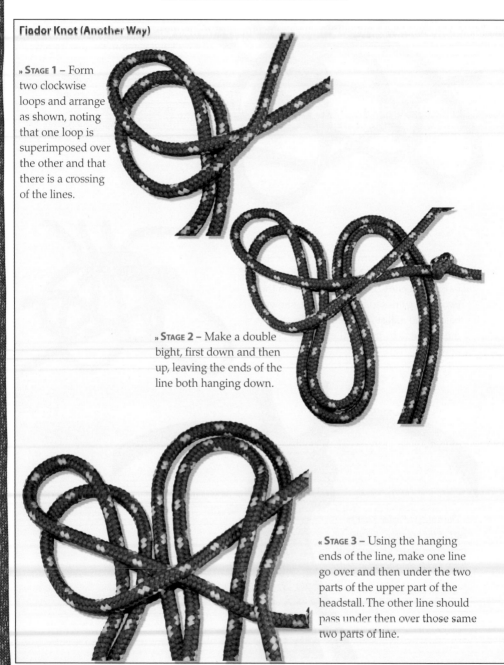

» **STAGE 2** – Make a double bight, first down and then up, leaving the ends of the line both hanging down.

« **STAGE 3** – Using the hanging ends of the line, make one line go over and then under the two parts of the upper part of the headstall. The other line should pass under then over those same two parts of line.

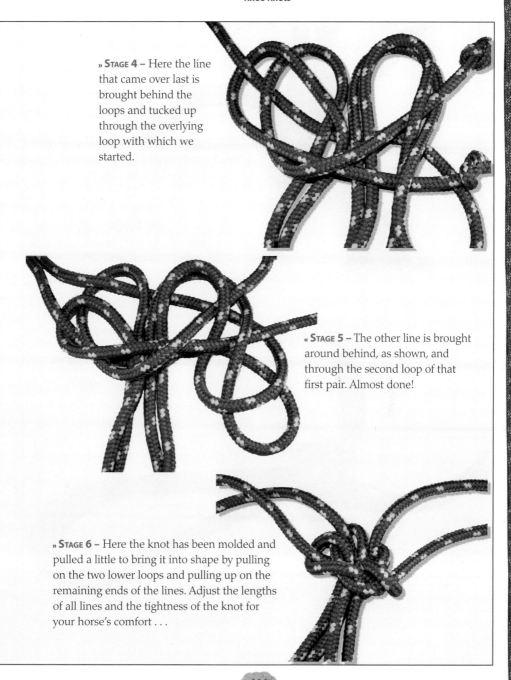

» **STAGE 4** – Here the line that came over last is brought behind the loops and tucked up through the overlying loop with which we started.

« **STAGE 5** – The other line is brought around behind, as shown, and through the second loop of that first pair. Almost done!

» **STAGE 6** – Here the knot has been molded and pulled a little to bring it into shape by pulling on the two lower loops and pulling up on the remaining ends of the lines. Adjust the lengths of all lines and the tightness of the knot for your horse's comfort . . .

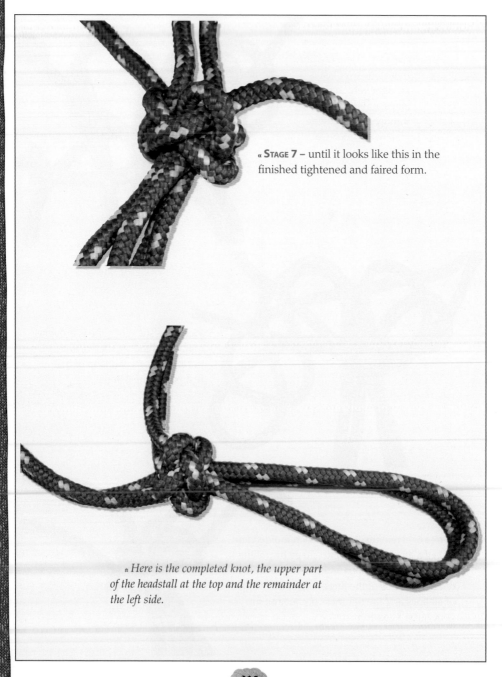

« **STAGE 7** – until it looks like this in the finished tightened and faired form.

ⁿ *Here is the completed knot, the upper part of the headstall at the top and the remainder at the left side.*

Fiador (Using Matthew Walker)

The Matthew Walker Knot may also be used to tie the Fiador, although it is a little more complex and takes extra time to make and to fair up. If you know the structure of the Matthew Walker, you will know that it is a series of Overhand Knots tied around each other. If you keep that in mind while tying this knot you should not get too lost! Here it is.

« **STAGE 1** – With the top-center of the line at the top of the page, tie a loose left-hand overhand knot around one leg of the line (left-hand overhand knots start and exit on the left side of the line).

» **STAGE 2** – Pass the other line behind the first line and then pass it across the front, right to left, up between the two parts of the top, then down through the first overhand to form the second Overhand Knot. Pull the line through but do NOT tighten yet.

▲ **STAGE 4** – Take the left line and bring it carefully up through both Overhand Knots . . .

▲ **STAGE 3** – Here is how it looks now that you have reached this step—if not, go back and do it again.

« **STAGE 5** – taking it around the front and then up through the previous two knots and through its own bight . . .

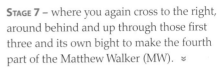

STAGE 7 – where you again cross to the right, around behind and up through those first three and its own bight to make the fourth part of the Matthew Walker (MW). ⌄

⌃ **STAGE 6** – then take the right-hand line and bring it up through the three knots and over to the left . . .

« **STAGE 8** – Here is how it looks now, with two loops below the knot and the top and end lines coming out of the top of the MW Knot.

STAGE 9 – Start fairing up the MW Knot, by passing each part over to the right like this, tightening a little at a time until . . . »

STAGE 10 – it looks like this. Now adjust the lengths so that you have the right size for your horse. »

≈ *The finished knot in place and adjusted for size, awaiting the remainder of the knotting for your mount's head*

Bosal Knot (aka Heel Knot)

The bosal is another part of the tack or leather (properly rawhide leather) fittings used to control a horse—a band put around the horse's nose (actually the nasal passages and jaw of the horse's head/skull). The Bosal Knot is the knot used on a bosal. Below is one made of rawhide, in three colors.

The Bosal Knot, also known as a Heel Knot because it is placed under the "heel" of the horse's head, is placed under the horse's chin, just behind its bottom lip. The bosal is supported in turn by a hanger or strap

behind the horse's ears, running down each side of its face to attach to the bosal strap. Attached to the side of the bosal are the reins, which run behind the horse's neck to the rider. If the whole assembly is used for training, it is usually known as a hackamore (from the Spanish term *jaquimá* meaning hanger), reins or lead rope, and bosal, and is made of softer rope. The Bosal Knot is usually round to oblate in shape and, when made with braided leather or with colored cord, is rather beautiful. It can be made with one, two, three, or more separate pieces of rawhide leather thong, some in different colors for a stunning finish. The details are hard to see

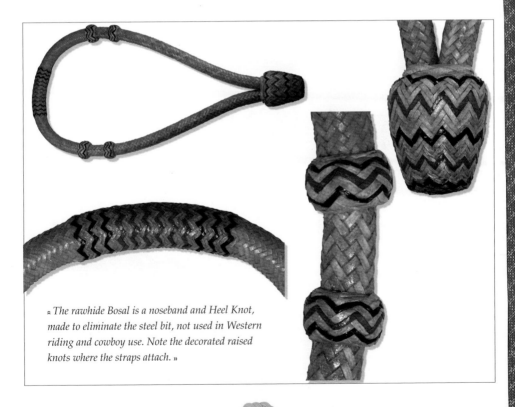

≈ *The rawhide Bosal is a noseband and Heel Knot, made to eliminate the steel bit, not used in Western riding and cowboy use. Note the decorated raised knots where the straps attach.* »

from a distance, even if you know where to look! Here are instructions for making a straightforward Bosal or Heel Knot.

Heel Knot (Bosal Knot)

This knot is usually made over a base that is raised or built up over the base layer by a process known as "raising a mouse." This is done either by making a single or a series of Turk's Head Knots under the location where the Heel Knot is to be made, or by adding strips of rawhide over the area of the knot to get the desired height above the surface. This moused area is then normally lacquered

over. In this series of photographs I have shown the handle of a tool known as a seam rubber on which the Heel Knot will be raised. Because the shape is already in place, there is no need to raise a mouse there. Make sure that if you are using leather strips to make the knot, the edges of your leather are beveled so that they lay flat on the final surface. With cord there is no need for such concerns, because the cord, being round, is as wide as it is thick. If you want the end to close fully, as in this case, try not to exceed six bights, because they will have difficulty in closing completely over the end.

« **STAGE 1** – Start with a 7L6B TH Knot (see Chapter 9).

» **STAGE 2** – Insert your second cord, here dark brown, and go under one, over one, under one, over one . . .

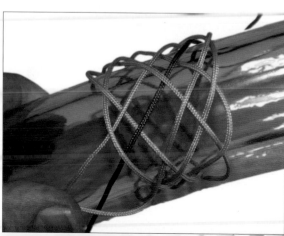

« **Stage 3** – under one, ready to turn the corner . . .

» **Stage 4** – to move down to the base of the knot, repeating under one, over one, under one, over one . . .

« **Stage 5** – under one, here gold . . .

« **Stage 6** and return to the top under, over, under, over, under, noting that we paralleled the gold cord to our left.

» **Stage 7** – Now pass under *two*, over one, under one, over one, under one . . .

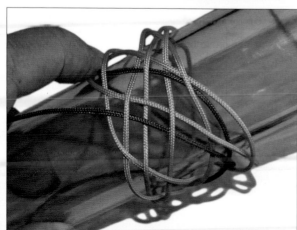

« **Stage 8** – noting here that we parallel the cord on our right . . .

« **STAGE 9** – then return to the top with another under two, over one, under one . . .

» **STAGE 10** – then over one, under one, ready to return to the bottom edge.

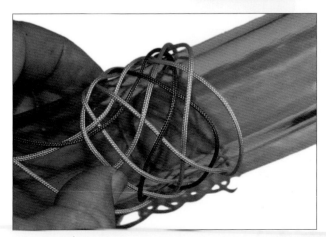

« **STAGE 11** – Pass under two, over two . . .

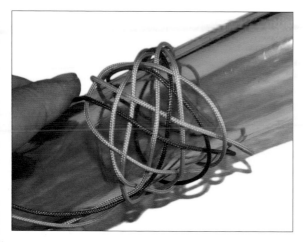

« **STAGE 12** – and follow that with under one, over one, under one, again passing parallel with half the cord on the right.

» **STAGE 13** – Turning the corner again, go under two, over two, under one, over one, under one.

« **STAGE 14** – Now we pass under two, over two, under one, over one, under two . . .

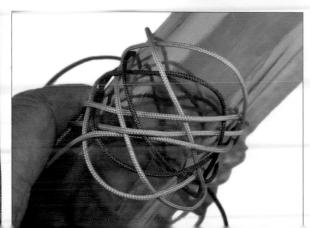

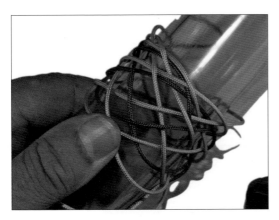

« **STAGE 15** – then under two, over two, under two, over one, under one.

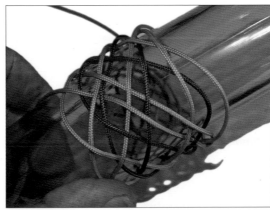

» **STAGE 16** – Now the return down is, again, under two, over two, under two, under one, over one . . .

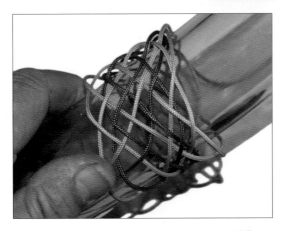

« **STAGE 17** – under two, over two, under two, over two, under one . . .

» **STAGE 18** – under two, over two, under two, over two, under one . . .

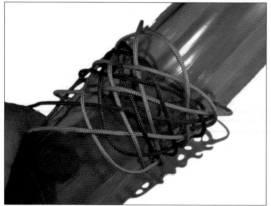

« **STAGE 19** – under two, over two, under two, over two, under one to finish.

» **STAGE 20** – Double the gold and the brown lines and start fairing.

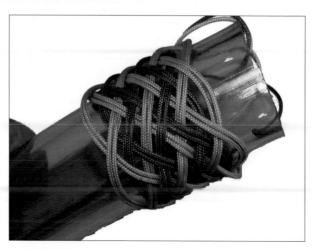

« *The finished Heel Knot applied to the end of a handle on a seam rubber, used in making the seams of canvas more flat*

As promised, here is the final appearance in this chapter of a Round Knot—the famous ten-strand round knot from *The Higher Power of Lucky* by Susan Patron—thanks Susan!

Ornamental Knots

What is the difference between an ornamental knot and a decorative knot? Perception. *Ashley's Book of Knots* contains a chapter *"Decorative Marlinespike Seamanship"* that covers not only items found at sea, but also curtain holdbacks, lanyards, and bell-pulls.

CHAPTER

10

He did not add leatherwork used in horse tack to that chapter, nor ply-split braiding anywhere else by name, although he did add Chinese Knotting to various other chapters, and also included a chapter on fancy knots and square knotting (also known as macramé). The term "Ornamental Knots" was used by John Hensel in his wonderful book of the same name. Most of the knots in his book focused on the expansion of the Carrick Bend and the square knot. It was his work that inspired me to understand knotting that could take on beautiful forms using only basic, simple structures. Ornamental knots are not strictly flat mats, globe shapes, or braids. One of my ornamental knotting mentors was Brian Field, a past president of the International Guild of Knot Tyers. Brian was a master at understanding flat knots and I have reproduced some of his works here, with my own instructions on how you can re-create them. Ornamental means then that the knot is part of the original work, while decorative means that the knot may be incorporated into another structure or it may be a separate entity, depending on how it is perceived.

Chinese Knotting and other Asian knots make up a large part of this chapter. To finish, I have included some of the canvas work and split-ply braiding work of sailors and fiber artists. There are many other forms of ornamental knots that I do not cover. Much remains for you to discover.

Few things can convey the concept of togetherness better than a decorative knot. An untied or incomplete knot represents disharmony. But when two strands act as one, gaining color and shape, as well as inexorable binding, they become united in spirit. Wander for a while among these decorative and ornamental knots; browse this sampling of work from around the world, in different fabrics, different colors, and different shapes. Harmony awaits!

CRUCIFORM KNOTS

These are really braided knots, made from short intersecting pieces, or arms, into the forms of crosses, including the "X," the Christian faith-based T-shaped cross, and even the Calvinistic cross with two sets of horizontal arms. I have reproduced some elegant pieces from Brian Fields, a former president of the International Guild of Knot Tyers (IGKT) using instructions amended from his fine work in an IGKT publication called *Concerning Crosses*. Another true devotee of the flat knot is Skip Pennock of Maryland. He also committed his patterns to a publication of the IGKT in 2002 and has been very encouraging in helping others make similar woven flat mats and crosses. Crosses can also be made as a solid piece, as we see later courtesy of Patrick Ducey of the Pacific Americas Branch of the International Guild of Knot Tyers. The shapes we share with you here of Celtic-based cross forms may be thought of as pagan, but really they are Celtic only and have long histories. Let's start the cruciform shapes with some regular X-shaped pieces.

These first few are from Brian Fields. A simple Carrick Knot Mat follows.

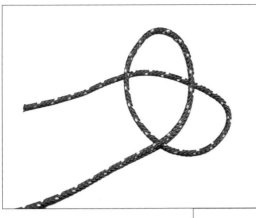

« **Stage 1** – Start with a clockwise round turn, which is then crossed over itself to form the base start of a Carrick Knot.

˅ **Stage 2** – Finish the Carrick Knot shape under, over, under, over, under.

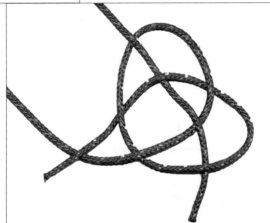

˅ **Stage 3** – Here the Carrick Knot shape is defined and doubling has been started.

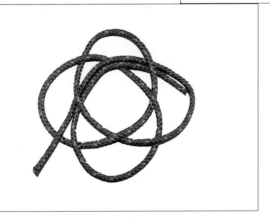

Note that the Carrick Mat Cross is built clockwise if you tuck the overhand knots as left-hand knots instead. Here the mat progresses counterclockwise as each right-hand overhand knot is made.

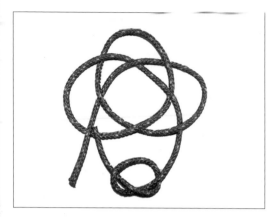

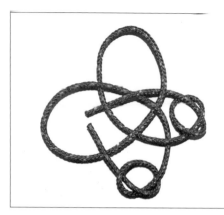

↟ **STAGE 1** – Using the Simple Carrick Knot Mat above as the start, make an overhand knot in the first arm . . .

↟ **STAGE 2** – then make a second overhand knot in the next arm counterclockwise . . .

↟ **STAGE 3** – then repeat for each of the vertices of the Cross.

↟ **STAGE 4** – The final knot, doubled in a fine red cord.

Here's a version of a Celtic Cross that has a Carrick Knot at each vertex, which gives a more robust look and additional stability to the piece.

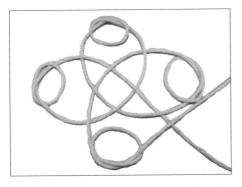

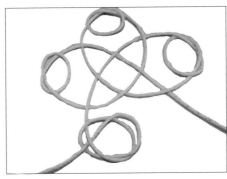

↟ **Stage 1** – The beginning single-pass Carrick Knot Cross.

↟ **Stage 2** – Bring the end of the Overhand Knot over, under, over, to start the half-knot . . .

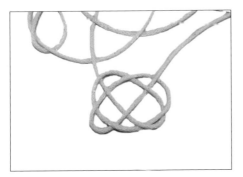

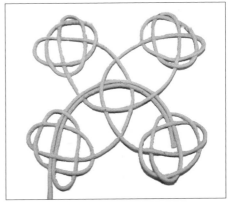

↟ **Stage 3** – then pass under, over, under, over to complete the Carrick Knot out of the overhand knot.

↟ **Stage 4** – Complete all four of the Carrick Knots for each vertex and start the doubling.

« **Stage 5** – Finish this handsome Carrick Cross Mat with three bights at the end of each arm.

Brian named this next version the Greek Cross. It is made with three pieces of cord and has three bights at each arm's end. It also resembles the shape of the emblem on the Swiss national flag. It may also be made with a single cord if you develop more bights along each arm, as seen in Skip Pennock's version next below.

« **STAGE 1** – Start in the middle of one cord with a counter-clockwise overhand loop . . .

« **STAGE 2** – then make a second similar loop on the right and a third loop on the left, but this one is clockwise and underhand.

« **STAGE 4** – Follow the same pattern of the first cord, with overhand and underhand loops, again ensuring the interlocking of the two cords.

« **STAGE 3** – Insert the second cord, here white, to match the turn and overhand loop, ensuring the over, under on the first cord.

« **STAGE 5** – The third cord after insertion in the same pattern. Note the doubled cords where the ends are longer than needed for single pass work (single pass is not recommended for this cross).

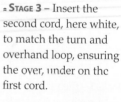

« **STAGE 6** – The final cross, doubled on each cord and then the whole faired.

This next design is a Four-Bight Square Greek Cross from Skip Pennock. Note that this cross is made with one cord:

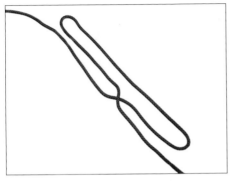

≈ **STAGE 1** – Start with a counterclockwise overhand loop and flatten it as shown.

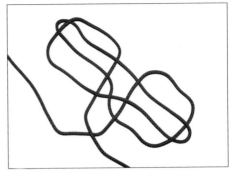

≈ **STAGE 3** – Form a counterclockwise loop over, under, over and a clockwise loop under, over, under, over the line from the counterclockwise loop.

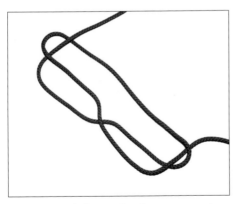

≈ **STAGE 2** – Tuck the overhand part over and under, with the underhand part going under then over.

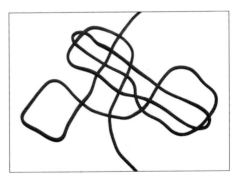

≈ **STAGE 4** – Form a counterclockwise overhand loop under, over, under, over.

» **STAGE 5** – Form a clockwise underhand loop then pass over, under, over, under, and return over, under, over, under, then under, over to cross the loop.

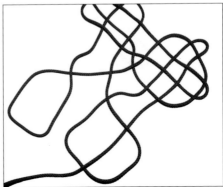

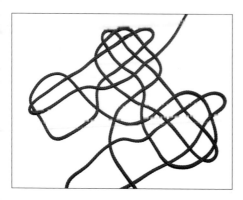

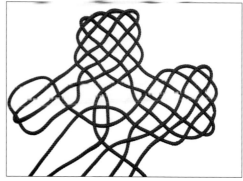

STAGE 6 – Back to the counterclockwise loop and move U, O, U, O, then return U, O, U, O and O, U the loop, returning across the loop O, U, O, O, U, O, U. Note the presence of two "X"s, one each side of the upper arm of the cross. Finish the next counterclockwise pass around the upper arm, as seen in the next stage.

STAGE 8 – Make the center loop U, O, U, O, U, O, U to the lower loop.

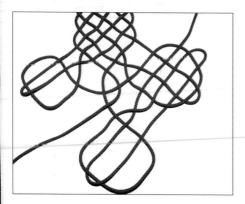

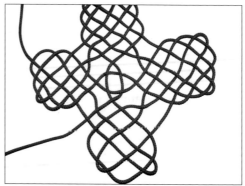

STAGE 7 – Here the cord at lower left has completed the counterclockwise pass around the upper arm and the other end of the cord is making U, O, U, U, O, U, O to complete the pass to top right of the photograph.

STAGE 9 – Now, U, O, O on the lower arm, returning up through the center with U, U, O, O the loop to the "X," and then complete the right arm of the cross clockwise, crossing the shape in the center to the left arm, where we form another center bight, following the O, U passes as shown. Be sure to follow the double pass under to form the fourth "X."

« STAGE 10 – Now we finish off the left and lower arms with a pass down through the center.

≈ *The four-bight version made with one cord and doubled*

Patrick Ducey (of the Pacific Americas Branch of the IGKT) made available, to the Branch and to all who would ask him, a printable grid that he worked out on his home computer using CAD. It is a three-dimensional cross, having depth as well as width and height, which can be made with a base or without, as shown here. There are four bights at the ends of each arm, and the passes can be easily seen in the version shown here.

There are many more cruciform shapes, dozens of cross-shaped mats and ornaments, which can be made using tatting, macramé, woven matting, or some form of single-cord or multi-cord weave or braiding. Ornate and intricate cruciform mats await your touch!

CHINESE KNOTTING

Chinese Knotting books fill an entire shelf in my knotting library. These knots take many different forms, but all derive from a set of basic patterns that can be shaped and formed into pieces with fanciful, mysterious shapes and colors, many of which have interesting stories behind them. Lydia Chen is one of my personal heroines for having almost single-handedly resurrected this art form and shared so much of her personal best with others in the world through her excellent books, such as *The Complete Book of Chinese Knotting*, written in Chinese, English, and that common language of us all, knots. Chinese Knotting is used to symbolize culture, tradition, family, nature, and the forces of the world around us like wind, earth, fire, and water. Lydia Chen almost single-handedly resurrected this art form with her dedication to excellence in art and the arts.

Many of the knots shown here have been made using a board, for ease of illustration when using a camera. Skilled devotees of Chinese Knotting will be able to make these knots in the hand, with no other aids than their nimble fingers. I highly recommend that, unless you are sitting with a teacher or instructor of Chinese Knotting who can guide your every move, try these knots first by pinning them to a board and then tightening them little by little to achieve the final shape. The final shape is all that will eventually be seen, so it is toward this elegant shape that you should steer when trying these more complex looped and wrapped structures.

There are four underlying methods of tying the fourteen basic Chinese Knots, according to Lydia Chen. They are:

Pulling and wrapping of outer loops, using those intertwined loops as an extension from the center;

Flat knots, developed from flat knots either as Reef Knots or as Granny Knots;

Overlapping outer loops, using the Carrick Bend form;

Using S-curves to make opposing half-loops on either side of a knot.

The fourteen basic knots she describes, together with photographs to illustrate their construction, are as follows.

Type A: Pulling and Wrapping Outer Loops

Cloverleaf Knot

You will find instructions for three types below. The first is the standard Cloverleaf Knot. It is formed by interlocking inserted loops to produce a knot that has interlocking center parts and outer loops that may be connected to other knots or to pieces of jewelry. Here is the sequence of making a standard Cloverleaf Knot:

« Stage 1 & 2 – Form two loops and insert the second one through the first.

≥ Stage 3 – Make and insert a third loop through the second one.

≥ Stage 4 – Make the end of the cord pass over, under, under, under . . .

≥ Stage 5 – then pass over, over, under, over to finish, pulling each loop tight around the preceding trapped loop. Then adjust everything, to bring the loops to the size you want or need.

⚬ A standard three-lobed Cloverleaf knot made with red cord

The Cloverleaf Knot is more of a challenge to make when joined with other Cloverleaf Knots or indeed with other unrelated knots. The challenge comes when you have to feed the end of the cord through instead of simply wrapping the loop around or tucking it through. Study carefully the turns that may have to be made when inserting the end of the cord instead of wrapping and tucking.

The following compound Cloverleaf Knot takes an added turn in, resulting in a more complex center that still retains the outer loops for further use.

⚬ **STAGE 1** – Make two loops and wrap around the first with the second.

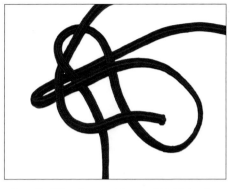

⚹ **STAGE 2** – Take the working end O, U the first loop, then O, O the second loop and again O, O the first loop.

⚹ **STAGE 4** – Continue counterclockwise as here (clockwise is OK also) O, U the second loop, O, O the third loop, O, O the first loop, held ready here for the return trip . . .

⚹ **STAGE 3** – Reverse the working end back through U, U, U, U, U, O the first loop, forming the third loop.

⚹ **STAGE 5** – U, U, O, U, U, U, U, O the first loop. Now it is time to start dressing the knot.

« **STAGE 6** – Here the knot is partly dressed, with the first through the fourth loops tightened a little, ready for the next round of adjustment. Make sure to dress each part flat when using flat cord, as shown here.

≈ The three-lobed compound Cloverleaf Knot with flat red cord

This third compound Cloverleaf Knot is built using a slightly different method in which you wrap around both parts instead of inserting through, as in the standard Cloverleaf. Notice the more complex center generated by this knot.

≈ **STAGE 1** – Starting with a bent loop, wrap another loop around it. T-pins definitely help!

≈ **STAGE 2** – Insert the working end through the first loop O, U, then O, O, O, O, O, O . . .

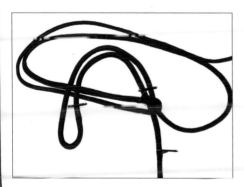

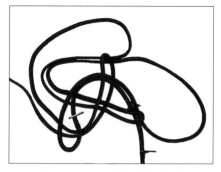

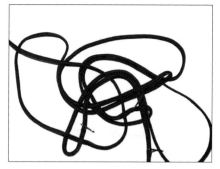

⁀ **STAGE 3** – returning U, U, U, U, U, U, U, then O to finish the second loop.

⁀ **STAGE 4** – The third loop moves again through the first, O, U, and then the second O, O. Move O,O, the third to pass U, O the first loop ear, then O, O, O, O to the upper left

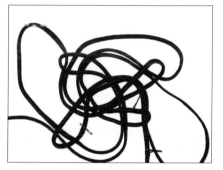

⁀ **STAGE 5** – returning U, U, U, U, O, U, U, U, U, O, U, O to finish. The third loop is thereby completed

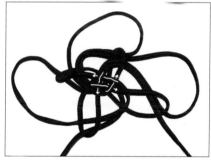

⁀ **STAGE 6** – Here I am starting to dress the knot. Beginning with left vertical down, tighten around to lower horizontal, then right vertical, to upper horizontal. Tighten gradually to achieve your desired tension. The gray arrows show the finishing square.

Constellation Knot (1 Type)

The Constellation Knot was invented by Lydia Chen. This star-shaped knot is an outstanding piece of art, both by itself and when linked with other knots. When complete it has an open center with loops around the edge. The center has interlocking ear loops, while the outer loops may be singular or compound and vary in number. Here is but one example, with multiple outer loops as a compound Constellation Knot.

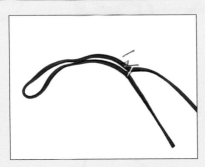

⚓ **STAGE 1** – First, make a bight, also known in Chinese Knot instruction books as a loop . . .

⚓ **STAGE 2** – then wrap a bight around that first bight, and pass a second bight through the first bight and around the second bight. We have now formed our first two outer loops on the perimeter, counterclockwise.

⚓ **STAGE 3** – Make a third bight and pass it through the first two bights only. At this point it is necessary to undo the bight by pulling the end of the bight strand through, passing it around the next two bights and then returning it through the first two bights. This forms the third outer loop,

⚓ **STAGE 4** – Make the next bight, passing it through the second and third bights, ready to be opened again to pass the working end by . . .

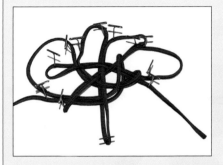

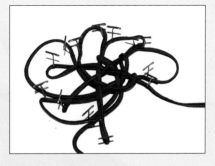

⊼ **Stage 5** – wrapping around the first, second, and fourth bights, returning alongside the inserted cord as before.

⊼ **Stage 6** – Form a sixth bight and pass it through the third and fourth bights, ready for wrapping . . .

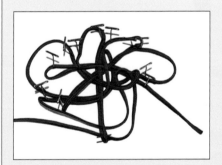

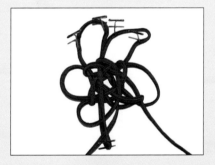

⊼ **Stage 7A** – around the fifth, then through the first bight, then wrapping around the second and third bights. Shown here, the cord end is pulled through the first two bights and then the wrapping, passing, and wrapping are completed.

⊼ **Stage 7B** – Here the knot is being gradually tightened, starting at the first bight by pulling gently on the lower or last clockwise leg of each "loop" on the outside. Then move on to the bight end of the second loop, the second loop, the third bight, the third loop, and so on, moving gradually counterclockwise around the star.

≈ Here is the finished compound five-loop Constellation Knot with ends available for forming the sixth.

Good Luck Knot

The Good Luck Knot is believed to bring just what its name implies—good luck. You can see images of the knot carved on a statue of the Asian Goddess of Mercy, Kuan Yin, which was created between AD 557 and 588, and later found in a cave in northwest China. Kuan Yin is sometimes depicted as having a thousand arms, each of which has an eye in the palm, allowing her to help as many people as possible and to seek out the suffering.

Making the knot is easier than it looks—it even lends itself to being made in the hand.

There are many variations of the knot, of which only one is shown here. The basis of the Good Luck Knot is the use of a series of loops wrapped over each other by crowning, which allows the center to be tightly gathered. Some people put a bead or precious stone into the center to enhance it. Try adding beads before you make the knot and then maneuver each bead to the center of a loop as you make the individual Crowns. Try this lovely knot as a brooch or as a necklace centerpiece and remember to remind yourself of the origins of the knot when you do.

Basic Good Luck Knot

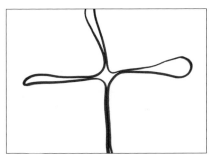

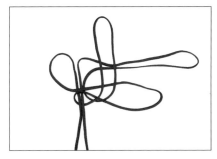

☆ **STAGE 4** – Bend the loop at the bottom up over the remaining loop . . .

☆ **STAGE 1** – Lay out three loops below the doubled cords, seen here as the upper pair.

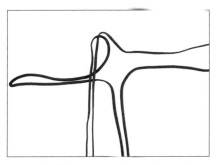

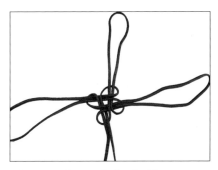

☆ **STAGE 5** – then tuck the final loop over the previous loop and then under the pair of cords.

☆ **STAGE 2** – Take the top pair and bend it down over the left loop . . .

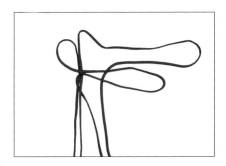

☆ **STAGE 3** – then take the left loop and bend it to the right over the pair of cords and the loop at the bottom.

☆ **STAGE 6** – Pull tighter and then turn the knot over, ready for the final step.

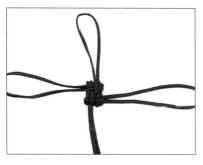

≈ STAGE 7 – Repeat the actions for
Stages 2 through 6 in turn, then adjust.

> » *The finished knot, after adjusting it
> for size and to ensure that all cords
> are properly flat, which is necessary
> when using this type of cord*

Good Luck Knot with Compound Outer Loops

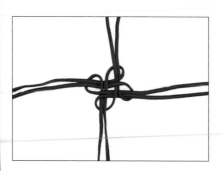

≈ STAGE 1 – Form the start of the standard
Good Luck Knot, but do not turn it over.

» **STAGE 2** Take the
lowest pair, the
cord ends here, and
wrap them up and
over the left loop,
turning to the right,
inserting the cords
through the upper
loop, over the left
leg, and under the
right leg.

» **STAGE 3 –** Take the left loop over
the previous pair of cords, over the
upper loop legs, then insert through
the legs of the right loop as shown.

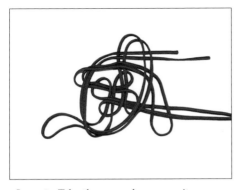

⌂ STAGE 4 – Take the upper loop, pass it over the previous loop legs, over the right loop legs, and then through the first pair of strands.

⌂ STAGE 5 – Take the right loop, pass it over the legs of the third loop, over the strands of the first pair and then tuck through the legs of the left loop. Check to see that you have one passed loop coming out of the loops as shown.

The lovely Compound Outer Loops Good Luck Knot

⌂ STAGE 6 – Gradually tighten the loop ends that were sticking out, starting north, then east, south, and west, pulling them away from the center. As you do so notice the lovely crossing strands in the center. Adjust each of the large outer loops to form the inner small loops by following the strand around piece by piece.

Pan Chang Knot

The Pan Chang Knot is one of the eight symbols of Buddhism. It communicates that religion's belief in a cycle of life with no beginning and no end. It was illustrated in a painting of the Emperor Xiaozhong (the second ruling member of the southern Song dynasty, which existed from AD 960 to 1279) that I believe is now in the Palace Museum in Beijing. The knot is also known as the Mystic Knot, and is believed to impart good fortune to those who wear and observe it. It is an intricate knot that forces the tyer to think in three dimensions. When I tied my first Pan Chang, I felt a tremendous sense of relief and joy. It is a knot with many blessings to bestow and I wish you joy of your own efforts. Be careful to set out the knot on paper with pins to begin with—tying this knot in the hand is possible, but only after much practice.

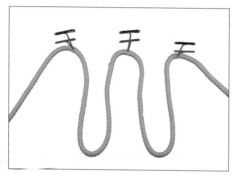

≈ **STAGE 1** – Begin by setting out the vertical wraps, started here with three, but this is not the upper limit.

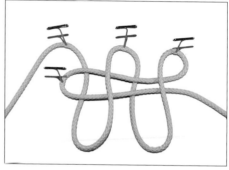

≈ **STAGE 2** – Make a bight with the right-hand end and pass it under, over, under, over to the left, leaving the end on the right.

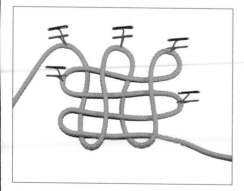

≈ **STAGE 3** – Repeat Stage 2 with a second bight.

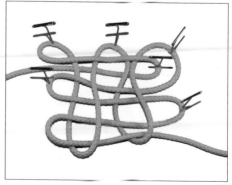

≈ **STAGE 4** – Using the left cord end, make a pass over and under four cords as shown.

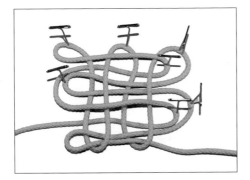

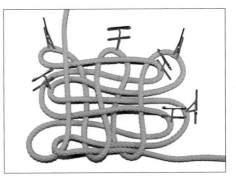

⌂ **STAGE 5** – Make a second pass/bight from the left, passing it over and under four cords again.

⌂ **STAGE 6** – Take the left cord and turn it vertically to pass under one cord and over three, then under one and over three again. Note that the upper end of the cord is now ready to return as in Stage 7 below.

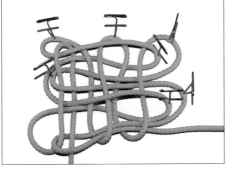

⌂ **STAGE 7** – Return down the knot, under two, over one, under three, over one, under one ready for the return up through the knot.

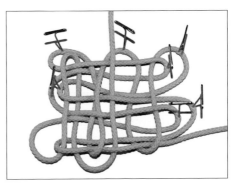

⌂ **STAGE 8** – Again we return to the top, under one, over three, under one, and over three, just as for Stage 6, and then ready for Stage 9.

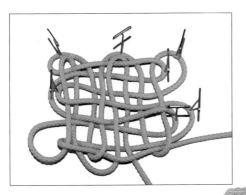

« **STAGE 9** – Again, do as we did for Stage 7, under 2, over 1, under 3, over 1, under 1 to exit. The knot is now ready to be faired.

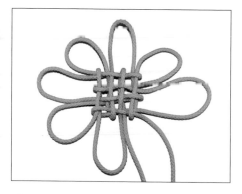

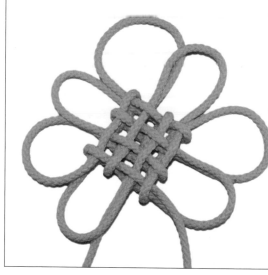

Stage 10 – Now pull out the two ends of each bight, leaving the bight to enclose the other cords that pass through it for each bight. Here we have seven loops out of the knot and one pair of strands. Keep tightening and fairing the knot, adjusting the size of the loops as needed.

Here we see the essential structure of the Pan Chang Knot, showing the structure of the face and reverse as over-under weaving with one cord.

Round Brocade Knot

The ring is a symbol of eternity in cultures worldwide, while the Chinese believe that the round parts of the knot bring completeness. This pattern is found on brocade designs that date to the Tang and Song dynasties. This knot is also made by inserting a series of loops through preceding loops or sets of loops, depending on how many loops the outer part will have. The center of the knot is raised and round and the loops to the perimeter may be varied, using this pull-and-wrap technique. The outer loops may be overlapped, compound, or compound and overlapped. Here is a simple round brocade knot.

Stage 1 – Start with a figure-eight loop . . .

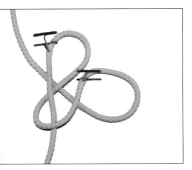

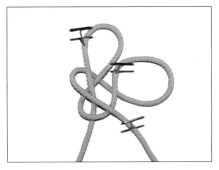

« **STAGE 2 –**
then form an
underhand
clockwise loop
and pass the
end of the
cord under the
crossing of the
figure eight.

⌐ **STAGE 3 –** Now wrap down over to the right,
ready for the next loop. The second loop is
again underhand clockwise and the end
is passed up to the right, passing this time
through the first loop of the figure eight.

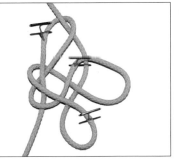

« **STAGE 4 –**
Now we pass
the end of
the cord over
everything,
parallel to
the standing
part, which we
move next.

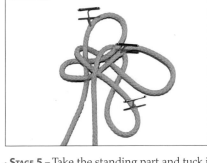

⌐ **STAGE 5 –** Take the standing part and tuck it
up through the loop it lies inside to make a
bight.

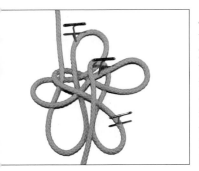

« **STAGE 6 –** Tuck
the standing
part over, over,
then under
two cords and
down through
the second
underhand
loop from
Stage 4 above.

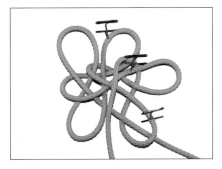

» **STAGE 7 –** Now we return
the end the way we came
through, to trap the
second underhand loop.

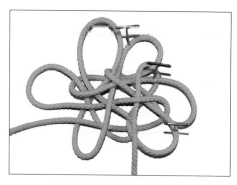

⌃ **STAGE 8** – Now again we pass the end of the cord over, over, under, under, as we did for Stage 7 above, passing the cord over into the first underhand loop. We are now ready to return the cord along the same path.

⌃ **STAGE 10** – Start to tighten and fair the knot, recalling that the left cord of a loop is connected to the right cord of the next clockwise loop, making a bight around the last previous pair counterclockwise.

⌃ **STAGE 9** – Return under and out to the left as shown.

» *The finished Round Brocade Knot with its lovely raised center, ready for sewing to fabric for decoration or for spraying with a fabric stiffener and adding a pin to make a brooch*

TYPE B: FLAT KNOTS

The Buddha Knot

This knot represents the heart of Buddha, showing virtue and giving good fortune to the wearer. Some varieties of the knot are also seen in Western culture, although a more pragmatic version, the Mast Head Jury Knot, is used to secure the head of a mast in the event one has to jury-rig it. I have never used the knot for this purpose and I hope never to have to do so! I prefer the name Buddha Knot, and the deep symbolism that it represents.

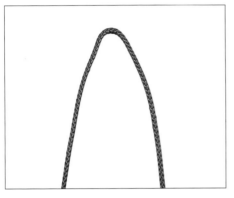

⌐ **STAGE 1** – Form a bight in the center of your line . . .

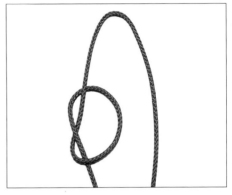

⌐ **STAGE 2** – then add an Overhand Knot, right-handed, to the left leg.

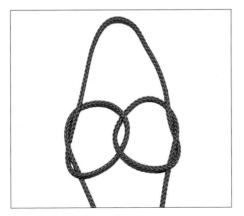

⌐ **STAGE 3** – On the right-hand leg, form a left-handed Overhand Knot, with the loop passing down through the center of the first Overhand Knot.

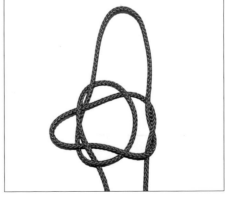

⌐ **STAGE 4** – Pass the loop of the right-hand knot through the crossing of the left-hand knot as shown . . .

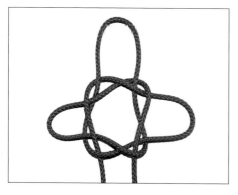

≈ **STAGE 5** – then pass the left-hand knot's loop through the right-hand knot's crossing parts.

≈ **FINAL APPEARANCE** – Pull each loop out to the side, balance the loops with the top loop, and your knot is complete.

« *This shows the Loopless Buddha Knot, finished by tightening and fairing the knot without adding the loops at each side after Stage 3 above.*

The Creeper Knot

Tucking a loop of cord into the middle of a pair of flat knots will quickly produce this knot, as shown below. The knot was invented by Lydia Chen. It is very readily added to other knots to create some wonderful shapes. If you wish to make the knot using a single cord end, I have shown how this can be accomplished also. The Creeper Knot is used where you want to add a series of "leaves" or creepers to a solid or a line. It is most enjoyable when used as the basis of a necklace or as an added embellishment on a bracelet.

ꙮ STAGE 1 – Form a square knot (also called a flat knot in Chinese Knotting) with a loop below it.

ꙮ STAGE 2 – Pass a bight up into the crossing parts of the square knot.

ꙮ STAGE 3 – Pull the bight up into the desired position, then adjust the size of the loops below the flat knot.

ꙮ STAGE 4 – The Creeper Knot may be added to a line, as here, or to a solid rod.

» STAGE 1A – To form the knot with just one end of the line, make a bight with an overhand counterclockwise loop below it to the left.

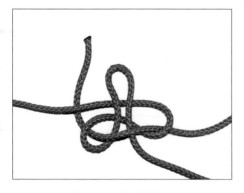

≈ **STAGE 2A** – Form a vertical bight, then pass the end of the cord up through the first bight, over the vertical bight and pass down into the first loop, then behind the legs of the first bight to the top.

≈ **STAGE 3A** – Finally, pass over the vertical bight and down into the first horizontal bight, and tighten and fair the knot.

≈ *The finished Creeper Knot, arranged parallel along a secondary cord. For a different look try reversing every other knot, loops up, loops down.*

The Double Connection Knot

This knot is found in many cultures. The Western version is called the two-strand Matthew Walker. It is formed by interlocking two Overhand Knots, both made in the same orientation. The Chinese use this knot in making necklaces and bracelets and other jewelry. It is also used in other Asian communities to show strength in unity from two separate sources. Without further ado, here it is.

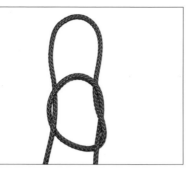

« STAGE 1
– Form a right-hand Overhand Knot around one leg of the bight. You could also start this as a slipknot.

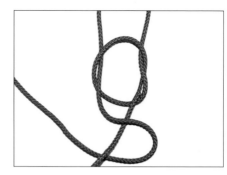

⌐ STAGE 2 – Wrap the left leg around the lower part of the right leg, below the knot.

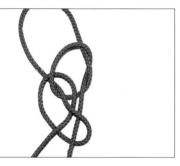

« STAGE 3 – Form a second right-hand overhand through the loop of the first Overhand Knot.

⌐ STAGE 4 – Start to roll the second knot around, so that its loop covers over the crossing of the first knot and the loop of the first knot covers outside of the crossing of the second knot. Pull both ends both directions away from the knot.

« *The Double Connection Knot, appearing as a single knot*

↟ *A row of Double Connection Knots. They may be made closer together or may have spaces left, as here, to hold semi-precious stones.*

The Flat Knot

The flat knot is what Western cultures have known as the Overhand Knot, which itself forms the basis of the square knot, made from two Overhand Knots. It forms a solid foundation to the Plafond Knot and to the Double Connection Knot. As I have pointed out previously, the Overhand Knot may be made either left-handed or right-handed. Be sure to follow the directions, because the orientation will change if you change from the left-handed to the right-handed version.

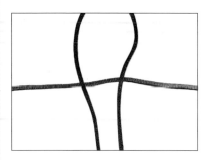

↟ **STAGE 1** – Form a bight with one colored cord, centering it on top of the knotting cord, here multi-colored.

» **STAGE 2** – For the first knot, wrap the left end over the base cord to the right, and then pass the right cord down over the left cord.

» **STAGE 3** – Wrap the right cord behind the base cord and tuck the end up through the loop made by the left cord.

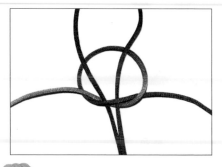

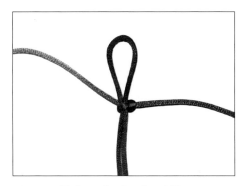

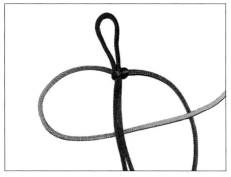

⌃ **STAGE 4** – Tighten the Overhand Knot, leaving a small bump on the right side of the base cord.

⌃ **STAGE 5** – For the second and subsequent knots, pass the cord that is opposite the bump behind the base cord, leaving a small bight on that opposite side as shown here. Leave the other cord behind the passed cord.

⌃ **STAGE 6** – Tuck the second cord over into the bight made with the first cord. Pull tight again with both cords, creating a bump opposite the first bump.

⌃ **STAGE 7** – Pass the cord that lies on the side opposite the bump behind the base cord, finishing on top of the second cord.

« **STAGE 8** – Again, tuck the second cord down through the created bight and pull both cords tight. Repeat from Stages 5 through 8 for the length needed.

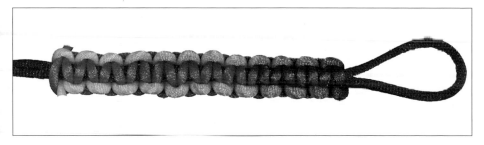

☙ *The flat knot tied as a series to form an Emperor Sinnet. The knot forms a great base for bracelets.*

The Plafond Knot

The Plafond Knot is simply made, requiring a small amount of dexterity if it is to be made in the hand. Lydia Chen says that this knot derives its structure from decorations found on panels located in the center of many domed Chinese temple and palace ceilings. Here are some basic methods for making a slightly longer form of the knot than the standard, rather square, Plafond Knot. The knot may be made with one cord, as shown here, or with two separate cords for a more colorful effect.

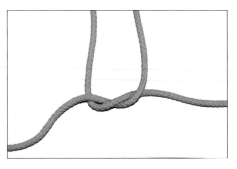

☙ **STAGE 1** – Form a bight and below it form a right-hand Overhand Knot.

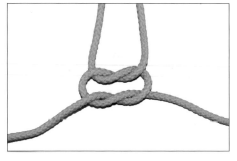

☙ **STAGE 2** – Form a left-hand Overhand Knot below the first Overhand Knot.

« **STAGE 3** – Form a right-hand Overhand Knot below the second knot. Note that you now have a Granny Knot, with a square knot below it.

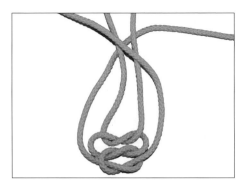

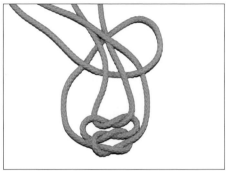

⌃ **Stage 4** – Take the right cord up over the front of the knot and the left cord behind the knot. Note that the cord exits the knot at the base on the top of the right side and beneath the left-side portion.

⌃ **Stage 5** – Take the cord at the back over the right cord, behind the starting bight and then over itself to pass to the left side.

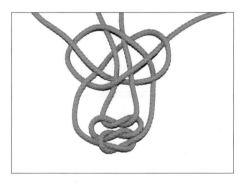

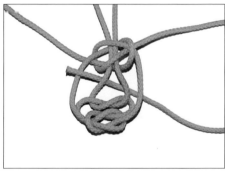

⌃ **Stage 6** – Pass the right cord under both parts of the left cord, passing over the legs of the bight, then tucking down into the loop of the left cord.

⌃ **Stage 7** – Continuing with the right cord, pass it behind itself, behind the legs of the bight and over the vertical cord of the left side.

» **Stage 8** – Here the right cord has been tightened to remove the slack. The left cord is now passed under itself, over the bight legs and down into the bight formed in the last step by the right cord.

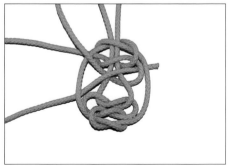

≈ **STAGE 9** – Here the left and right cords have been tightened to remove the slack. Note that the top and bottom of the knot now have a balance of one square knot and one Granny Knot each.

≈ **STAGE 11** – The right cord has now been pulled down into place and the knot is ready for the last part.

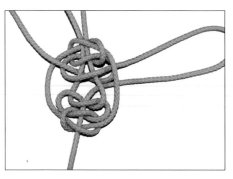

≈ **STAGE 12** – Pass the left cord down in front to parallel the right cord. Tighten and fair the knot.

≈ **STAGE 10** – Pass the right-side cord behind the right leg of the first bight and down through the middle of the lower knots, under their three crossings.

» *The Long Plafond Knot includes one more flat knot each side, bringing some greater balance to the knot. This knot may also be made horizontally.*

TYPE C: OVERLAPPING OUTER LOOPS

The Button Knot

This knot forms a button from a single or even two cords. The button produced is at once intricate, decorative, and yet completely functional. When inserted into a loop, the button was difficult to loosen, and I take it as a symbol of permanence. I take great satisfaction in making these delightful little knots.

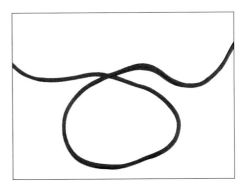

⌐ **STAGE 1** – Form an overhand clockwise loop in the center of your cord.

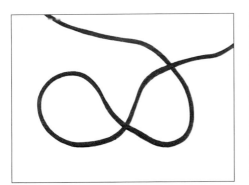

⌐ **STAGE 2** – Take the lower edge of the loop in your left hand, palm downward, and turn it upward and to the left, palm upward now, to form the figure-eight loop.

⌐ **STAGE 3** – Move the left part of the figure-eight loop up under the left cord.

⌐ **STAGE 4** – Wrap the right cord counterclockwise over this last loop.

⌐ **STAGE 5** – Continue with the right cord counterclockwise, pulling it under the right part of the figure-eight loop.

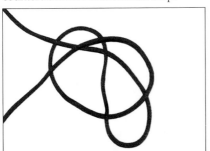

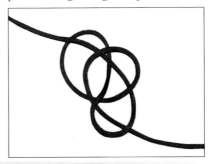

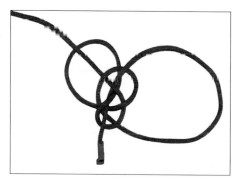

≈ **STAGE 6 –** Continue moving the right-hand cord over two, under two, over three to exit at lower left.

≈ **STAGE 7 –** Bring the left cord around counterclockwise . . .

≈ **STAGE 8A –** passing it over one, under two, and then over three cords. Note that it exactly opposes the right-hand cord exit.

≈ **STAGE 8B –** Holding the top loop, gently pull the two cords down, pulling the two loops into place within the knot.

» *The finished Button Knot, here forming a loop, although it may also be formed into a true button by pulling the cord structure downward to make the top loop a pass over the top of the knot instead of a loop.*

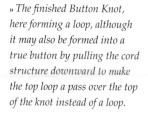

The Double Coin Knot

The Chinese coin with a square hole in the center is a distinguishing mark of coins of the "knife money" areas, like the Shanxi province. The original "coins" were in the shape of model knives, until the shape of the coin was banned by Emperor Qin Shi Huangdi, who replaced them with the round coins with square holes that we know today. The hole is there so that the coins may be tied onto a string. The Double Coin Knot symbolizes two such coins overlapping each other and having a square center, symbolizing prosperity and longevity for the Chinese. In other decorative applications the knot is known as the Carrick Bend or the Josephine Knot. Try using two cords or more to accentuate this fine and simple knot.

≈ **Stage 1** – Starting at upper right, form an underhand clockwise loop and pass the end of the line clockwise under the loop formed, taking the end of the line over the first part of the line.

≈ **Stage 2** – Pass the right-hand cord over, under, over, under, down and to the left. The knot is now ready for fairing.

» *The finished Double Coin Knot in a single, simple cord.*

Type D: S-Curves That Make Opposing Half Loops

The Cross Knot

This intertwining of a single 'S-shaped" curve allows the front and back of the knot to carry different symbols. The method is probably one of the simplest to master and yet may present its own challenges by popping open if not made sufficiently tight. The Cross Knot also symbolizes the Chinese character for the number ten. The cross formation has also been said to represent the Christian faith, although the knot is known to have existed long before the dawn of that religion.

⁂ **STAGE 2** – Tuck the right leg behind and then over the left leg of your bight.

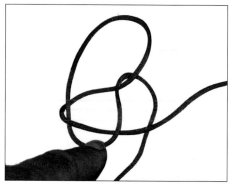

⁂ **STAGE 3** – Take the left leg up over two cords into the upper bight, then down behind the bight and the right leg.

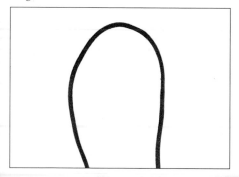

⁂ **STAGE 1** – Form a bight in the center of your cord.

» **STAGE 4** – Take the right leg and wrap it over the left leg, passing up through the left leg's bight, to exit on the left. Tighten and fair the knot.

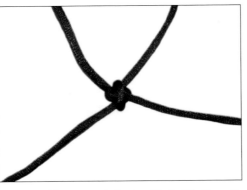

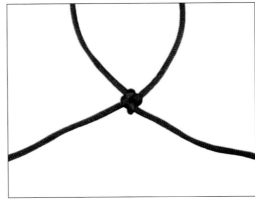

≈ *Here we see the front and back of the Cross Knot—simple and yet readily formed to create a fascinating circle of tens.*

The Double Cross Knot or Tassel Knot

The knot takes the form of intertwined "S-shaped" cords, in a doubled or layered manner. It appears, at first sight, to be a Cloverleaf Knot; the difference is that it is formed with the two ends of one cord passed around the shape, rather than for each of four or more loops to be formed and wrapped over each other as in the Cloverleaf. The knot is frequently found in the beak of a phoenix, a symbol of good luck.

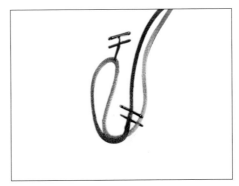

≈ **STAGE 1** – Start in the middle of your cord and make a bight. Pass the two ends of the cords, overlapped as shown, up and to the right.

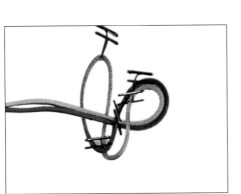

« **STAGE 2** – Form an underhand clockwise loop, being sure to keep the cords aligned as shown.

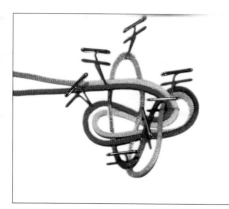

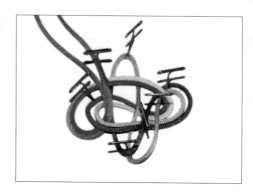

≈ **STAGE 3 –** Pass the cords behind the first bight's legs, then up through the loop made in Stage 2, and pass them over the bight.

≈ **STAGE 4 –** Now make a counterclockwise overhand loop.

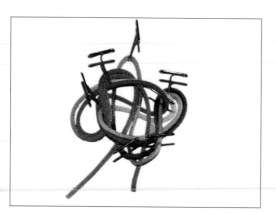

≈ **STAGE 5 –** Pass the ends down through the knot as shown, being sure to tuck them each side as shown.

≈ **STAGE 6 –** Pull out the loops on each side and at the top (the first bight) and bottom (the two ends) to firm up the knot. Adjust the crossings over and under, to get the final look shown below, front and back

≈ *The finished front and back of the Double Cross or Tassel Knot*

I hope that this brief introduction to Chinese Knotting has tickled your palate and raised your awareness of this beautiful form. Know that it is not remotely comprehensive, in part because the knots are formed in ways that allow formation of many creative structures not covered here. The loops around each knot encourage linking, which makes possible compound knots with entwined parts. Their combined and singular effects are amazing and worthy of great study.

KOREAN KNOTTING

Korean Knotting forms, thanks to masters including Kim Jee-Hin who have shared their work, are now enjoyed throughout the world. Color plays a vital role in Korean Knotting. Red, blue, yellow, black, and white form the five basic colors, with combinations of those colors making up green, dark blue, scarlet, purple, brown, and many other colors in the form of braids. The stronger colors are used in men's clothing, the basic colors or *yang* are used in royal adornments, and the softer colors or *yin* are used in women's clothing and accessories. Korean Knotting can be difficult to differentiate from Chinese Knotting, yet it has a distinct flavor, adorning wedding dresses and clothing, and recently as lanyards on cell phones. Typical Korean Knotting decoration is made with a finer thickness of cord than Chinese Knotting decoration. Round cord (*dongdahoe*), or flat cord (*gwangdahoe*), is made and dyed from raw silk. Today, many other forms of cord may be used, but the best is made from raw silk using dyes made with plant extract. Also, the names used to describe Korean Knotting derive less from abstract notions such as longevity and abundance, but from objects in nature and everyday life.

Of course, Korean Knotting plays a cultural role but it also plays an important family role in uniting, figuratively and in life, the essence of the nation.

There are thirty-six basic Korean Knots, too many to describe here. What follows is a smaller selection. I encourage you to pursue the subject more by browsing the works of master tyers Kim Hee-Jin, author of *Maedup; The Art of Traditional Korean Knots*, and Kim Sang Lan, author of *Decorative Knot Craft*. The knots presented here are listed in order of simplicity, rather than in alphabetic order.

THE DOUBLE CONNECTION KNOT (DORAE MAEDUP)

This is a most straightforward knot and, when made in two contrasting colors, perhaps one of the easiest to look upon and understand. If you have a need to make a start on any project with two cords, this surely must be the knot for you!

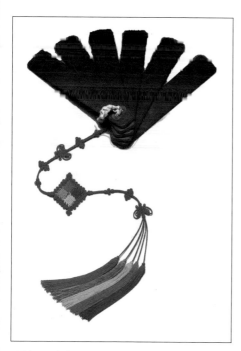

≈ *This musical instrument is a wooden clapper from the Joseon dynasty of Korea, now held at the Foundation for the Preservation of Cultural Properties, Seoul, Korea.*

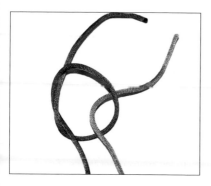

≈ **STAGE 1** – Take two cords side by side and tie a left-handed Overhand Knot in one of them.

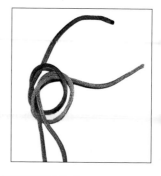

» **STAGE 2** – Tie a left-handed overhand in the second cord also, being sure to tie around the standing part of the first cord, wrapping around the base of the first knot, then passing the second cord up through its own loop and the loop of the previous knot, as shown.

« **STAGE 3** – Loosely at first, and then with a little more persuasion, push the knots together and then pull their cords as one apart on each side of the knot. In slippery cord this will result in the knots opening to accommodate each other and to tighten around each others" crossing parts.

≤ *Here we show a string of Double Connection knots. They can be made a little distance apart as here or tied immediately adjacent to each other.*

THE CHRYSANTHEMUM KNOT (GUKHWA MAEDUP)

This traditional emblem of Korean Knot craft, tied in plum and mauve cords, is similar in construction to the Pan Chang Knot of Chinese origin. In Korean literature it is apparently a symbol of autumn and eternity when tied with these colors. It is named the *Gukhwa* Knot in Korean (as near as can be pronounced in English) and is usually tied in the hand. This practice of tying knots in the hand can be difficult for a beginner to master,

so I show the instructions for making it by pinning it to a board. It will usually be made with two loops, to each side, and is shown here with two loops, although it is always possible to make it with a larger number if tradition is not required. Look also at the instructions for the Chinese Pan Chang, which are the same, if slightly differently worded. I like the mixture of dark and light colors in this knot, which allows for greater interpretation of the intermingling of life forces. I have used not plum and mauve—but two colors of Autumn that are familiar to me, golden and dark brown, to represent the autumnal change from summer's green to winter's white.

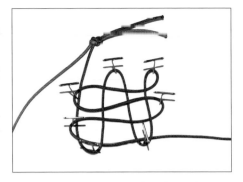

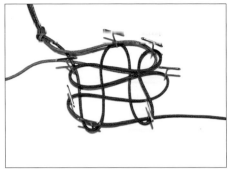

‡ **STAGE 1** – Join two colors of cord together using the Double Connection Knot. Next make a letter "W" as here, finishing at top right with an underhand clockwise loop, leading in to make a letter "E." For the letter "E" insert a bight under, over, under, over and hold it in place with a pin. Repeat for the next stroke of the letter. Your cord should now look like the photograph.

‡ **STAGE 2** – We now turn our attention to the other cord, which is inserted as a bight that wraps around the first cord. The wrap is made over the tops of all the strokes of the letter "W" and then returns under all those same strokes. The wrap sits above the top stroke of the letter "E," but do not worry too much about precise placement at this time.

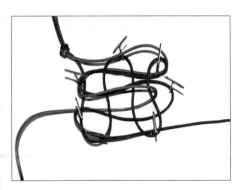

‡ **STAGE 3** – We now again pass a bight wrapping over the top of the strokes of the letter "W," returning again to the left under those same strokes. The next stages are vital.

‡ **STAGE 4** – Make a counterclockwise overhand loop at lower left of the knot. Pass the end of this cord under, over, under, over the back of the letter "E" bights in the first cord only. Your second cord should also pass over all of its own color parts.

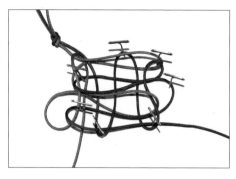

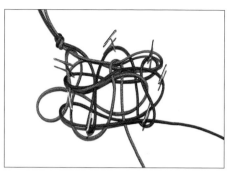

⚡ **Stage 5** – We now return down the first stroke of the letter "W," passing under, under the second color cord, followed by over, under the first cord, then again under, under the second cord and over, under the first cord.

⚡ **Stage 6** – We now repeat the pass of Stages 4 and 5, going up under, over the first color, then over, over the second color, then again under, over the first color and over, over the second color. The return is made under, under the second color, over, under the first color, over, over the second color, and over, under the first color. Now we must adjust! The horizontally oriented loops for each side of the knot are the two opposing corners with two cords entering or leaving, plus the two horizontal overhand and underhand loops at the other two corners for the first four. Then the four loops, forming the center horizontal bight to each side of the square, make up the remaining four sections.

« *The finished Chrysanthemum Knot shows the same structure as the Chinese Pan Chang but is made with two cords instead of one, thereby allowing the shape of the knot to be seen more clearly.*

THE GINGER KNOT (SAENGJJOK MAEDUP)

Known as a universal splice, this favorite of the East is found as ginger root (a tuberous root) in so many food dishes throughout Asia, it is hard to imagine many without the wonderful spicy aroma. Whether as shaved ginger added to sushi or as powdered root in curries, ginger is a great favorite. The Ginger Knot is said to resemble the ginger root, gnarly and a little irregular.

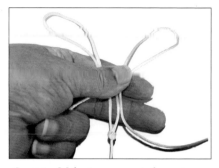

⌃ **STAGE 1** – Make two separate loops in your two pieces of cord.

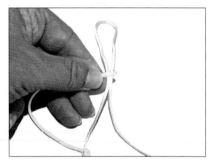

⌃ **STAGE 2** – Insert the right loop through the left loop and close up the left loop to trap the right loop.

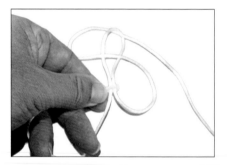

⌃ **STAGE 3** – Form a third loop alongside the second loop, using the second cord, and insert it through the second loop.

⌄ **STAGE 4** – Reach down through the third loop and hold the first cord, pulling it up through the third loop as shown here.

⌄ **STAGE 5** – Take the end of the first cord and slip it under the parts pulled up through the third loop, then fold the first cord back on itself to make the fourth loop.

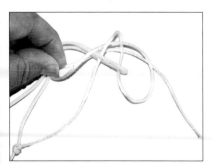

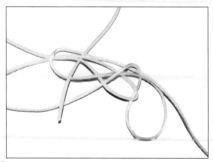

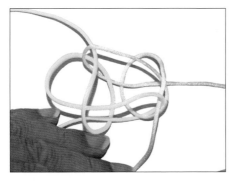

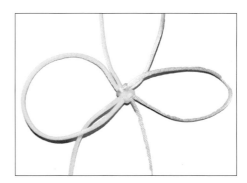

≈ **STAGE 6** – Start to pull out the loops to the sides and cords top and bottom, to close up the diamond in the center.

≈ **STAGE 7** – Close up the loops and the shape starts to look like this. Move around each loop in turn to close the loops to the desired size.

« *The finished Two-Loop Ginger Knot adjusted to size. Note the diamond in the center.*

« *Here is the same knot made with a single cord, so that a third loop is closed at the top.*

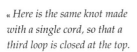

THE CHICK KNOT (BYEONGARI MAEDUP)

This knot is intended to resemble the view of a baby chick when seen from above by the parent bird. I think it is a delightful way of introducing new beginnings and a new view of a part of the world we are rarely privileged to see. The body of the chick is a Chrysanthemum Knot; the legs are Ginger Knots.

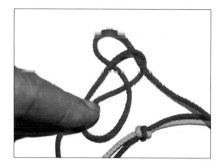

⚬ STAGE 1 – First, take two cords of the same color, or use one cord and center it. Here the Double Connection Knot has been used on two cords so that the structure may be clearly seen. Form two loops with one cord, about ten inches away from the Double Connection Knot or the center, and slip the second loop into the first loop as shown.

⚬ STAGE 2 – Slip a third loop into the second loop and tighten the second loop to hold the third loop in place.

» STAGE 3 – Pull the first loop leg and the starting cord together up into the third loop.

⚬ STAGE 4 – Pass the end of the cord through from behind to be caught by that loop from Stage 3.

» STAGE 5 Pull the first loop and the start cord down through, making a fourth loop as shown. Note the end of the cord is at upper right and the start of the cord is at upper left.

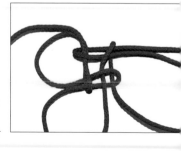

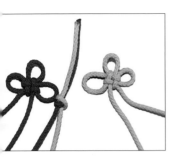

« **STAGE 6** – Tighten the knot's loops and repeat the action for Stages 1 through 5 for the other cord (other end of the cord if you are using one cord) to produce your two Ginger Knots as shown. See also comment in Stage 9 below.

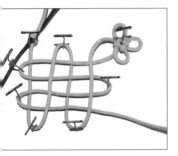

« **STAGE 8** – Pass a second bight under, over, under, over.

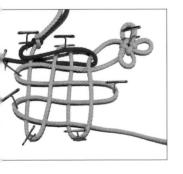

« **STAGE 9** – Now, working with the other end of the line, pass the cord over then under four cords. The Ginger Knot will also need to be passed under, or you may wish to wait to make the Ginger Knot in the second cord until after Stage 10.

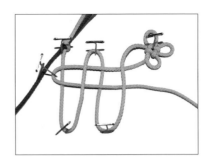

≈ **STAGE 7** – Starting with the yellow cord, make a letter "W" and locate the Ginger Knot at the upper right of the "W." Then pass a bight of the remainder of the yellow cord under, over, under, over as shown. Be sure to include a clockwise underhand loop after the Ginger Knot.

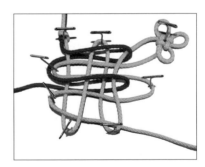

≈ **STAGE 10** – Pass the end of the second cord over and under four again.

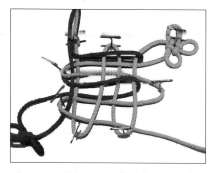

⬍ STAGE 11 – Take the end of the second cord under and over the first cord, then over both parts of the second cord, then under, over the first cord again, finally passing the second cord over both parts of the second cord at the top left of the figure.

» STAGE 12 – Pass the end of the second cord under two parts of the second cord, over and under the first cord, then under two parts of the second cord again and finally over and under the first cord again.

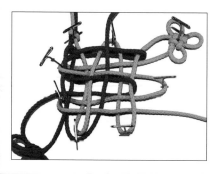

⬍ STAGE 13 – In this penultimate stage, pass the second cord again under, over the first cord, over two parts of the second cord, again under, over the first cord and then over two parts of the second cord.

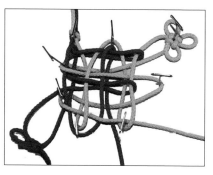

⬍ STAGE 14 – Finally, before tightening, pass the second cord under two parts of the second cord, over, under the first cord, under two parts of the second cord and lastly, over, under the first cord. Tighten the knot by pulling outward on each of the Ginger Knots and the Double Connection loop and two end cords. There are also two red loops and two yellow loops that lie flat between the Ginger Knot and either the Double Connection or the end cords. Pull out each of these flat-lying loops to make six loops or pairs of cords in total. Adjust the position of the Ginger Knots by pulling the cord through each, one at a time.

≈ *The finished Chick Knot, looking a little gangly and just how I might imagine a chick would appear*

THE DRAGONFLY KNOT (JAMJARI MAEDUP)

This delightful little knot is a big favorite with children, who like the idea of having their own dragonfly! If a finer cord is used they also will make a very pretty pair of earrings. This ornament represents courage, strength, and happiness in Japan, a land where the dragonfly is revered. It is appropriate then that in Korea it is a symbol of victory. The combination of the Lotus Bud Knot, the Double Connection Knot, and flat knots gives great opportunity for this knot to be tied readily by young people who would like more of a challenge. The use of the Dragonfly Knot in Korea is largely ornamental, not being regularly combined with other *Maedup*.

477

▲ **STAGE 1** – Find the center of the cord, or use two cords, and tie a Double Connection Knot. If using two cords, leave a short length for the dragonfly's tail.

▲ **STAGE 2** – Tie four more Double Connection Knots for the body. You may need to adjust their position later to ensure that they all touch each other. That action will form part of the adjustment at the end.

▲ **STAGE 3** – Tie the right-hand cord over and tuck under the left-hand cord to make an Overhand Knot. Note that the left-hand cord exits at the right under the right-hand cord.

▲ **STAGE 4** – Tuck the cord exiting under the knot on the right back toward the left under both cords. When it exits under, tuck it under.

⌃ STAGE 5 – Take the left exiting cord, pass it over all and then tuck it behind the knot and pass it up through the Overhand Knot to exit at the top.

⌃ STAGE 6 – Take the remaining cord from the left side and tuck it up over the front of the knot, again passing up into the Overhand Knot, parallel to the first cord.

⌃ STAGE 7 – Tighten the knot formed and then adjust the wings.

⌃ STAGE 8 – Make a second set of wings in the same manner, adjusting them also to match. To finish, tie a Lotus Bud Knot to form the head.

« *The delightful Dragonfly Knot, a very pretty addition to a picture frame or to your hat, handbag or other clothing accessory*

THE LOTUS BUD KNOT (YEONBONG MAEDUP)

Formed as a series of clockwise circles closing in on each other, the Lotus Bud Knot is slightly different from the Bo'sun's Lanyard Knot, which it resembles. It is said in Korea to resemble a lotus bud, a symbol of rebirth, in its open form. Revered throughout the world, the lotus is and was a symbol of rebirth, in that it falls to the water and rises again the next day. A lotus of one thousand petals is said to be sacred and the blue lotus is treasured because of its rarity. There are only two true lotuses in the world, the Asian and the American. The Asian lotus is pink, blue, or white, whereas the American lotus is yellow. The method of making the Lotus Bud knot shown here may be adapted to the use of two cords of differing colors, allowing for a wonderful array of shading in the finished piece.

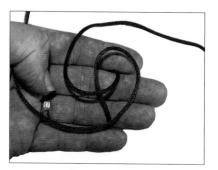

STAGE 1 – Tuck the center of your cord behind your hand and allow the ends to exit as shown. Wrap the lower cord clockwise to the left of the upper cord and wrap the upper cord clockwise to the right of the lower cord.

STAGE 2 – Form a diamond by continuing the circle under each preceding loop, the lower cord under the upper loop and the upper cord under the lower loop. The lower cord exits on the left, while the upper cord exits on the right.

STAGE 3 – Take the right cord over, under, under, and up into the left side of the diamond, while taking the left cord over, under, under, and up into the right side of the diamond, passing each other in the center.

STAGE 4 – Draw up the two cord ends to form small loops around the knot and slip it off your fingers. Continue forming by squeezing the knot into shape, while tugging gently on the two cords.

☙ The finished Lotus Bud Knot in a single cord and, below, a two-color Lotus Bud Knot. ☙

THE ONE MIND KNOT (DONGSIMGYEOL MAEDUP)

I have found no explanation as to why this knot is called One Mind Knot, although clearly all strands have one mind in making their way through the knot! In Western treatments this is the Sailor's Cross or Good Luck Knot, as it is also in Chinese Knotting. As you will see from the photographs, it is not essential to keep all cords exactly flat and together during the making of the knot, although there is less time spent adjusting if the cords do lie together! The initial construction of holding all loops together is not an easy task; it will help to pin it to a board the first few times you make it. Once the four loops have been crowned over each other, it is straightforward and the knot holds together well. This is a particularly good knot to use as a brooch or pendant and it should be sprayed with a fabric stiffener to help hold the cords in place.

≋ **Stage 1** – Take two contrasting cords together and form a cross structure, having equal length arms left, right, and top.

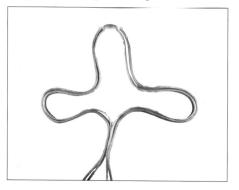

≋ **Stage 2** – Set your thumb on top of the cords" center and wrap the two ends of the cords up and over your thumb.

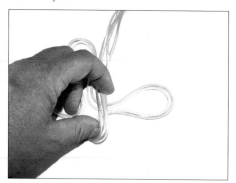

≋ **Stage 4** – Tighten the crossings of your Crown Knot and lay the whole cross in its current orientation as shown.

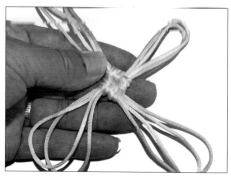

≋ **Stage 5** – Cross the two sets of cords down over your thumb again, continuing to crown the arms clockwise and ending up with the tuck under the two end cords, as for the first stages.

« **Stage 3** – Now wrap the right arm, the top arm, and the left arm over the other cords. The left arm, when wrapped, will have to be tucked through where your thumb is and under the two sets of cords from the base.

⚹ **STAGE 6** – Here is the knot before being faired and straightened with each color in its place, here with pale lemon inside and golden outside. Note the cords that lie between each of the arms of the cross. These cords must be pulled out to form small loops in the finished piece.

⚹ *The finished article in two colors, with the inner loops pulled out to make them more of a contrast with the arms of the cross*

THE PLUM BLOSSOM KNOT (MAEHWA MAEDUP)

The Plum Blossom is a symbol of health, happiness, long life, prosperity, and the natural journey of life, all represented by the five petals of the Plum Blossom Knot. The six strands of the center overlap each other to show continuity. The knot is shown here made with two cords, but may be made with one that has been centered. The center of such a cord lies where the Double Connection Knot lies. When two or more Plum Blossom Knots are combined, the second and subsequent knots will have only four petals.

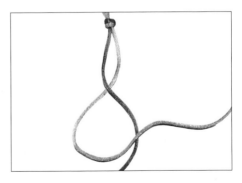

⚹ **STAGE 1** – Pass the right-hand cord behind and then in front of the left-hand cord.

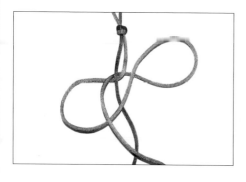

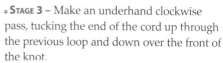

« STAGE 2 – Make a clockwise underhand turn and pass the end over the back and down in front of the left-hand cord.

≈ STAGE 3 – Make an underhand clockwise pass, tucking the end of the cord up through the previous loop and down over the front of the knot.

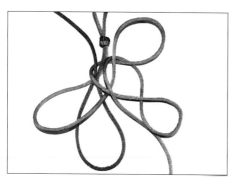

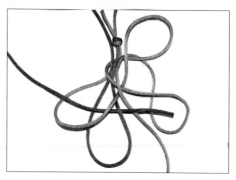

≈ STAGE 4 – Pass the left-hand cord back on itself, forming a bight. Bring the end of the cord counterclockwise around to the lower left.

≈ STAGE 5 – Pass the left-hand cord over two, under two, and over two to the right.

« STAGE 6 – Pass the left-hand cord under three cords, then over and under from the right to the left.

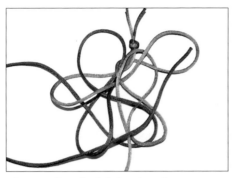

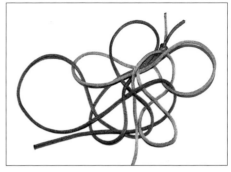

▲ **STAGE 7** – Pass the left-hand cord over one, under one, and then over six strands to the right.

▲ **STAGE 8** – Return under six strands and over two. Pull the two pale blue loops on the right, the two dark blue loops on the left, and the Double Connection Knot at the top, pulling down on the end strands.

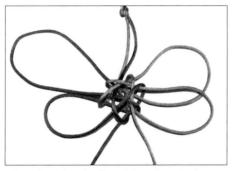

▲ **STAGE 9** – After the first tightening, the knot should begin to form this shape.

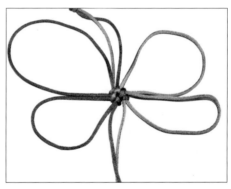

▲ **STAGE 10** – After tightening the center of the knot, the overlapping six center strands look like this, with the outer loops overly large and requiring adjustment in a counterclockwise direction, one by one, to bring the knot to shape.

« *The finished Plum Blossom Knot, here with an upper knot of a Double Connection*

» *Seen from the rear, the Plum Blossom Knot appears to "rotate" in the opposite direction.*

THE RING KNOT (GARAKJI MAEDUP)

The Ring Knot is known to Western tyers as the Turk's Head Knot. This one is a four-bight, three-part Turk's Head, tied as a ring and then formed into a ball, an unusual and welcome step. The Ring Knot is formed on the fingertip and is called the Ring Knot for that reason. It may be formed like the Turk's Head into a cylinder, a flat mat, or, as here, into a ball.

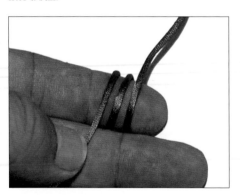

≈ **STAGE 1** – Wrap the cord twice around your first finger.

≈ **STAGE 2** – Slip the right-hand loop across the left-hand loop to make an "X" in front.

« **STAGE 3** – Tuck the right-hand end of the cord to the left and then pass it over and under as shown from left to right.

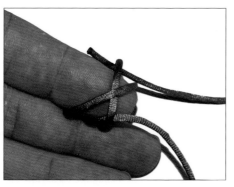

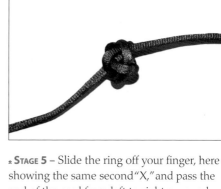

⌃ **STAGE 4 –** Rotate the ring toward you at the top to show the second "X" and pass the end of the cord from right to left over and under as shown.

⌃ **STAGE 5 –** Slide the ring off your finger, here showing the same second "X," and pass the end of the cord from left to right over and under. The cord being held on the left is the starting cord. Note that the passed cord now lies alongside and to the right of the starting cord, like a pair of parallel railroad tracks.

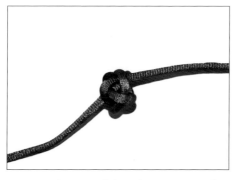

⌃ **STAGE 6 –** Start paralleling the starting cord, to make a Double Ball Knot.

⌃ **STAGE 7 –** The doubling shown in progress, with the paralleling of the original cord clearly shown, to the right.

« *The finished Ring Knot, formed as a ball, may be moved along the cord by tightening and loosening the structure gradually to enable the knot to be shifted. It cannot slide along the cord. The ball shown here has been doubled.*

THE SPECTACLES KNOT (ANGYEONG MAEDUP)

This is an interesting knot when tied in pairs like this. The addition of color is a twist on the usual methods of tying the knot by itself in one cord. Here is the series of steps to make the Spectacles Knot.

≈ **STAGE 1** – Start with a Double Connection or other joining knot to bring the two cords together, facing away from you, then tie an Overhand Knot above them.

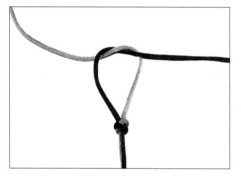

≈ **STAGE 2** – Tie an Overhand Knot, here tied left over right and under.

≈ **STAGE 3** – Next, tie a second, third, and fourth Overhand Knot above each of the previous knots, being sure to always tie them with the same crossing each time, here left over right. Cinch them up a little to make the next steps easier.

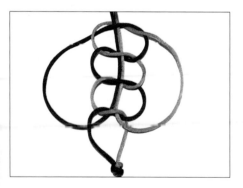

. **STAGE 4** – Note that the two cords in the last stage come out of the knot, one above the cord on the right and one under the cord on the left. Take the cord on top and insert it on top of the first loop near the base, then pass it up under each of the crossings of the Overhand Knots, four crossings in all. Repeat for the other cord, but start from underneath and then insert parallel to the first cord as shown final here.

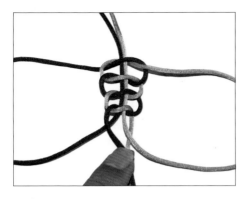

⌁ Stage 5 – Tighten each of the Overhand Knots, bringing the excess cord into the two side loops.

⌁ Stage 6 – Pull most of the excess side loop cord up through the knots, leaving a small-size loop on each side.

« Stage 7 – Take the upper crossing parts, one in front and one behind, and wrap them down by pushing or inverting the crossing parts to the bottom of the four Overhand Knots.

» Stage 8 – Repeat the stage above with the second crossing pair of cords, now become the top pair. Bring this pair of cords outside everything and down to the bottom of the set of four pairs, as shown here, and then gently pull up on the cord ends exiting the top of the knot. Tighten each cord in turn, following it through the knot.

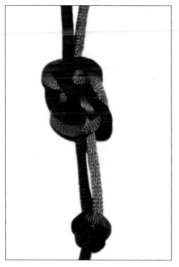

⋆ *The finished Spectacles Knot as a pair—whimsical, isn't it? Here a Double Connection Knot has been used on each end of the spectacles" "arms" for balance.*

⋆ *Final Stage: After tightening the knot it should look like this, with rolling sides and top and a diagonally arranged center set of crown crossings.*

THE WING KNOT (NALGAE MAEDUP)

This rather intriguing knot is made to look like an insect's wing, in the same way that the Dragonfly Knot is made. It may be added to a series of other knots to indicate dreams or flight. Here is the Wing Knot, made by itself.

⋆ **STAGE 1** – Make an Overhand Knot, being sure to identify the side on which the cord exits under the other parts.

« **STAGE 2** – Wrap the cord that exits under the knot under the upper loop, and wrap the cord that exits the upper side of the knot over the top of the upper loop.

▲ **STAGE 3** – Pass the cord from the back over the knot and down through the overhand crossing.

▲ **STAGE 4** – Pass the cord from the front around behind the knot and down into the crossing of the Overhand Knot.

« *The front view of the finished Wing Knot*

» *The back view of the same knot*

JAPANESE KNOTTING

Samurai warriors were responsible for much Japanese Knotting, (*Hanamusubi*). They created *Kumihimo*, the art of making and wearing braiding. Braids, flat and round, were used to hold together their armor when they went into battle. The significance of the knots used cannot be understated, for they represented life itself and, if undone, so might the warrior become undone. On the other hand, *Mizuhiki* (the use of paper-covered wire to form animal, bird, food, and spirit shapes) was used to decorate gifts in ways that showed the grace and temperament of the giver. I show you here how to make two simple knots used as adornments for gifts— they may be made with *Mizuhiki* or with round braids in *Kumihimo*. Let's start with the dragonfly. Apart from the Japanese reverence for the dragonfly, they also have a strong affinity for the garden, organized or simply fenced and always under control or guidance.

A garden being a place of simplicity, peace, and contemplation, it behooves the gardener to make life easy and gentle. Few nails or other harsh metal objects are used, instead preferring the use of bamboo tied with cords and rice-straw wrapping instead of plastics.

THE DRAGONFLY

This method of making the dragonfly seems somehow more natural and true to form, at least as far as making anything in cord may be thought of as more natural! The dragonfly itself is a symbol of courage, strength and happiness in Japanese culture. It was also a symbol of martial success, because the words "dragonfly" and "victory" in Japanese apparently sound alike to the Western ear. However, the dragonfly is also seen in Western culture as something sinister or harmful. In Swedish folklore, the dragonfly is said to be the devil's assistant in weighing people's souls. I like the Japanese version and I offer it here as a token of good strength and happiness for you.

▲ **STAGE 1** – Make the head of the dragonfly first, using the same Lotus Bud used by other Asian knotters.

▲ **STAGE 2** – Next, the wings are made as the Good Luck Knot or Jury Mast Knot. Here the first pair of cords is tied in an Overhand Knot using the left side cords, leaving enough cord for the wings to be formed.

⚹ **STAGE 3 –** Then tie the right side, making sure to tuck a bight for the wings and to pull only what you need through the knot. Tighten the knot to form the dragonfly's thorax.

⚹ **STAGE 4 –** Now tie square knots over the body, formed by the outer two of the cords, for the abdomen. Leave the tails of the outer cords for the dragonfly's tail.

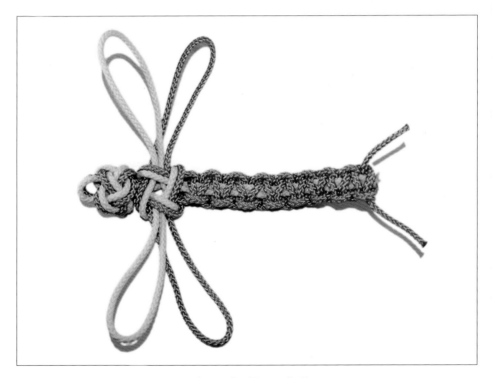

⚹ *The completed Dragonfly Knot*

THE CRANE

Certainly when I was a child, I saw the value placed on the crane as a symbol of love and long-lasting affection, because we all knew how to make a crane using origami. It was not until later in my life that I found out how to make the crane in cord—what an elegant surprise! The giving of a thousand cranes is said to be a gift that will bring great good luck to the giver and to the recipient. Here is the same opportunity for you.

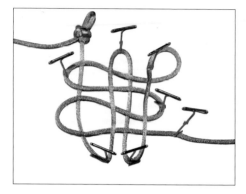

≈ **STAGE 1** – Start with the Lotus Bud Knot to form the head of the crane. Now we start the body and wings by making the Pan Chang Knot—first the "W" for the top, then the letter "E" on the right side. That completes the action with the right-hand cord.

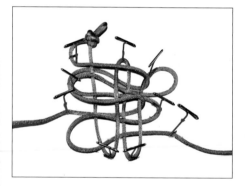

≈ **STAGE 2** – Using the left-hand cord we now pass over all the top cords to the right and then under all to the left. Repeat for the next part of the letter "E" that we formed in Stage 1 above.

≈ **STAGE 3** – Now we turn the corner counterclockwise at the bottom and go up, under one, over three, under one, over three.

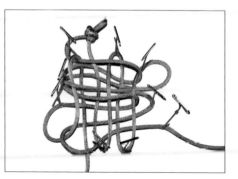

« **STAGE 4** – Now pass down the figure under two, over one, under three, over one, under one.

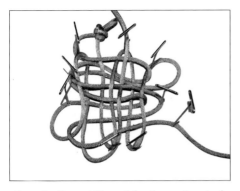

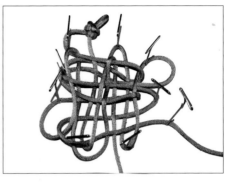

⌃ **STAGE 5** – Repeat Stage 3 for the next part of the letter "W" to pass under one, over three, under one, over three.

⌃ **STAGE 6** – Repeat Stage 4 for the last part of the letter "W," going under two, over one, under three, over one, under one.

» *The Japanese crane, symbol of honor, loyalty, and longevity. May your life be blessed with 1,000 cranes!*

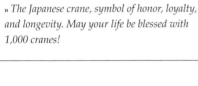

« **STAGE 7** – Now adjust all the loops and the center to make a tight knot in the center and large loops at the top gradually getting smaller toward the bottom. The first knot, the Lotus Bud, is the head and neck of the crane.

Apply a fabric stiffener to the cord if it is loose or slippery.

MACRAMÉ

People who lived through the 1960s and 1970s in the United States, Europe, and other parts of the world will recognize the Arab word for fringe, even if they did not realize what it was they are saying. *Mukrameh* is indeed the English pronunciation of the Arabic word for fringe, with which the edges of those fabulous rugs were woven. The knots that form the body of the rug were varied also, but the sections that have been copied the most in this art form are the fringes, where the knotting itself is the art form. You might almost think of this as a fringe art! I was first introduced to Arabic rugs when sailing on a dhow across the Gulf of Aden as a small child from what was then British Somaliland to Aden. The stern of the ship

was littered with rugs and the edges were all decorated with fringes, although I had no personal knowledge of what they would later signify to me as an adult. The art of macramé as it is practiced today employs four or five simple structures that are repeated over and over to create a large-scale pattern, sometimes with bright coloration, sometimes just with plain cords and some with a mixture of the two. Simpler is better in my opinion, but the masters of the art use color to enhance their work. No more simple plant-hangers for them—they now create wall hangings of great simplicity and elegance that grace the halls of museums worldwide.

Samples of macramé abound still, and yet some of the better pieces perhaps have not been seen by all. Here are a few of my favorite pieces, made by the author and knot-tyer Geoffrey Budworth.

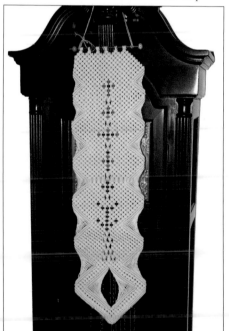

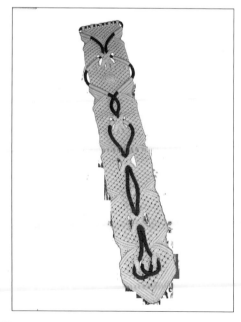

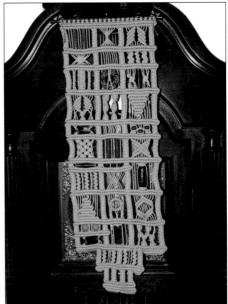

Made with some blue and red pony beads on white polyester braided cord, this simple bead and square knot piece enhances the effect of the square knotting and Half Hitching rather nicely.

This square knot and rope piece sets off the qualities of the knotting by adding a striking contrast of colored line to bring out the effects of shape and contour. The line is brightly colored enough to add visual interest without overwhelming the piece.

This close-up view of the gold square knots shows how evenly the individual knots have been made. Note also the interesting use of larger square knots in the center diamonds, utilizing the lateral threads derived from the Half-Hitching work and leaving the vertical threads to form half-moon crescents under the cover of the square knots.

The addition of multiple colors and textures again shows off the beaded and knotted work to allow the eye to explore the variety of surfaces, colors, and textures of the piece.

The basic knots of macramé are few: the Ring Hitch the square knot, the Granny Knot (or Double Overhand), the Carrick Bend, and the Half Hitch. Here are photographs of each of them, together with examples of how they may be joined or attached to other knots to make a piece of macramé work. Beads and other embellishments may be added as you progress.

Ring Hitch

This knot has been named in countless knot books as the Lark's Head, which name was taken, incorrectly, as a literal translation (a machine translation, if you will) from a

French knotting work under the name of *tête d'alouette*. It is more properly named the Ring Hitch and is commonly used to start needle hitching and macramé work from the top of the work as a form of suspension when mounted on a rod or frame. Here I show it on a hoop, but it could equally be started from a header cord or from a straight cord or rod. For some bottle coverings it is even possible to remove the initial cord after applying a fabric stiffener to the knots, for an interesting start in midair, as it were!

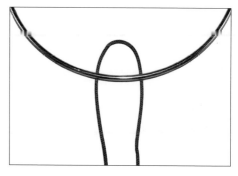

⁊ **STAGE 1** – For pendant cords, the cords that hang down at the start of macramé work, first find the center of the cord and bring a bight behind the attachment point like this.

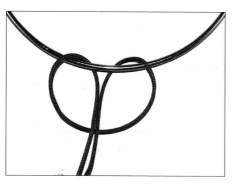

⁊ **STAGE 2** – Now simply pull through the hanging cords and tighten. Be sure that you always put the bight behind the starting rod or cord and that the bight is then wrapped over the top of the rod to finish behind as here.

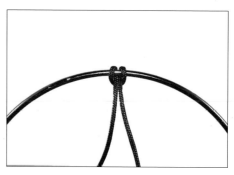

⁊ **STAGE 3** – The series of pendant cords is attached to the wire frame to begin the work.

⁊ *The start of a macramé cover to a lampshade, made with Ring Hitches and hanging down for square knotting, Half Hitching, or Granny Knotting*

Square Knot

This knot of Boy Scout fame has earned a reputation as a knot of little strength. This is true, but strength is immaterial in decorative knotting. Boy Scouts do use the square knot as the emblem for their merit badges and it is rightly used for holding the ends of fiber bandages together if no tape or pins are available. It comes to the fore in macramé work because of its regularity and ease of joining to other parts. It is also invaluable when making a Solomon's Bar (square knots over a pair of support cords) for children's bracelets. There is a superb example of square knotting on display at the Los Angeles Maritime Museum, made by one Captain Nicholas, which measures approximately seventy-two inches in width and over 144 inches in height. A rough estimate of the number of knots puts this piece at somewhere over 170,000 knots! The square knot is also used, in a slipped form, for tying shoelaces—use the Granny Knot and your laces will be up and down the shoe instead of side-to-side!

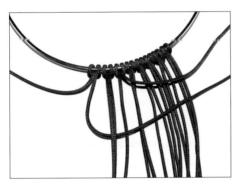

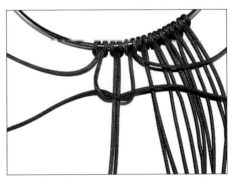

↗ **Stage 1** – Take the second pair as a core and the fifth from the left and the second from the left cords by wrapping the second cord behind the pair; wrap the fifth cord behind the second, ready for Stage 2 below.

↗ **Stage 2** – Now wrap the fifth cord over the pair to the left and tuck the end down through the loop made by the second cord.

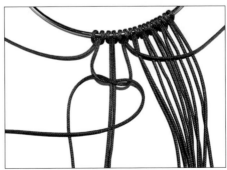

» **Stage 3** – Tuck the right cord behind the pair and the left cord behind that.

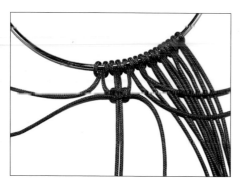

« **Stage 4** – Take the left cord up over the pair and down into the loop formed by the right cord, then pull tight. Repeat with the next set of four cords, then switch cords for the next row of knots. Repeat as necessary. Try also knotting as right-over-left first followed by left-over-right, so that the "top bight" of the knot switches sides in alternating rows.

ₔ *This shows a series of square knots formed and being formed and the progression of building multiple knots in one piece. Note how the cord pairs keep switching, so that a triangle in progress is formed.*

Granny Knot

This knot is also known as the False Knot, Calf Knot, Booby Knot, and Lubber's Knot, but it remains a staple of decorative knotting because it enables the production of twisting flat knots instead of the straight Solomon's Bar. The twisting flat knots are also known as the Bo'sun's Twist in some of the children's knotting books. It is simple to form and has a lovely tendency to cast the most interesting shadows.

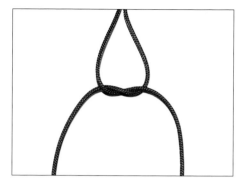

« **Stage 1** – Tie the left cord over the right (or the right over the left if you prefer) and tuck it up in the air again.

« **Stage 2** – Repeat Stage 1 by tying the left over right again (or right over left if that is what you did in Stage 1), and again leave the end tucked up in the air. Repeat until satisfied.

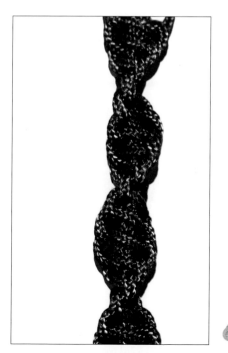

« This photograph shows the Granny used to good advantage in creating twisted sections of flat or overhand knots when tied over a second pair of cords.

Carrick Bend

This rather interesting knot seems to give beginning knot-tyers a great deal of trouble. The interlocking form of two intertwined loops is formed by using the over-under technique. However, many people when starting out seem to find the number of over-under pairs to be overwhelming. Perhaps a brief but steady examination of these photographs will help. In macramé work the Carrick Bend is known as the Josephine Knot. The name Josephine Knot came from tatting and was invented by Mme Therése do Dillmont of France in about 1906 from her *Encyclopedia of Needlework*, which is still available today! Try forming the knot with a doubled cord or perhaps adding beads to the two centers of the knot.

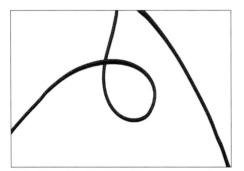

≈ **STAGE 1** – Form an overhand counterclockwise loop with one cord. Note that the cord ends in an eight o'clock position.

≈ **STAGE 2** – Bring the second cord from a two o'clock position, under the first loop, then pass over the eight o'clock tail of the first cord in a clockwise direction.

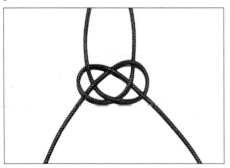

≈ **STAGE 3** – Continue clockwise to pass the cord over the first loop, under itself and over the bottom half of the first loop to exit at the four o'clock position.

≈ *The finished Josephine Knots in a piece of macramé*

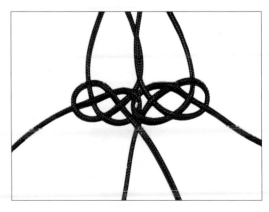

Half Hitch

The Half Hitch we have seen previously, although perhaps not as it is used in macramé work. It acts to cover pendant cords that would otherwise be exposed, enabling the pendant cords to form a pattern like that seen above in the Gold Square Knot piece.

Tatting

Tatting follows one of the simplest of forms in knotting, and yet achieves great complexity when wrought into patterns with cotton threads. I cannot hope to do justice to tatting in such a small volume as this, so I will show only a few simple elements to encourage you to explore this art further. I highly recommend it to those of you who value delicate tracery.

One of the more well-known or famous (in my mind) decorative coverings, which I recall distinctly from that part of my childhood spent at my grandmother's house, is that of the anti-macassar. The name alone fascinated me and the patterns were even more fascinating. It is a kind of furniture doily or cover, intended to keep the (nasty) macassar oil, with which the gentlemen of the Victorian and Edwardian day treated their hair, off the precious coverings of the sofas and armchairs. Macassar oil was named for the area of the Island of Celebes in Indonesia where the oil was made from the *ylang-ylang* tree. The area is now known as Ujang Padang. Covers for furniture were made from crochet-work, embroidery, or tatting. Sometimes we find the most interesting pieces of history in the most apparently mundane of places!

The basic stitches of tatting are the half stitch and the double stitch. After that, everything else is a matter of forming circles, loops, half-rounds, and other shapes, each of which is made with the same stitches linked to and through each other to form the beautiful tracery reminiscent of bobbin laces (such as Honiton lace) or needle lace from the great French masters (such as Alençon lace, also known as *point d'Alençon*). Strictly speaking, tatting is, of course, a knotted lace, not made either with bobbins or with needles but made with a refinement of the netting needle. When incorporated into a fine mesh fabric, the quick passerby would not really know the difference, although the knowledgeable lace-maker would certainly be able to tell.

« *This cross was made by my friend and fellow knot-tyer, Lily Morales.*

CANVAS WORK

Because canvas was so plentiful aboard sailing ships, it was used not only for sewing sail bags, ditty bags, and canvas clothing, but also for decorative work. The fringed edges of canvas work would receive attention in the form of macramé, while the canvas itself was woven with ribbons and other attachments that were intended to enhance its appeal and utility. It was much used on the Admiral's barge and in other lordly decorative tasks. It

≈ This canvas ditty bag, with open thread work on the sides, was made by Tony Doran of Surrey, UK. Note that the canvas used is stripped of the weft yarns and the remaining warp yarns are tied together in bundles or tied to each other in the form of Solomon Bar and Square Knotting work — an object to be admired, rather than used aboard ship!

is upon the edges and open weaves of the work that we focus here, leaving the addition of ribbons and other sewing-related tasks to others to explain in some greater detail. The work here shows an example of how the edges may be decorated with tasselings and square knotting.

PLY-SPLIT WORK

My good friend Maggie Machado, a practicing devotee of this style of cord-work, introduced me to the few pieces I have shown here. I bow to her superior knowledge and abilities in this art form, and I include here some of her own creations for your enjoyment. Look for a great selection of ply-split work by Portland teacher Linda Erickson, master crafter Peter Collingwood (now, regrettably, deceased), and world master Erroll Pires to see more of this fascinating craft.

Ply-split work may have started with the construction of making camel girths (straps) for use in crossing the Thar Desert of northwestern India. It is also found in Colombia and in Israel. There are three basic techniques: Plain Oblique Twining (POT), Single Course Oblique Twining (SCOT), and Two-Layer Oblique Twining (TLOI). This last technique created small pockets where it is said that gold pieces or coins could be hidden from view. The technique also allowed for the creation of a two-sided pattern.

Split-ply twining is, as its name suggests, a way of splitting the twine to make a woven product, instead of the usual form of weaving one cord over and under another, where neither cord is being split but woven. The action of splitting the cord brings the cords all to one side of the piece, resulting in a triangular woven piece, with one side

≈ This camel of the Indian subcontinental deserts appears to be showing off the magnificent split-ply work! [Photograph from indolinks.com without permission]

» The work of Maggie Machado of Oregon, USA, making cords into handsome key fobs

of the triangle forming an edge of the fabric. The direction of splitting then reverses to allow the cords to be split to the other side of the strap fabric. The building of triangular sections of split cords allows for a very strong fabric that is used to make a long, narrow strap that can withstand much pulling and tugging without stretching unduly or snapping. Camel girths were made from four-ply cords in cotton or jute, the most readily available fibers around that had the required stiffness and strength. Patterns soon developed by using different-colored cords.

To start twining, the cord is divided in two over a buckle, a rod, or another piece of cord, which acts as the base or hanger for the piece. One half of the cord is the active part and the other is the passive part. The passive part of the cord is opened in the center, thus splitting the ply, and the active cord is passed through it. No knotting, just feeding one line through another. This is not a simple task— far from it! The colors are usually selected so that one side of the finished piece is one color or one pattern when complete and the other side has its own unique pattern. Wool yarns are sometimes substituted for the cotton or jute, to make softer, more forgiving fabrics or even fabrics that, depending on the tension applied to individual cords or yarns, may have a texture, including curves and re-entrant hollows. Many split-ply weavers make their own cords, so that they can pick and choose the tightness of the lay, the placement of the colors and the material of which the cord is made. Hemp, paper, wire, and seagrass have all been used as the base twine in split-ply work, some with more success than others!

List of Contacts

Knot tyers and decorative cords: R & W Rope Warehouse, 39 Tarkiln Place, New Bedford, MA 02745 USA
1-800/260-8599 www.rwrope.com

Traditional Ropes and tools: Des & Liz Pawson of Footrope Knots
501 Wherstead Road, Ipswich, Suffolk, IP2 8LL, UK
+44 (0) 1473 690090 http://despawson.com

Knotting tools: Don Burrhus, Knot Tool Co., P.O. Box 740485, Orange City, FL 32774 USA
www.knottool.com

Colored cords: KJK Ropeworks, Town Living Farmhouse, Puddington, Tiverton, Devon EX16 8LW UK +44 (0) 1884 860692 www.ropesandcords.com

Hi-Tech and Exotic ropes: Liros Ropes, Poststrasse 11, D 95100, Lichtenberg, Germany
+49 (0) 9288 71-0
www.liros.com

Traditional Fibre suppliers: Scottish Fibres, 23 Damhead, Lothianburn, Edinburgh FH10 7EA Scotland UK
+44 (0) 131 445 3899
www.scottishfibres.co.uk

Hemp lines: Touwfabriek Langman BV, P.O. Box 225, NL-3860, AE Nijkerk, The Netherlands
+31 (0) 33 246 19 86
www.langmanropes.com

Horse ropes: Horse Rope Connection, Hirsch Industries Inc.,
1-877/377-4224
www.horseropeconnection.com

Lacrosse cords: Jimalax Lacrosse Mesh Headquarters, 2117 S 48th Street, Ste 109, Tempe, AZ 85282 USA
1 888/401 5002
www.jimalax.com

Leather supplies and tools: Tandy Leather Factory Inc., 1900 SE Loop 820, Fort Worth, TX 76140 USA
1-800/433-3201
www.tandyleatherfactory.com

Rope: Columbian Rope Company, 145 Towery Street, Guntown, MS 38849 USA
1-800/629-0151
www.unicordcorp.com

Glossary

Armorial	Having to do with heraldry, the description, devising, and regulation of coats of arms
Back	The side of the finished knot that, during construction, is behind the parts already passed. Note, this applies also to passing behind another line.
Bell-rope	A decorated hanging handle used to move the clapper of a ship's bell.
Bight	A bend in a piece of line made without crossing one part of the line over itself.
Binding	(noun) A rope device for bringing two or more spars or sticks together.
	(verb) To bring two sticks or spars together by tightly passing a rope or line around the objects and knotting them.

Bosal	A rawhide noseband used in Mexico for hackamore gentling (training) of a horse.
Braid(ed)	(noun) An interlacing weave of yarns forming the basic structure of a rope, line, or cord, the number of yarns varying from one to six or more (see Chapter 4).
	(adjective) The appearance of a braided line.
Braided line	A rope, line, or cord that has been braided
Cable	A left-laid line, ten inches or more in circumference, made with three strands, each strand being a right-laid rope.
Coir	The fiber husk surrounding the coconut seed of the coconut palm (*Cocos nucifera*), used in making hard-wearing twine, cords, and line.
Doubling	The action of passing the working end of the cord alongside and parallel to a previously laid cord, thereby forming an expansion of the thickness of each pass from one cord to two cords.
Exotic cords	Cords made with plastic compounds that have been treated further from the raw polyamide, polyester, polyethylene, or polypropylene to increase their strength.
Fair	(verb) A process of pulling a knot into the desired shape, gently and without stressing the line, to ensure that the final shape is what you intended.
	(adjective) The appearance of a finished piece that shows all parts lying alongside each other neatly, with no gaps, twisted or missing cords, no visible splices, or snags, no glue-blobs, evenly spaced sections between adjacent crossings, and neatly lined-up intersections consistent with the knotting.
Fibrillated	The result of making shorter lengths of polymer or plastics fibers appear hairier, resembling natural fibers.
Fibers	The individual threads or filaments of which rope, line, and cords are made.
Fid	A (usu.) wooden tool used to separate the strands of a rope or line in the activity of splicing that rope or line to itself or to another. See also Swedish fid.
Flat knot	A knot that is created with a woven structure that, when laid on a flat surface, does not excessively protrude above the general surface of the knot.
Flax	The plant (*Linum usitatissimum*) from which the fibers are extracted and twisted to make a fine thread, twine, or small line. The thread is most often used to make linen fabric and the seeds of the plant are crushed to make linseed oil.
Fraying	The action of the end of a twisted or braided line that, when released from its confining, whipping, or sealing, tends to splay out the yarns and threads as to become unruly and spoiling the lines.

Front	That side of the finished knot that, during construction, is nearest to the tyer.
Grafting	Wrapping the warps of cord around the weft cord, or wrapping the weft cord around the warp cords.
Hackamore	A rope or leather fitting that is used to exert pressure on a horse's nose when training the horse.
Hackled	Cleaned of debris, bark and other impurities in a natural fiber by drawing repeatedly across a brush with close-set spikes of metal prior to spinning the fibers for rope making.
Halter	A strap forming part of the hackamore that holds the bosal in place.
Hawser	A right-laid rope used in holding a ship or in controlling its parts, such as yards, sails, etc. Hawser-laid refers to a rope being right-laid or Z-laid.
Hemp	The plant (*Cannabis sativa*) from which fibers are extracted and twisted or woven into rope, line, cord, or twine.
Hockle	A round turn in a piece of rope, line, or cord that is formed when a laid or braided line is twisted along its length to form a tight circle that is very damaging to the fibers or wires in the line.
Hollow fid	A round metal bar, pointed at one end and with a hollow recess at the other, used in splicing braided line.
Jute	The plant (*Corchorus capsularis* OR *C. olitorius*) from which fibers are extracted and twisted into rope, line, or cord.
Knittle	A bundle of cord wrapped in a figure-eight pattern and bound around its center, thereby allowing the cord to feed out from one end without tangling.
Lacquer	The sap of the East Asian tree (*Rhus verniciflua*) that is mixed with alcohol or other solvent to form a liquid that dries to form a hard, protective coating. Sometimes also made with shellac instead of sap, which lac is derived instead from insects.
Ladder	The formation found in making a knot whereby the previously passed parts of the knot form two parallel lines and the lines crossing them are alternately under or over both parallel lines; ladders are typically completed by passing the working end between the parallel lines.
Laid line	Line that has been formed by twisting the parts together, typically left-laid strands from right-laid yarns, those strands twisted together to form right-laid line.

Lanyard	A length of (usu.) decorative cord used to suspend or retain a badge, tool, or other object to prevent its loss. Lanyards may encircle the neck or may be attached to a belt or other suspension device on the clothing of the wearer.
Lashing	(noun) A series of tight wraps of rope, line, or cord intended to substitute for nails or other metal fittings in keeping two objects (usu. spars or sticks) close together and structurally safe; used in erection of scaffolding in some parts of the world.
	(verb) The act of forming a lashing.
Leads	The several parts of a knot that cross each other in forming the knot.
Leather lace	A narrow strip of leather cut from the perimeter of an animal hide as a continuous piece using a sharp, vertically mounted blade.
Loop	A simple crossing of one part of a line over another part in somewhat close proximity to form an enclosure.
Manila	The plant (*Musa textilis*) from which fiber is extracted and twisted to make rope or line.
Marlinespike	A tapered steel or iron tool used in splicing wire ropes.
Nippers	A steel tool having hardened opposing cutting blades used in cutting wire and metals.
Overhand	The manner of moving one line past another by crossing atop the other line; the opposite of underhand.
Pass	(noun) A single portion of the line used that crosses between two readily distinguished places in a knot (one side to the other, for example). A knot may have more than one pass.
	(verb) To cause the line to be moved through the knot from one place to the next.
Plait	A decorative weaving of cords to form a (usu.) flat strap or band having a series of regular or irregular crossings (see also Chapter 4).
Plaited line	A woven (over and under) form of yarns that are formed of alternately twisted fibers to form a rope, line, or cord.
Pleaching	The action of interweaving the vertically growing branches of a small tree or bush to create an open trunk-like latticework of branches.
Pointing	Covering the end or a part of a line to prevent fraying or abrasion, particularly when used repeatedly in one location where friction will occur.

Polyamide	A synthetic polymer made by linking an amino group from one molecule with the carboxylic group of another one; commonly known as Nylon.
Polyester	A synthetic resin in which the polymer units are linked together with ester groups; commonly known as Dacron®.
Polyethylene	A synthetic resin made by polymerizing ethylene; also known as polythene and commonly known as poly.
Polymer	A synthesis of small groups of molecules grouped together.
Polypropylene	A synthetic resin that is a polymer of propylene, a gaseous hydrocarbon; commonly known as yellow rope.
Pricker	A steel or brass tool having a dulled and tapered point, used to insert under a cord for tightening.
Rawhide	Stiff untanned leather that has been treated by repeated pulling through a narrow slit in a piece of wood.
Rein	The long, narrow strap or cord used on a hackamore or a steel bit to control a horse's movements from the saddle.
Ret	The action of soaking in water; lye is added to ret natural plant fibers free of pithy matter.
Seizing	The act of binding two or more parts of rope, line, or cord together with (usu.) twine or thinner cord.
Sinnet	A decorative weaving of cords to form a flat, round, or rectangular strap or band having a series of regular or irregular crossings (see also Chapter 4).
Sisal	A plant fiber extracted from the large fleshy leaves of the Mexican agave (*Agave sisalana*) and twisted into twine, cord, line, and rope.
Skiving	The action of evenly thinning a (usu.) strip of leather from its maximum thickness down to nothing in a wedge shape. Skiving is performed to enable the joining of two pieces whose ends have been thinned or skived.
Snags	Small sections of fibers lifted from the surface of a cord or sections of defective cord.
Splicing	The action taken to join one line to itself or to another by separating the strands of a twisted line (or by expanding and enclosing the parts of a braided line), such that the strands (or another section of that braided line) may be joined securely by tucking or squeezing the parts together. Splicing relies on friction for its strength.

Spun	(adjective) See fibrillated above.
Standing end	That part of a line used in knotting that generally does not require to be moved during the making of the line; opposite of working end.
Swedish fid	A V-shaped length of thin steel, tapering from one end and having an inserted handle at the other, used to pass a cord or to insert a strand when splicing. Also known as a hollow fid (see also different description of *hollow fid* above).
Tanned hide	An animal hide that has been chemically treated (usu. with tannic acid) to prevent deterioration or decay.
Tape	A paper to which adhesive has been applied on one side; usually supplied in rolls of a certain width.
Turk's Head	A type of knot in which a (usu.) single cord is wrapped over and under itself to form what appears to be a continuous braid or plait having separate parts and no ends; usually abbreviated TH Knot, there exist many different patterns of forming the wrappings and the subsequent knot is described by the number of bights to its extremes and the number of crossings between those bights, known as leads.
Twisted line	Line that has been formed by rotating the yarns or fibers about their longitudinal axis; a line formed by such action.
Underhand	The manner of moving one line past another by crossing beneath the other line; the opposite of overhand.
Varnish	The resin of the cypress tree (*Tetraclinis articulate* and others) dissolved in one of several solvents that, when applied to wood, dries to a hard finish.
Whipping	The action resulting from making multiple wraps of a twine around the end of a piece of larger rope or line to prevent that line from fraying.
Working end	That part of a line used in making a knot that performs the principal movement during creation of the knot; opposite of standing end.
Yarns	The twisted fibers that form the base units of laid and twisted lines; the base units of yarns are twisted into strands or are used as twisted fibers subsequently woven in groups or singly to form braided line.

Bibliography

The following list of books is an abbreviated list of the essential books that the author has used, now owns, and feels are worthy of your seeking out from your own resources, your local library, or from the Internet where that resource is available to you. These books have served as a fulfilling guide and as an essential resource when trying new techniques, revisiting old techniques and when seeking help on technical questions. They are arranged by author, alphabetically by last name.

Author	Title	Publisher	Date
Bowling, Tom	The Book of Knots	Hardwick & Bogue	1876
Ambuter, Carolyn	The Open Canvas	Workman Publishing	1982
Ashley, Clifford Warren	The Ashley Book of Knots	Doubleday Doran	1944
Auld, Rhoda L.	Tatting; the contemporary art of knotting with a shuttle	Van Nostrand Reinhold Company	1974
Babcock, Joan R.	Micro-Macramé Jewelry; Tips and techniques for knotting with beads	Joan Babcock Designs	2007
Barnes, Charles and David P. Blake	Creative Macramé Projects	Dover Publications Inc.	1972
Beavis, Bill	Sailors" Crafts	George Allen & Unwin	1981
Benns, Elizabeth and Gina Barrett	Tak V Bowes Departed; a 15th century braiding manual examined	Soper Lane	2005
Beverley, Deena	New Crafts Stringwork	Lorenz Books	1997
Brady, William	The Kedge-Anchor or A Young Sailor's Assistant	William Brady	1847
Budworth, Geoffrey	Challenging Knots	Lorenz Books	2000
Budworth, Geoffrey	The Ultimate Encyclopedia of Knots and Ropework	Hermes House	2003
Burgess, Joseph Tom	Knots, Ties, and Splices	George Routledge & Sons	1884
Burrhus, Don	The Globe Knot Cookbook	Don Burrhus	2008
Burrhus, Don	Turks Head Cookbook	Don Burrhus	2006
Burrhus, Don	Turks Head Cookbook Volume Two	Don Burrhus	2007
Carey, Jacqui	200 Braids to Twist, Knot, Loop, or Weave	Interweave Press	2007
Carey, Jacqui	Japanese Braiding, The Art of Kumihimo	Search Press	1997
Carey, Jacqui	The Braider's Bible	Search Press	2007
Cha, Dia and Norma J Livo	Teaching with Folk Stories of the Hmong	Libraries Unlimited	2000

Author	Title	Publisher	Date
Chatelaine, Amber	How to Macramé with Small Cords	Craft Course Publishers	1975
Chen, Lydia	Fun with Chinese Knotting	Tuttle Publishing	2007
Chen, Lydia	The Complete Book of Chinese Knotting; A compendium of techniques and variations	Tuttle Publishing	2007
Day, Cyrus Lawrence	The Art of Knotting and Splicing	United States Naval Institute, Annapolis, Maryland	1955
Dusenbury, Teri	Tatting Hearts	Dover Publications Inc.	1994
English, Alan and Roosalind Silvester eds	Reading Images and Seeing Words	Rodopi	2004
Field, Brian	Brian E. Field's Breast-Plate Designs to Make and Wear	International Guild of Knot Tyers	1985
Field, Brian	Concerning Crosses	Brian E. Field	1996
Gardner, Martin	Hexaflexagons, Probability Paradoxes and the Tower of Hanoi	Cambridge University Press	2008
Grant, Bruce	Encyclopedia of Rawhide and Leather Braiding	Cornell Maritime Press	1972
Graumont, Raoul M. and John J. Hensel	Encyclopedia of Knots and Fancy Rope Work	Cornell Maritime Press Inc.	1939
Hall, Bobi	Macramé Magic	Craft Course Publishers	1975
Hall, Tom	Introduction to Turk's-Head Knots	Tom Hall	1996
Hall, Tom	More Western Tack Tips	Tom Hall Braiding	2000
Hall, Tom	Turk's-Head Workbook	Tom Hall	1996
Hall, Tom	Western Tack Tips	Tom Hall	1987
Harrison, P.P.O.	The Harrison Book of Knots	Brown, Son & Ferguson	1964
Harvey, Virginia I.	Split-Ply Twining	HTH Publishers	1976

Author	Title	Publisher	Date
Hee-Jin, Kim	Maedup; The Art of Traditional Korean Knots	Hollym	2006
Howard, Frank	Segel-Kriegsschiffe 1400 – 1860	Bernard & Graefe Verlag	1979
Hurley, William M.	Prehistoric Cordage; Identification of impressions on pottery	Taraxacum, Washington	1979
Journal, The Young Ladies	Complete Guide to the Work Table	E. Harrison	1887
Kemp, Peter Ed	The Oxford Companion to Ships and the Sea	Oxford University Press	1976
Kliot, Jules& Kaethe	Kumihimo Techniques of Japanese Plaiting	Lacis Publications	1977
LaBarge, Lura	Do Your Own Thing with Macramé	Watson-Guptill Publications	1973
Latter, Lucy R.	Knotting, Looping, and Plaiting	George Philip & Son, Ltd.	Unk.
Leuszler, Marilyn	Macramé for Enthusiasts	Craft Publications Inc.	1975
Lewis, Bob and Jackie Day Clark	To Knot or Not to Knot	Crown Crafts Publications Inc.	1975
Mason, Kate	Make Your Own Friendship Bracelets	Troll	1993
Meehan, Aidan	Celtic Design Knotwork; The secret method of the scribes	Thames and Hudson	1991
Meilach, Dona Z. and Dee Menagh	Exotic Needlework	Crown Publishers	1978
Miles, Roger E.	Symmetric Bends; How to join two lengths of cord	World Scientific	1995
Muller-Wille, Ludger as translated by William Barr	Franz Boas Among the Inuit of Baffin Island 1883 - 1884	University of Toronto Press	1998
Murasugi, Kunio and Bohdan I. Kurpita	A Study of Braids	Kluwer Academic Publishers	1999

Author	Title	Publisher	Date
Nares, Lt. George S., R.N.	Seamanship	Gresham Books	1979 facsimile of 1862
Neubecker, Ottfried with J.P. Brooke-Little	Heraldry Sources, Symbols and Meaning	McGraw-Hill Book Company	1976
Osornio, Cesar Lopez and Francisco Meeks	Manual de Trenzado	Libros de Hispanoamérica	2008
Osornio, Mario A. Lopez	Trenzas Gauchas	Libros de Hispanoamérica	2009
Owen, Rodrick	Braids	Interweave Press	1995
Pennock, Skip	Decorative Woven Flat Knots	International Guild of Knot Tyers	2002
Phillips, Mary Walker	Step-by-Step Macramé	Golden Press	1970
Quick, Betsy D and Judith A. Stein	Ply-Split Camel Girths of West India	Museum of Cultural History, UCLA	1982
Richir, Gabriel	L'Appel du Large	Musee Industriel de la Corderie Vallois	2008
Rosenow, Frank	Canvas and Rope Craft for the Practical Boat Owner	W. W. Norton and Company	1987
Rosenthal, Ed	Hemp Today	Quick American Archives	1994
Salmeri, Alessandro	Como Hacer Nudos	De Vecchi	2007
Sang Lan, Kim	Decorative Knot Craft	David and Charles	2006
Schevill, Margot Blum, Janet Catherine Berlo and Edward B. Dwyer eds	Textile Traditions of Mesoamerica and the Andes	University of Texas Press	1991
Silver, Lynette	Making Friendship Bands	Milner Dodgem Books	1994
Simmons, Denni and Glen, with Doreene and Clint Clement	Macramé Elegance	Macramé Elegance, Provo, Utah	1975
Simpson, J.A. and E.S.C. Weiner, preparers	The Compact Oxford English Dictionary, New Edition	Clarendon Press	1994

Author	Title	Publisher	Date
Smith, Hervey Garrett	The Marlinespike Sailor	John de Graff Inc.	1981
Sondheim, Erich	Knoten, Spleisen, Takeln	Verlag Klasing & Co.	1953
Steinke, Robert H.	Harness-Making; A step-by-step guide	J.A. Allen	2004
Steven, G.A.	Nets – How to Make, Mend, and Preserve Them	Read Country Books	2005
Sunset Books editors	Macramé Techniques and Projects	Lane Publishing Co.	1975
Svensson, Sam as translated by Inger Imrie	Handbook of Seaman's Ropework	Adlard Coles Ltd Granada Publishing	1983
Woodcock, Thomas and John Martin Robinson	The Oxford Guide to Heraldry	Oxford University Press	1988
Zischka, Ulrike	Stickmustertucher	Staatliche Museen PreuBischer Kulturbesitz	1978

Index